D1602529

PALGRAVE STUDIES IN THEATRE AND PERFORMANCE HISTORY is a series devoted to the best of theatre/performance scholarship currently available, accessible, and free of jargon. It strives to include a wide range of topics, from the more traditional to those performance forms that in recent years have helped broaden the understanding of what theatre as a category might include (from variety forms as diverse as the circus and burlesque to street buskers, stage magic, and musical theatre, among many others). Although historical, critical, or analytical studies are of special interest, more theoretical projects, if not the dominant thrust of a study, but utilized as important underpinning or as a historiographical or analytical method of exploration, are also of interest. Textual studies of drama or other types of less traditional performance texts are also germane to the series if placed in their cultural, historical, social, or political and economic context. There is no geographical focus for this series and works of excellence of a diverse and international nature, including comparative studies, are sought.

The editor of the series is Don B. Wilmeth (EMERITUS, Brown University), Ph.D., University of Illinois, who brings to the series over a dozen years as editor of a book series on American theatre and drama, in addition to his own extensive experience as an editor of books and journals. He is the author of several award-winning books and has received numerous career achievement awards, including one for sustained excellence in editing from the Association for Theatre in Higher Education.

Also in the series:

Loss and Cultural Remains in Performance

The Ghosts of the Franklin Expedition

Heather Davis-Fisch

LOSS AND CULTURAL REMAINS IN PERFORMANCE

An earlier version of "Aglooka's Ghost: Performing Embodied Memory" was published in *Performing Arts Resources* Vol. 28, *A Tyranny of Documents: The Performing Arts Historian as Film Noir Detective* (Theatre Library Association, 2011) as "Aglooka's Ghost: Apparitions in the Archive."

First published in 2012 by
PALGRAVE MACMILLAN®
in the United States—a division of St. Martin's Press LLC,
175 Fifth Avenue, New York, NY 10010.

Where this book is distributed in the UK, Europe and the rest of the world, this is by Palgrave Macmillan, a division of Macmillan Publishers Limited, registered in England, company number 785998, of Houndmills, Basingstoke, Hampshire RG21 6XS.

Palgrave Macmillan is the global academic imprint of the above companies and has companies and representatives throughout the world.

Palgrave® and Macmillan® are registered trademarks in the United States, the United Kingdom, Europe and other countries.

ISBN: 978–0–230–34032–9

Library of Congress Cataloging-in-Publication Data

Davis-Fisch, Heather, 1979–
    Loss and cultural remains in performance : the ghosts of the Franklin Expedition / Heather Davis-Fisch.
        p. cm.—(Palgrave studies in theatre and performance history)
    Based on the author's dissertation (doctoral)—University of Guelph.
    ISBN 978–0–230–34032–9 (alk. paper)
        1. Franklin Expedition (1845) 2. Northwest Passage—Discovery and exploration—British. 3. Search and rescue operations—Northwest Territories. 4. Search and rescue operations—Arctic regions. 5. Ede, Charles, 19th cent. Zero, or Harlequin light. 6. Collins, Wilkie, 1824–1889. Frozen deep. I. Title.

G660.D28 2012
820.9'3216327—dc23   2012010278

A catalogue record of the book is available from the British Library.

Design by Newgen Imaging Systems (P) Ltd., Chennai, India.

First edition: September 2012

10 9 8 7 6 5 4 3 2 1

Printed and bound in Great Britain by
CPI Antony Rowe, Chippenham and Eastbourne

Contents ❧

Images

Acknowledgments ❧

I t is my great pleasure to thank a number of people who have shaped this
book. This project began as a PhD dissertation in the School of English
and Theatre Studies at the University of Guelph, generously supported
through a Social Science and Humanities Research Council (SSHRC) doc-
toral fellowship and an Ontario Graduate Scholarship. I am deeply indebted
to my advisor, Alan Filewod, for his challenging questions about spectatorship, performance, and theater history, his rigorous mentorship, and his
unfailing enthusiasm for this project. Daniel O'Quinn, Michelle Elleray,
and Ute Lischke provided thoughtful criticism, shaping my research and
writing practices and sharing their areas of expertise. Mark Fortier, Stephen
Johnson, Smaro Kamboureli, Paul Mulholland, Susan Nance, and Ann Wilson
offered thought-provoking feedback and made insightful suggestions about
further development of this project. I would also like to thank my fellow
graduate students at Guelph, who were invaluable resources and caring
friends. In particular, Ben Authers and Erin Elliott volunteered to read sections of this book and provided much-needed practical advice.

I was the fortunate recipient of a postdoctoral fellowship funded by
SSHRC, which enabled me to research and write this book. I would like
to thank my colleagues in the Department of Theatre and Film at the
University of British Columbia for their support and Jerry Wasserman,
in particular, for his generous mentorship and encouragement. I also owe
great thanks to my colleagues in the English and Theatre departments
at the University of the Fraser Valley for allowing me to defer my teaching position in order to embark upon postdoctoral research and for providing kind words and encouragement during my writing process. Brad
Whittaker, Director of Research Services and Industry Liaison at UFV,
also provided generous financial support that assisted me in publishing this
work. I would also like to thank Samantha Hasey of Palgrave Macmillan
for taking a chance on this project; Don Wilmeth, my series editor, for his
supportive feedback; and an anonymous reviewer, for precise and challenging suggestions for revisions.

While completing this book, I have had the pleasure of meeting a number of skilled and knowledgeable librarians and archivists who provided invaluable assistance. I would like to thank Christine Windheuser and Kay Peterson from the National Museum of American History (Smithsonian Institution) for helping me locate documents within the voluminous collection of Charles Francis Hall's fieldnotes. Naomi Boneham, Lucy Martin, and Shirley Sawtell provided helpful archival and library assistance during my visit to the Scott Polar Research Institute at Cambridge. I would also like to thank Richard Espley, assistant librarian at the National Maritime Museum at Greenwich, and Fiona Jenkins, curator of the Charles Dickens Museum, for their help during my visits.

There are also a number of personal debts I must acknowledge. Amy Jones, Alicia Kerfoot, Heather Russek, Mary Sweatman, and Richie Wilcox have patiently listened to me talk about this project for the last six years. My parents, Keitha and Michael Davis, my brother Ian, Kimberly, Gary, and Andrew Fisch and Tamara Hatton have encouraged me over the years and have provided support for this project in too many ways to list. Finally, my husband Scott's unconditional love and generosity, particularly in his willingness to share our marriage with John Franklin for the last four years, have gone far beyond what he signed up for: thank you for reminding me that there is a world outside of the nineteenth century.

Introduction: Jane Franklin's Dress: Archives and Affect ✑

On January 12, 1854, the Admiralty informed Lady Jane Franklin that as of March 31 of that year, her husband Sir John Franklin—who had disappeared in 1845 while attempting to chart the Northwest Passage—would be removed from its active service list. Although ships were still searching for Franklin and the 128 men under his command, the Admiralty's decision effectively declared the missing men dead. After recovering from the shock the letter had "inflicted on [her] already shattered health," Lady Franklin wrote a pointed response to the secretary of the Admiralty: "You will not expect from me, Sir, to claim from the Admiralty the Widow's pension which you remind me is granted under certain regulations.—I believe that my husband may yet be living where your expeditions have never looked for him" (20 January 1854). In a private letter to her sister in-law, Jane explained her refusal to accept the Admiralty's decision, claiming, "It would be acting a falsehood & a gross hypocrisy on my part to put on mourning when I have not yet given up all hope—Still less would I do it in that month & day that suits the Admiralty's financial convenience" ("Letter to Mrs. Wright," qtd. in Woodward 286). Not only did Lady Franklin refuse to accept her widow's pension or dress like a widow, she also, according to a letter written by her stepdaughter Eleanor Gell, "changed the deep mourning she had been wearing for years for bright colours of green & pink as soon as the Adm^y notice was gazetted" (qtd. in Woodward 285). Jane Franklin's change of clothing both represented her challenge to the Admiralty's decision and signified that while she had mourned her husband's long absence by dressing in black, she refused to mourn his death until she had evidence it had indeed occurred.

By putting on pink and green clothing, Jane Franklin conjured up a ghost. Her body, clothed as a married woman rather than a widow, brought another body—her husband's living one—into presence. Because a woman of Lady Franklin's standing would never flaunt convention by refusing to mourn her deceased husband, her clothing functioned as a "complex piece of social semaphore" that declared her husband alive (Spufford 119). Her performance made this statement despite the fact (unknown at the time to Jane or the Admiralty) that John Franklin had died in 1847. Knowing, as we do now, that her husband was dead, Lady Franklin's performed denial of her widowhood produces a shiver of uncanniness, capturing a moment at which John Franklin was both actually dead and imaginatively alive at the same time. Oddly, when one attempts to identify this ghostly presence, two specters appear: John Franklin as living, not dead, and Jane Franklin as wife, not widow. Witnesses noted the eeriness of the performance: Eleanor Gell was so shocked that she told an aunt she "trembled" for her stepmother's mind, adding that Jane was "fast losing public sympathy by her strange conduct" (McGoogan, *Lady* 331).[1]

The story of Lady Franklin's unusual clothing prompts methodological questions regarding the evidentiary value of performance, memory, and affect in generating historical narratives. Frances Woodward, the first to publish the story, is clear that the anecdote is hearsay, prefacing it with "if Eleanor [Gell] is to be believed" (285). Mrs. Gell's letter is the only evidence that Jane responded to the Admiralty's decision in this unconventional way and is uncorroborated: Woodward does not cite Gell's letter in her notes or bibliography; later works reference Woodward, not Gell's original letter; neither the Scott Polar Research Institute in Cambridge, which holds much of the correspondence related to the Franklin search, nor the Derbyshire archives, which hold the Gell family papers, possesses the letter. Tracing the story of Jane Franklin's pink and green clothing leads to an archival dead end, leaving simple questions unanswerable: it is unclear when she wore the clothing, whether it was a one-time occurrence or a habit, or whom she wore the dress or dresses for. While these questions appear trivial, answering them is essential if one hopes to reconstruct Lady Franklin's sumptuary protest.

Despite the uncertainty surrounding the details of the performance— indeed, it is unclear whether it happened at all—the story has a remarkable staying power: whether it occurred or not, it has been remembered. It appears in many accounts of the Franklin search as an accepted fact. Pierre Berton, for example, writes that "in a bold act of defiance, as ludicrous as it was symbolic, she scorned Victorian convention by throwing off her widow's black mourning [...] and appeared in brilliant pink and green" (*Grail* 264).[2] The story's endurance epitomizes the concerns of this project: while the performances this book examines each address the disappearance of the Franklin expedition, they are linked not only by thematic but also by structural concerns with loss. The remains of these performances prohibit thorough reconstruction, instead enticing one to examine how they expose the tensions between material remains and memory, to contrast historicism with historical materialism, to distinguish between mourning and melancholia, and to consider the roles played by surrogation and substitution in coping with loss. Engaging in a sustained consideration of these questions allows one to explore both how performance functioned as a way for the public to understand and document the particular losses that followed the Franklin expedition's disappearance and the theoretical and methodological concerns arising when performance responds to extratheatrical experiences of loss.

The questions raised in examining Jane Franklin's pink and green clothing illustrate David Eng and David Kazanjian's provocative comment concerning the relationship between loss and remains: "as soon as the question 'What is lost?' is posed, it invariably slips into the question 'What remains?' That is, loss is inseparable from what remains, for what is lost is only known by what remains of it, by how these remains are produced, read, and sustained" (2). Lady Franklin enacted a relationship between loss and remains, tacitly claiming that without physical remains, her husband remained alive. Her clothing evoked her husband's absence and temporarily denied the reality that there was neither a married woman nor a living husband, only a widow and a corpse. Her performance expressed a specific relationship between absence, loss, and remains by enacting an imaginary but emotionally real relationship to her husband. Jane Franklin's performance not only embodies the relationship described by Eng and Kazanjian but also constitutes a discrete set of performative remains, preserving how John Franklin's absence was understood by evoking, through its moving power, an individual experience of loss. What is remarkable is that the story's power survives independently of its archival authority: whether Jane wore the dresses or not, the story of her refusal to mourn endures because of the affect it continues to evoke.

The tension between archival instability and affective endurance apparent in the story of Jane Franklin's dress characterizes any number of theatrical and nontheatrical performances: the problems of determining precisely what happened on the stages of the past are familiar to scholars of theater and performance history. I contend, however, that performances responding to the loss of the Franklin expedition constitute a limit case that sheds light on how performance studies can intervene in the production of historical knowledge. While these performances exemplify the historiographical tension between loss and remains that generate many of the questions motivating the work of theater and performance historians, they also engage this tension thematically, structurally, and epistemologically: this is a consequence of the particular circumstances surrounding the expedition's disappearance. The case of the Franklin expedition poses critical problems for those who attempt to read the past through its physical, tangible remains. It is unique in the annals of polar exploration history not because it ended in disaster but because it left almost no records: only one document from the expedition was ever recovered, and it provides little information about what befell the expedition. Material remains—personal effects, debris from the ships, corpses—were strewn across the central Arctic, yet when one attempts to piece these relics together to produce a coherent narrative of disaster and retreat, they are secretive and contradictory: attempts to reconstruct what happened are either partial or reliant upon imagination.

Many historians have neglected to consider the performative remains produced by the Franklin expedition, remains that survived not because they contributed to knowledge of the "facts" of what happened but because of their ability to generate affective attachments. Paying these remains the attention they deserve means shifting perspective, asking how the past was experienced rather than simply asking what happened. Considering the performative remains produced in the wake of the expedition's disappearance will not help reconstruct the past: it does not establish where Franklin's ships sank, reveal who engaged in survival cannibalism, or confirm causes of death. By looking at performative remains, however, one can better understand how the search for the expedition was justified and what the search parties' motivations were; how survivors, the British public, and Inuit came to comprehend the failure of the expedition; and how the lost men were remembered and mourned: in short, by looking at performance, one can understand how those affected made sense of their losses. This book proposes that examining the performative remains produced in the wake of the Franklin expedition's disappearance generates critical insights, not only concerning these events as performance, but also regarding how performance emerges, in particular historical circumstances, as a repository of cultural history and an epistemology of loss.

The theatrical and nontheatrical events examined in this book do not constitute an exhaustive list of all performative responses to the expedition's disappearance; rather, they are a curated collection, selected because they make visible the strange workings of affect and enactment, surrogation and substitution, and memory and disappearance, which are central both to how the Franklin expedition's disappearance was understood and to theater and performance historiography. These performances also bring the intercultural implications of the expedition's disappearance into sharp relief: interrogating performance practices provides a sense of how cultural anxieties regarding the differences between civilization and savagery, cultural adaptation and social transgression, strangers and allies were understood on the ground by Britons, Americans, and Inuit. Finally, these performances, like the story of Jane Franklin's dress, are fundamentally and appropriately marked by elision and erasure: the story of the Franklin expedition's disappearance is, above all, characterized by absence, ambiguity, and mystery.

WHAT HAPPENED TO THE FRANKLIN EXPEDITION?

Attempts to reconstruct what happened to the Franklin expedition break down because the material remains of the expedition produce, rather than alleviate, ambiguity. Despite this, I feel compelled to outline what is known of what happened, both to situate readers unfamiliar with the expedition and to contextualize the performances with which I am concerned. The third Arctic expedition under Sir John Franklin's command—comprising HMS *Terror*, Franklin's ship under the direct command of James Fitzjames, and HMS *Erebus*, under the command of Francis Crozier—left England on May 19, 1845, dispatched to complete the elusive Northwest Passage. Hardly the Admiralty's first choice for commander, the fifty-nine-year-old Franklin had not been to the far north in almost twenty years.[3] Other than Franklin, only six officers had Arctic experience: these were Crozier; Lieutenant Graham Gore, of the *Erebus*; Charles Hamilton Osmer, the purser and paymaster; Dr. Alexander McDonald, the assistant surgeon on *Terror*; and James Reid and Thomas Blanky, the icemasters on *Erebus* and *Terror*, respectively (Cyriax, *Sir* 38). Despite the officers' inexperience and the riskiness of the expedition, no formal agreement was made for relief expeditions and Franklin declined his friend John Ross's private offer to volunteer for a search if no word arrived by January 1847: the expedition had no expectation of assistance from home (Cyriax, *Sir* 51).

After *Erebus* and *Terror* left England, they stopped at the Orkney Islands and then the Whalefish Islands, where five men were discharged. Letters and journals sent home with these men indicate that the crews and officers were in high spirits and optimistic. Commander Fitzjames wrote on June 10 of the "immense stock of good feeling, good humour, and real kindliness of heart in our small mess" (*Journals* 13). His final entry, written on July 6, revealed that Inuit thought "it to be one of the mildest seasons and earliest summers ever known" (27); Fitzjames believed they had "a good chance of getting through this year," but hoped they would not

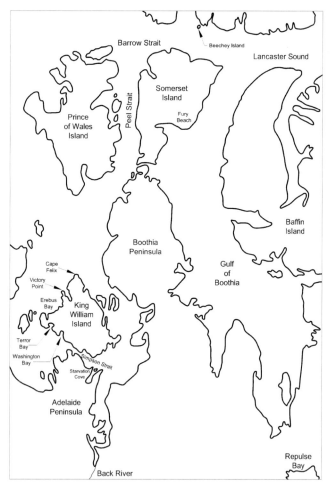

Image 0.1   Map: The Central Arctic

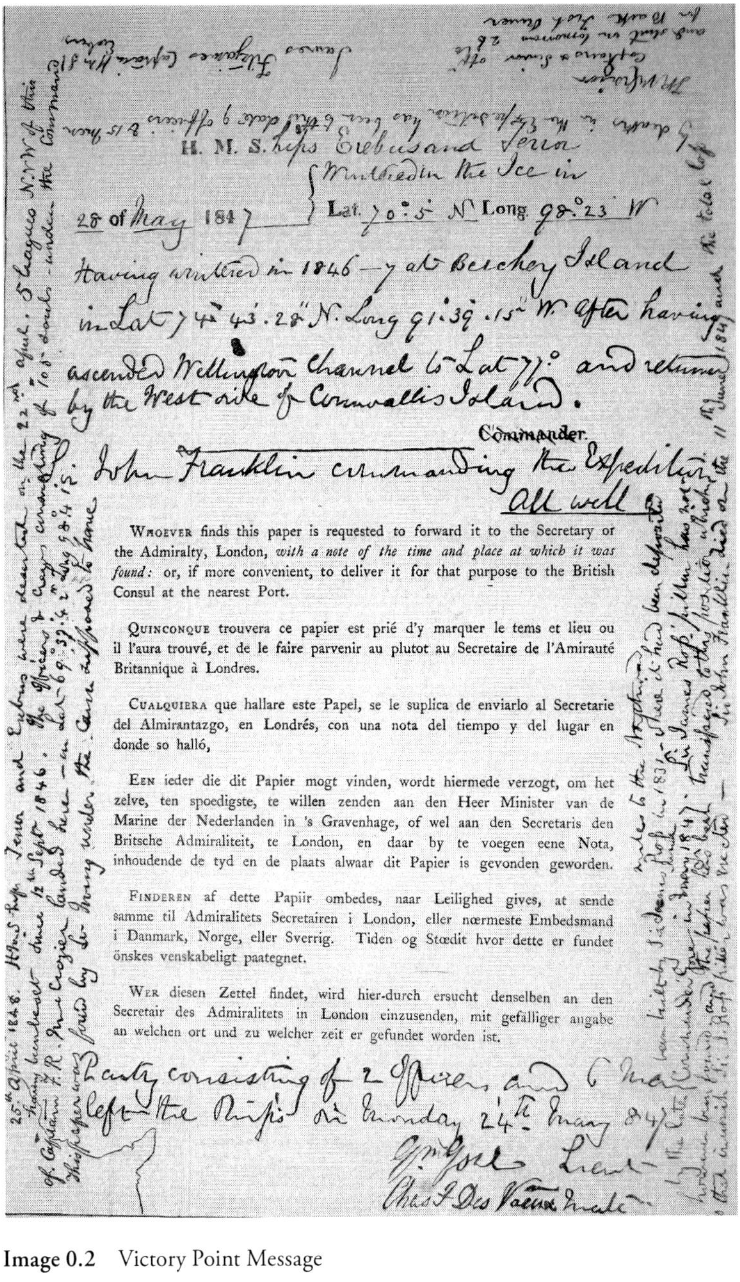

H. M. S.hips *Erebus and Terror*

{ Wintered in the Ice in

28 of May 184 7 } Lat 70.5 N Long 98.23 W

Having wintered in 1846—7 at Beechey Island

in Lat 74° 43' 28" N. Long 91° 39' 15" W after having

ascended Wellington Channel to Lat 77° and returned

by the West side of Cornwallis Island.

Commander.

John Franklin commanding the Expedition.

All well

WHOEVER finds this paper is requested to forward it to the Secretary of the Admiralty, London, *with a note of the time and place at which it was found*: or, if more convenient, to deliver it for that purpose to the British Consul at the nearest Port.

QUINCONQUE trouvera ce papier est prié d'y marquer le tems et lieu ou il l'aura trouvé, et de le faire parvenir au plutot au Secretaire de l'Amirauté Britannique à Londres.

CUALQUIERA que hallare este Papel, se le suplica de enviarlo al Secretarie del Almirantazgo, en Londrés, con una nota del tiempo y del lugar en donde so halló,

EEN ieder die dit Papier mogt vinden, wordt hiermede verzogt, om het zelve, ten spoedigste, te willen zenden aan den Heer Minister van de Marine der Nederlanden in 's Gravenhage, of wel aan den Secretaris den Britsche Admiraliteit, te London, en daar by te voegen eene Nota, inhoudende de tyd en de plaats alwaar dit Papier is gevonden geworden.

FINDEREN af dette Papiir ombedes, naar Leilighed gives, at sende samme til Admiralitets Secretairen i London, eller nærmeste Embedsmand i Danmark, Norge, eller Sverrig. Tiden og Stœdit hvor dette er fundet önskes venskabeligt paategnet.

WER diesen Zettel findet, wird hier-durch ersucht denselben an den Secretair des Admiralitets in London einzusenden, mit gefälliger angabe an welchen ort und zu welcher zeit er gefundet worden ist.

Party consisting of 2 Officers and 6 Men
left the Ships on Monday 24th May 84 7

Wm. Gore Lieut

Chas F Des Vœux Mate

Image 0.2 Victory Point Message

as he wanted "to have a winter for magnetic observations" (28). On July 26, the expedition met the British whalers *Prince of Wales* and *Enterprise* in northern Baffin Bay. Franklin and a few officers dined aboard the *Enterprise* before the whalers lost sight of the explorers on July 28 (Cooke and Holland 174; Woodman 1). The whalers were the last Europeans to see Franklin and his men alive.

The expedition wintered at Beechey Island in 1845–46 and it was there that the first three of the expedition's deaths occurred. The graves of petty officer John Torrington, marine private William Braine, and seaman John Hartnell were discovered in August 1850, when British and American search expeditions found the winter site.[4] Strangely, Franklin left no indication of where he was heading when he left Beechey Island: it was standard naval practice to leave a record behind and Franklin's failure to do so surprised search parties. This neglect can be explained in two ways: first, upon seeing an opening in the ice, Franklin was in such a hurry to get underway that he didn't take the time to deposit a message—this hypothesis is supported by reports that the Beechey Island site was littered with abandoned gear. The second explanation is that if Franklin was planning to follow his orders from the Admiralty, he may have felt a message was unnecessary, since ships dispatched to follow him would have carried a copy of them.

The lone written record recovered from the expedition relates what happened next (see Image 0.2). In May 1847, a surveying party led by Lieutenant Gore deposited at least two identical forms at Victory Point and Gore Point on King William Island. Almost a year later, the Victory Point message was retrieved and Commander Fitzjames added a second message around the margins of the page. The first message read:

> 28 of May 1847 H.M.S.hips Erebus and Terror Wintered in the Ice in Lat. 70.5°N Long. 98°.23'W Having wintered in 1846–7 at Beechey Island in Lat 74°.43'28"N. Long 91°39'15"W.[5] After having ascended Wellington Channel to Lat 77° and returned by the West-side of Cornwallis Island. Sir John Franklin commanding the Expedition. All well. Party consisting of 2 Officers and 6 Men left the ships on Monday 24th May 1847.

The addendum was as follows:

> 25th April 1848 HM Ships Terror and Erebus were deserted on the 22nd April 5 leagues NNW of this having been beset since 12th Sept. 1846. The Officers and Crews consisting of 105 souls under the command of Captain F.R.M. Crozier landed here—in Lat. 69°37'42" Long.98°41' This paper was found

by Lt. Irving under the cairn supposed to have been built by Sir James Ross in 1831—(4 miles to the Northward)—where it had been deposited by the late Commander Gore in June 1847. Sir James Ross' pillar has not however been found and the paper has been transferred to this position which is that in which Sir J Ross pillar was erected—Sir John Franklin died on the 11th June 1847 and the total loss by deaths in the Expedition has been to this date 9 officers & 15 men.

Crozier also added the postscript: "and start tomorrow, 26th for Backs Fish River."

The first message indicates the route the ships took to reach Beechey Island in 1845 and their position off the coast of King William Island in 1847. While the ships were beset, at least one surveying party—the party led by Gore that deposited the messages—reached the island. It is likely that Lieutenant Irving was the other officer in this group, as it was he who retrieved the paper in 1848. The remark "All well" has been subject to much scrutiny because so little time passed between when it was left and Franklin's June 11 death, raising the question of whether Fitzjames had failed to mention that Franklin's health was declining or whether Franklin had died suddenly.

The second message reveals that the situation deteriorated between May 1847 and April 1848. The ships remained trapped in the ice and the pack pushed them south. Franklin, Gore, seven unnamed officers, and twelve men died that winter. The ships had been away for just under the three years for which they were provisioned. While the men might have been placed on reduced rations in anticipation of another summer and winter in the Arctic, it is unlikely that these deaths were caused by starvation. Owen Beattie suggests that the canned food carried by the expedition was of dubious quality and that lead-soldered cans caused poisoning that contributed to the deaths at Beechey Island (123–24).[6] Beattie ultimately concluded, however, that while "lead played an important role in the declining health of the entire crews," particularly affecting their decision-making abilities, "There is no single reason why the expedition failed; it was a deadly combination of factors" (161). When Beechey Island was searched in 1850, a number of open cans were found: this suggests that the officers suspected the food was questionable and stopped consumption of it. While this would have resulted in further reduced food supplies, scurvy and other vitamin deficiencies likely posed a more urgent threat than food shortages: after three winters, the lack of fresh meat and the inevitable deterioration of the ships' stores of lemon juice mean that most or all men would have suffered from scurvy (Cyriax, *Sir* 155).

While one can speculate that the declining health of the crews led to the 1848 abandonment, it remains unclear why Crozier abandoned the ships so early in the season or why he decided to take his men south to the Back River, rather than north to Fury Beach, where there was a cache of provisions left by Parry's 1824 expedition and a better chance of meeting whalers (Wright 242–45). When the men reached King William Island, they left a large cache of supplies on the coast, perhaps because they did not want to risk losing all their supplies if the ships sunk (Lamb 276),[7] perhaps because it became clear that the men were too weak to carry all they had planned to (Cooper 125). Lieutenant Irving retrieved the 1847 record and, after Fitzjames and Crozier added their messages, the record was reburied. Crozier led his men south, perhaps hoping to lead them through a rich hunting ground (Cooper 121; Woodman 107; Cyriax, *Sir* 151). As the health of the men deteriorated, a makeshift hospital camp was likely set up near Terror Bay and a detachment of thirty or forty men continued travelling southeast (Cyriax, *Sir* 136). This group met Inuit near Washington Bay and their leader—called Aglooka by Inuit—told Inuit they were trying to get to Repulse Bay, asked them for food, and performed a "pantomime" that indicated his ship had been crushed by ice. The same group of Inuit later found a campsite where they discovered evidence of cannibalism. There were approximately thirty bodies and graves at this campsite. Inuit stories of the site are divided on its location: some place it at Terror Bay, suggesting that this was the "hospital camp"; others place it further southeast, on the mainland near Starvation Cove. At some point a group of men, perhaps from the "hospital camp," attempted to return to the ships: in 1859, Francis McClintock's search expedition found a sledge with two bodies in it, pointing north toward the abandoned ships, at Erebus Bay; he believed that these two men were left behind because they were too weak to continue (269–70). Graves, skeletons, and personal items were found by British and American search parties and by Inuit along the coast of King William Island and at the mouth of the Back River, suggesting that the final survivors crossed the Simpson Strait by boat to the Adelaide Peninsula, where they finally died.

These details emerged between 1854 and 1869 as search parties uncovered remains and interviewed Inuit. In 1854, Dr. John Rae met an Inuk named Innookpoozheejook who wore a gold cap band.[8] He told Rae that the cap band came from the place where "a large party of 'Kabloonans' [non-Inuit] [...] had died of starvation" (*Arctic Correspondence* 274).

Rae bought the cap band but did not believe that the story was about the Franklin expedition, thinking he was far from where Franklin's ships had disappeared. A month later, Rae arrived in Repulse Bay, where Inuit were waiting with British relics to sell. They told him stories that had been circulating for a few years, which he collated for the Admiralty and the Hudson's Bay Company. Rae's report told of the meeting between Inuit and white men at Washington Bay and included the shocking allegation that Franklin and his men had, according to Inuit, resorted to cannibalism. When Rae returned to England that fall, he was ostracized for believing second-hand Inuit testimony and for daring to suggest that British naval heroes would commit cannibalism.[9]

Jane Franklin responded to Rae's report and the Admiralty's refusal to dispatch further investigative expeditions by enlisting Charles Dickens to refute the allegations of cannibalism and by raising funds for a private expedition to search King William Island. Lady Franklin recruited Francis Leopold McClintock, a veteran of three search expeditions, and in 1859, McClintock and his men searched King William Island and found the first "hard" evidence of what had happened. McClintock heard Inuit stories of a ship being wrecked and sinking and of white men falling down dead as they marched toward the Back River (262–63) and discovered caches of artifacts left by the retreating men, but it was his second-in-command, William Hobson, who made the most famous discovery, locating the Victory Point record. When McClintock returned to England, the issue of what happened to Franklin and his men was considered officially resolved. The Victory Point record provided the date of Franklin's death, exonerating him personally from accusations of cannibalism. Inuit testimony, when it was believed, and the trail of artifacts retrieved from the King William Island coastline told of a disastrous attempt to reach the Back River and convinced most people that there were no living survivors. McClintock was knighted for his discoveries. Lady Franklin turned her attention to proving that her husband's expedition had completed the final link of the Passage and to commemorating him through a public monument. Isolated calls for more searches—for buried written records or for final survivors—were for the most part ignored.

A few later expeditions, most notably Charles Francis Hall's of 1860–62 and 1864–69, unearthed new details. Hall interviewed Inuit who had found the mutilated corpses; while this confirmed Rae's reports of cannibalism, the assertions were largely ignored in Britain. In the 1980s, Owen Beattie found skeletons on King William Island that had been intentionally dismembered, providing scientific support for Inuit stories of retreating men carrying human body parts with them as a portable food source (59–62). Hall also recorded a number of Inuit stories concerning contact with Franklin expedition survivors; he, unlike many of his contemporaries, took Inuit stories seriously as evidence of what happened and ensured that these stories entered the archive.[10] These records are invaluable, since Hall recorded Inuit memories of contact and discovery shortly after they occurred. As we will see, however, Hall's notes often include factual inconsistencies, making it impossible to precisely determine where and when some events occurred.

Certain events are relatively indisputable: Franklin's ships wintered at Beechey Island in 1845–46, where three men died; they traveled to the northwest coast of King William Island and were beset by ice on September 12, 1846; in May 1847, an exploring party left the ships and deposited a message; on June 11, 1847, Franklin died; by the time the ships were abandoned in late April 1848, an additional twenty men had died. Sometime between 1848 and 1850, a group of survivors met Inuit near Washington Bay and their leader told Inuit that their ship (or ships) had been crushed by ice; after this, Inuit found bodies at a campsite that suggested some men had resorted to cannibalism; some men attempted to make their way back to the ships; some of the final survivors made their way south, and may have reached the mouth of the Back River before finally dying. Inuit stories fill in many details about how the survivors looked and what they did: because of language and cultural differences, these stories tend to provide more qualitative than quantitative information. But gaps remain. While one can hypothesize about why Crozier ordered his men to abandon their ships and why he decided to head toward the Back River, one cannot reconstruct his motives. One cannot determine precisely where the campsite with the cannibalized bodies was or what led some men to consume human flesh. One cannot establish a precise timeline of the events that followed the abandonment or a detailed map of where the men went or where each died. These impossibilities mean that the Franklin mystery has both engaged and frustrated historians concerned with determining precisely what happened.

HISTORICAL REMAINS

Sarah Moss has argued that the impossibility of establishing what happened to the expedition is "the key to Franklin's apotheosis"; the lack of written records constitutes a "persistent absence that gives his story its immediacy" (139). According to Moss, the narrative of Franklin's final expedition is unique, not because of the scale of the disaster, but because it "remains fragmented," in contrast to other polar disasters—most notably Franklin's 1819–22 Coppermine expedition and Robert Falcon Scott's 1910–13 Terra Nova expedition—which produced conclusive narratives (139). In the 1820s, Franklin earned the nickname "the man who ate his boots" after the first expedition he commanded was crippled by starvation and culminated in the deaths of eleven of twenty men. Attempting to increase their chances of survival, Franklin's men and officers separated into two groups, with surgeon John Richardson taking responsibility for a party that included midshipman Robert Hood and Iroquois guide Michel Teroahauté. The men began to turn against Teroahauté when he brought them "wolf meat" to eat: they consumed it but later suspected it was human flesh. After Hood died of what Teroahauté claimed was a self-inflicted gunshot to the head, the survivors were convinced Teroahauté was responsible, accused him of murder, and executed him.[11] Richardson's group found Franklin's party (who had been subsisting on lichens and boot leather) and the men, on the verge of death, were saved by Dene hunters. What differentiates the Coppermine expedition from Franklin's final expedition is that what happened to the Coppermine expedition became widely and conclusively known. When Franklin returned to England, his published account of his travels—a "Gothic tale of adventure, starvation, cannibalism, and murder in a harsh and brooding land," according to Pierre Berton—cemented his fame (*Grail* 74).[12] Robert Falcon Scott's Terra Nova expedition, like Franklin's final one, ended in failure and death, but what happened to it, like Franklin's first expedition, became known. Scott and four others reached the South Pole on January 17, 1912 only to discover that Roald Amundsen's party had arrived there a month earlier. Two men died on the return journey, and the remaining three set up camp to wait out a blizzard; trapped by the snow, they ran out of supplies and died. In November 1912, a search party found the men's journals and final letters in their tent; these documents make what happened clear. Many of these papers are on display at the Scott Polar Research Institute in Cambridge and examining them provides visitors with a sense of narrative closure and emotional catharsis, elements lacking when one examines the personal items retrieved from the Franklin expedition, also on display.

　The impossibility of establishing precisely what happened to Franklin's men has not stopped popular historians from attempting to reconstruct events. Even David Woodman's impressive *Unravelling the Franklin Mystery*, which makes extensive use of Inuit oral history to challenge standard accounts of what happened, is ultimately a reconstruction. The impetus behind these works is what Walter Benjamin terms historicism, the attempt to tell "the sequence of events like the beads of a rosary" (255). While "historicism contents itself with establishing a causal connection between various moments in history," historical materialism breaks with linear causality and instead seeks to approach the past by seizing "hold of a memory as it flashes up at a moment of danger" and grasping "the constellation which his own era has formed with a definite earlier one" (Benjamin 263, 255, 263): in other words, historical materialism takes into account the historian's present affective and ethical engagements with the past. By interrogating the moments when the past erupts into the present, one may come closer to articulating how the past was experienced.

Greg Dening takes up Benjamin's argument, implying that the methodological protocols of historical materialism might illuminate histories of intercultural performances. Dening, critiquing how "being accurate became equated with being true and [...] history became equated with historical facts," distinguishes between historical actuality and historical reality: "By 'actuality' I mean what happened as it is known for its balance of the circumstantial and the determined, in its typicality as well as its particularity, known for its multivalent meanings. By 'reality' I mean what happened as it is reductively known, by its determinants, known in its simplicity of meaning, set in some hierarchy of acceptability" (*Performances* 55, 60–61). Dening's emphasis on "actuality" over "reality" resonates with Benjamin's concept of historical materialism in its call for complexity rather than reduction, for connections over causality. Dening terms his method "ethnographic history," defining it as "an attempt to represent the past as it was actually experienced in such a way that we understand both its ordered and disordered natures" (*Bligh* 5). My decision to ask how what happened to the Franklin expedition was understood and experienced rather than what happened to the expedition is very much inspired by Dening's plea to represent the past as it was actually experienced, rather than reduce it to a linear, singular narrative. Shifting the question, from "what happened?" to "how was what happened experienced and why was it remembered?" provides an opening through which one might address the material, historical, and psychological conditions that determine how performative remains are preserved and acknowledges that the remains of past performances are always and necessarily fragmented.

Historical writing, according to Dening, constructs a relationship between the past and present through the act of interpreting remains:

> The relics of the past, the only ways in which the past survives, *are* cargo to all the present moments that follow [...] All relics of the past, even if they disappear

with the note of a song or the sight of a mime, have a double quality. They are marked with the meanings of the occasion of their origins and they are always translated into something else for the moments they survive. Historical consciousness is always built out of that double meaning. (*Performances* 46–47)

It is only by both identifying the process through which the remains—the cargo—of the past were collected and preserved and acknowledging one's complicity in this process that one can make sense out of the double nature of the remains of the past. This recognition—that "history" is constructed by the process of preserving, reading, and interpreting the cargo of the past—is critical when the remains in question are embodied rather than strictly material or archival, as is often the case in examples of performance, particularly intercultural performance.

The Franklin expedition left two forms of cargo: material items—personal effects, corpses, the lone document—that refuse to produce reliable reconstructions, and performances—Jane Franklin's clothing, pantomimed gestures, reenactments—that testify to experiences. These two sets of remains correspond to the distinction Diana Taylor draws in the first chapter of *The Archive and the Repertoire*. Proposing that performances are preserved in two ways, Taylor uses the term "archive" to refer to textual and material remains, the supposedly permanent artifacts of practices, and "repertoire" to refer to the corpus of embodied and socially transmitted memory, to the supposedly ephemeral, and to performance as practice (19–20). Taylor points out that the two systems operate together, sometimes in opposition and sometimes interdependently (21). This is particularly the case when examining how performances endure over time: performances often move from the repertoire to the archive as time passes, eventually becoming "stable" and "permanent" as written records documenting embodied performances, not as lived performance practice. The process of textualizing embodied and gestural performances transforms performances into cargo, into the texted remains of experiences.

This transformation does not constitute a dead end: while one cannot witness the performances of the past, their remains are not necessarily cold, distant documents. Often, as in the case of the story of Lady Franklin's dresses, the performances of the past survive in texts that continue to generate affect, bringing the past into the present and linking readers to the performers of the past, complicating the distinction between archive and repertoire. This engagement with the past occurs, Rebecca Schneider suggests, through the body: the tension between archive and repertoire, between remains and reappearance, can be resolved by rethinking how the

body stores memory and knowledge. Implicitly placing competing definitions of performance—as "twice-behaved behavior" (Schechner 36) and
as that which "cannot be saved, documented, or otherwise participate in
the circulation of representations" (Phelan 146)—in dialogue, Schneider
claims one can understand performance *as* an act of remaining by questioning the logic of an archive that defines performance as "that which
does not remain" (100) and by admitting that remains "do not have to be
isolated to the document, in the object, to bone versus flesh" (103). The
ability of the body to both transmit and store memory, to function as a site
of both remaining and reemergence, is central to Schneider's argument
that performance is both repetition and disappearance:

> This body, given to performance, is arguably engaged with disappearance
> chiasmatically—not only disappearing but resiliently eruptive, remaining
> through performance like so many ghosts at the door marked "disappeared".
> In this sense performance becomes itself through messy and eruptive reap-
> pearance, challenging, via the performance trace, any neat antinomy between
> appearance and disappearance [...] Indeed performance in this light can be
> figured as both the act of remaining and a means of disappearance. (103)

Schneider argues that the body is not only a vessel that transmits social
memory, but also an archival repository where memory is catalogued and
stored.

Schneider illustrates Taylor's assertion that performance is not only
a "vital [act] of transfer, transmitting social knowledge, memory, and a
sense of identity through reiterated" behavior" but also "functions as an
epistemology [...] a way of knowing" (2–3). While Schneider's argument
emerges from questions raised by contemporary performance art and
Taylor's from those raised by performances that endure in the repertoire,
the questions raised by performances that responded to the loss of the
Franklin expedition are a bit different. In the cases I examine, the repertoire has been contained, over time, by the archive; bodies no longer transmit these performances or the embodied knowledge they once contained.
This project attempts to address a question latent in both Schneider's and
Taylor's arguments: how can one locate and recuperate the repertoire—the
embodied performances of the past—in and from the archive? Engaging
with this question allows one to reflect upon the moments at which performances were created and at which they were "translated into something
else for the moments they survive" (Dening, *Performances* 46–47). By
locating moments when embodied, performative remains persist in the

archive, one may identify how the past "flashes" up in the present through the mechanisms of affect, taking up the challenge posed by Benjamin's concept of historical materialism.

THE EFFIGY AND THE GHOST

Many were affected by the Franklin expedition's disappearance: the sailors who abandoned their ships to trek south, the men who searched for them, the families who waited at home, the Inuit encountered by survivors, the British public who imagined the end of the expedition in cannibalism. Why focus on performances—arguably ephemeral events—as the remains of these experiences of loss?[13] I have alluded to the idea that theater and performance history, because of their disciplinary concerns with interpreting the embodied remains of the past, provide methodological frames for addressing how performative remains endure differently than material remains. But this leaves the question of why performance emerged, as I argue it did, as particularly suited to expressing the experiences of loss that followed the disappearance of the Franklin expedition? Examining the structural parallels between psychoanalytic theories of loss—melancholia, mourning, and trauma in particular—and definitions of performance as an act of substitution or surrogation reveals that the psychological losses that resulted from the disappearance of the Franklin expedition were expressed and experienced through the same structures of substitution and surrogation that characterize theatrical performance. This contention becomes particularly apparent in tracing the appearances of two theatrical figures—the effigy and the ghost—in performances that responded to the expedition's disappearance.

The term loss "functions as a placeholder," naming "what is apprehended by discourses and practices of mourning, melancholia, nostalgia, sadness, trauma, and depression" (Eng and Kazanjian 2). Loss, unlike absence, is always "situated on a historical level and is the consequence of particular events" (LaCapra 712). Because loss emerges historically, it is always retroactive: "Something of the past always remains, if only as a haunting presence" (LaCapra 700). However loss is practiced or enacted, it demands either the recovery of the lost object or its replacement by a surrogate (LaCapra 708). The desire for recovery and the quest for replacement are aligned with practices of melancholia and mourning as responses to catastrophic losses. In "Mourning and Melancholia," Freud distinguishes between these two responses not because of their causes—as both can emerge from similar experiences—or their symptoms—as extreme mourning resembles melancholia—but because of their duration. While mourning moves toward completion, melancholia is marked by a continued engagement with the lost object: "in melancholia the past remains steadfastly alive in the present" (Eng and Kazanjian 4). Linking loss to trauma, LaCapra writes that melancholia is an "arrested process in which the depressed, self-berating, and traumatized self [...] is possessed by the past;" whereas mourning brings "the possibility of engaging trauma and achieving a reinvestment in [...] life" (713).

LaCapra notes that mourning is characterized by "working through" whereas melancholia is characterized by "acting out" (713). In melancholia, the individual refuses to seek a substitute for the lost object and cannot move forward, instead he "acts out" his relationship to an object that shifts from being lost to being absent, abstract rather than tangible. In mourning, the individual re-enters life after "working through" the trauma of loss and transferring desire from the lost object to a substitute. Lady Franklin's decision to don bright clothing to protest the Admiralty's declaration of her husband's death is an instance of melancholic acting out: she refused to accept her husband's death and move forward as a widow, instead acting out a relationship to her living husband. Later, after her husband's death was confirmed, she mourned his death, working through her loss by commemorating her husband's memory and moving on to new engagements with life. Linking "acting-out" and "working-through" to performance, LaCapra suggests that melancholia and mourning become visible through action. In melancholic "acting-out," the past is "performatively regenerated or relived as if it were fully present rather than represented in memory and inscription, and it hauntingly returns as the repressed" (716). In contrast, mourning performs "a relation to the past that involves recognizing its difference from the present—simultaneously remembering and taking leave of or actively forgetting it" (LaCapra 716).

While Freud and LaCapra tend to pathologize melancholia, Eng and Kazanjian suggest it can be a productive response to loss. Drawing attention to Freud's later acknowledgement in *The Ego and the Id* that "the work of mourning is not possible without melancholia" (qtd. in Eng and Kazanjian 4), they suggest that by "mourn[ing] the remains of the past hopefully" and engaging in a "creative process, animating history for future significations as well as alternate empathies," one can establish the "acting and ongoing relationship with history" that is described by Walter Benjamin as historical materialism (1). The processes LaCapra describes—of melancholia generating a continual engagement with the past and of mourning causing the individual to seek surrogates through which the past can be set aside—emerge as culturally, historically, and psychologically productive in performances that responded to the disappearance of the Franklin expedition. This becomes apparent when one considers structural parallels between mourning and melancholia, theatrical processes of substitution and surrogation, and the figures of the ghost and the effigy.

In order to address how theatrical substitution addresses and stages loss, one must first redefine mimesis as the basis of theatrical representation. Alice Rayner makes the bold argument that mimesis is not the ability to imitate, as Aristotle suggested, but is more precisely the capacity to substitute; the act of substitution "constitutes not only an essential element of theatricality but also its centrality both to the representation of the world and to the consequent behavior that orders the world" (129). Rayner contends that "it is the very capacity to substitute one thing for another, to reconstitute a lost object in a present object, to transform the material objects of the world into imaginary objects, and the imaginary into the material, that characterizes the foundation of mimesis. This sense of mimesis is not a matter of visible reflection or mirroring [. . .] It is, rather, the point in a psychic topography where the experience of loss generates the demand for a substitute" (129). Theatrical mimesis is based not on the imitation of actions but on the ability to substitute one object (such as the actor's body) for a missing object (a character). Substitution produces doubles: words, images, characters, and objects that both are and are not what they pretend to be; Rayner calls this the "paradox of the double (consciousness)" (115). An object on stage, as theatergoers intuit, "is never not itself, yet it is rarely wholly itself. This double negative—not not itself, yet also other than itself—is the fundamentally theatrical element of an epistemological stance" (115).

Rayner expresses an idea that feels familiar to theater scholars. It is, however, remarkable for its scope: Rayner argues that *all* theater acts to fill perceived losses through substitution, and that this process of substitution is essential to how theater creates meaning. The significance of her argument in relation to the Franklin expedition emerges in her description of what happens when the illusion of theater brushes against the reality of death. Rayner illustrates this using the example of the posthumous performance of Tadeusz Kantor's *Today is My Birthday* in which his chair—that he famously sat in, on stage, during performances—was present on stage throughout the performance:

> While the double is present, the reality of loss is affectively inaccessible. [. . .] The desire to keep others alive, even while knowing they are gone, gives substitutes—the mimetic doubles made by metonymy, displacement, and

metaphor—their power to preserve the imaginary attachment. The double provides the site of return, a site for memory as well as a site of denial, a site to which ghosts return again and again. The knowledge of his death and the experience of the loss are separate even when the empty chair marks Kantor's former place. It is not until the substitute is removed from the stage that the chair becomes fully empty, when the knowledge and the experience coincide. It is through the mimetic double that the imaginary attachment is maintained. (131–32)

Rayner's reading of Kantor's performance resonates with Jane Franklin's unusual choice of clothing and many other performances engendered by the disappearance of the Franklin expedition. Lady Franklin's pink and green dress functions as Kantor's chair, holding open a place for the missing body, even while it acknowledges—because of its implied protest—the likelihood of his death. The dress makes the double—the still-living Franklin—present and allows for temporary denial of his absence. This eeriness, the ghostly doubling that Rayner sees as essential to the work of the substitute, is central to her definition of mimesis.

Memories of the Franklin expedition often surface as ghost stories. Ghosts or frightening spirits play important roles in Inuit stories of encountering Franklin survivors. One example occurs in Cathy Towtongie's recollection of her grandmother's story of Inuit seeing the men: "They were a raggedy bunch and their clothing was not well made. Their skins were black and the meat above their teeth was gone; their eyes were gaunt. Were they *tuurngait*—spirits—or what?" (qtd. in Eber xi). Ghosts also appear in British theatrical representations of the expedition. A theatrical equivalent to Towtongie's story arose in Charles Dickens's performance in the 1857 drama *The Frozen Deep*: the play generated a heightened affective response because spectators experienced the double vision Rayner describes, seeing the ghost of the dead Franklin in the living Dickens's performance.

Marvin Carlson argues that ghosts frequently appear in the theater: in actors' performances, in repertoires, in design choices. Theater is "the repository of cultural memory, but, like the memory of each individual, it is also subject to continual adjustment and modification as the memory is recalled in new circumstances and contexts" (2). The reason theater activates communal memory is that it recycles a culture's past through performance: ghosts appear when audience members recognize that they are seeing what they have seen before. Rayner goes further than Carlson, arguing that theatrical ghosting is not merely the citation of past performances, but that the ghost is critical to the phenomenological structure of the theatrical event: "The theater itself gives appearance to the unseen, the hidden, and to the chronic return of the theatrical event from nothing into something. Theater is the specific site where appearance and disappearance reproduce the relations between the living and the dead, not as a form of representation, but as a form of consciousness [...] In this sense, the ghost is not at all a metaphor for something else but an aspect of theatrical practice" (xvi–xvii). Rayner intentionally defines the theatrical ghost in ambiguous terms: she argues that "making full use of the terms *ghost* or *haunting* involves [...] their remaining in the realm of uncertainty [...] The ghost is known only by its affective presence, when one asks from a state of wonder, What am I seeing, how does this happen, where is this coming from, this 'thing' happening before my eyes? If words are successful in naming the ghost, there is no ghost" (xxiii). When the Franklin expedition disappeared, it left both remains and ghosts: eventually these ghosts called out to be acknowledged, represented, and released. Rayner argues that in the theater, and I would argue this is the case in many nontheatrical performances as well, the dead "speak through us even if they don't speak directly to us"; as a mode of perception, theater produces an encounter with the dead, which is "both necessary and inevitable" can only be done "'in effigy,' the second time around. It is then that the fake, the substitute, the double, achieves its truth, and ghosts are released from their hauntings" (184–85). The appearance of ghosts in the performances considered here draw attention to the lingering engagement with the past and the inability to successfully substitute that characterize melancholia. Rayner's concept of mimesis—the ability and desire to substitute present objects for lost ones—links the performances that responded to the Franklin expedition's loss to one another. Viewing mimesis not as imitation but as substitution is furthermore essential to understanding how performances respond to cultural losses and function as a form of affective historical knowledge.

Joseph Roach, like Rayner, argues that performance is fundamentally a substitution, offering "a substitute for [...] an elusive entity that it is not but that it must vainly aspire both to embody and to replace" (3). Roach claims that surrogation—a particular form of substitution—allows an individual or a group to address losses that arise as a result of "actual or perceived vacancies [...] in the network of relations that constitute the social fabric" (2). The process "rarely if ever succeeds" because "collective memory works selectively, imaginatively, and often perversely" (2). Problems arise when a surrogate is unable to fill a role completely or surpasses the lost one he is replacing, when a surrogate is a divisive choice, or even because the process of surrogation is often an uncanny one. Roach explains: "The very uncanniness of the process of surrogation, which tends to disturb the complacency of all thoughtful encumbents, may provoke many unbidden emotions, ranging from mildly incontinent sentimental-ism to raging paranoia" (2). The heightened emotions generated by sur-rogation explain Eleanor Gell's response to Jane Franklin's pink and green dresses: the dresses marked Jane, the public representative of her husband's interests, as an eerie surrogate for him.

Surrogation allows a culture to not only respond to loss but also to define itself in relation to other groups. Roach argues that circum-Atlantic societies "invented themselves by performing their pasts in the presence of others. They could not perform themselves, however, unless they also performed what and who they thought they were not" (5). Candidates for surrogation are "tested at the margins of a culture to bolster the fiction that it has a core" (6). Situating surrogation as a marginal phenomenon allows one to consider how performances demonstrate the range of ways that British and Inuit cultures not only responded to the loss through perfor-mance but also used performance to situate themselves in relation to one another. The disappearance of the Franklin expedition generated consider-able cultural anxiety for the British, particularly because of the allegations of cannibalism and the fact that Inuit—not British—discovered what hap-pened. For Inuit, the appearance of strangers in their land, the discovery of caches of valuable European goods and mutilated corpses, and the seasonal changes that appeared to come with the arrival of the strangers prompted social and economic changes that necessitated and produced performances of cultural self-definition.

Rayner claims theatrical substitution works through the figure of the ghost and processes of ghosting or haunting; Roach makes the parallel suggestion that surrogation frequently operates through the figure of the effigy and the process of effigying. Roach begins by considering effigy as a verb meaning "to evoke an absence, to body something forth" (36). The effigy produced by this process "fills by means of surrogation a vacancy created by the absence of an original" (36). It is most productive, most eerie, and most uncanny when it is a living embodiment: "Such effigies are made by performances. They consist of a set of actions that hold open a place in memory into which many different people may step accord-ing to circumstances and occasions" (36). Roach uses a range of examples linked with funerary and end-of-life practices to illustrate how the effigy, like Rayner's ghost, gains power at the margins of life and death. The effigy holds open a place where past events are remembered and reacti-vated, brought to temporary life; like ghosts, effigies emerge at the margins of life and death, when personal and cultural losses become profound or unmanageable. Through substitution and surrogation—similar, often overlapping, but not interchangeable phenomenon—the ghost and the effigy become visible in performance.

(INTER) CULTURAL PERFORMANCES

In the years that followed Franklin's 1845 disappearance, the Arctic functioned as what Mary Louise Pratt terms a "contact zone," a social space "where disparate cultures meet, clash, and grapple with each other, often in highly asymmetrical relations of domination and subordination —like colonialism, slavery, or their aftermaths" (4). By using the term contact zone rather than frontier or colony, Pratt "invoke[s] the spatial and temporal copresence of subjects previously separated by geographic and historical disjunctures" and foregrounds "the interactive, improvisational dimensions of colonial encounters so easily ignored or suppressed by diffusionist accounts of conquest and domination" (7). Euro-American incursions into the Arctic do not, until at least the early twentieth century, fit neatly into existing models of colonial dominance. The Euro-American presence was neither pervasive nor permanent; there was no attempt until the early twentieth century to exercise political control in the region (Fossett, *In Order* xv). Even the Hudson's Bay Company, which had the longest permanent presence in the region, kept its trading posts to the south of Inuit territories until the early 1900s; the company's traders had some contact with Inuit but did little to change Inuit life. The Arctic was not imagined as a source of material or human resources: the British obsession with Arctic exploration was discursively constructed as a purely scientific enterprise, not explicitly linked to the colonization of the region's peoples or to the extraction of natural resources. The relative lack of Euro-American economic and political interest produced social relations between Inuit and *qallunaat* (non-Inuit) visitors that were substantially different from those between Euro-Americans and other indigenous groups.

The archival remains of the performances considered in this study overwhelmingly reflect European and American perspectives. A range of attitudes toward race and culture appear in these texts: while some erase the role Inuit played in the search for the Franklin expedition, others make a concerted effort to represent Inuit actions and worldviews. Even when primary documents attempt to represent Inuit performances "truthfully," the fact remains that they only allow proximity, never complete access, to what actually happened. Greg Dening articulates the problems inherent in interpreting intercultural performances of the past through such documents:

> The relics of the Native Polynesian past have all been transformed into relics of the Stranger European past. There is nothing—not a written down experience, not a myth, or a legend, not a material artifact, not an archaeological site—that does not, by the expressions of it, by the collection and preservation of it, and/or by the interpretation of it and inclusion of it in a Stranger's discourse, require critical reading to separate the Stranger's cargo from the Native's past. (*Performances* 57)

The critical reading practice Dening calls for—to separate the Native performance from the Stranger's record—is a fraught one. It is a skeptical reading practice: one must keep in mind that records of performances—by British and Inuit performers—may always include changes, erasures, and elisions, incorporated accidentally or intentionally, noticeably or silently. It is tricky to establish reception, particularly because a single performance always engenders various and contradictory responses at the time of performance; the responses that survive—in newspaper reviews or personal responses, for example—always only represent a sample of the range of responses. When reception occurs across cultural and linguistic borders, the problems become more pronounced, particularly when differing worldviews produce contradictory understandings of epistemology and history. It is essential to acknowledge that British and American tendencies to privilege written documents over orally transmitted knowledge during the search for Franklin and the epistemological and cultural ruptures that resulted from twentieth-century attempts to colonize Inuit undoubtedly mean that some indigenous stories of performance have been lost over time. Furthermore, applying theoretical paradigms that help to illuminate British and American responses to loss through performance—such as psychoanalytic theories of loss, semiotic performance codes, or the operations of surrogation and substitution—often fails to account for the cultural and historical specificities of Inuit cultures or for the temporary, hybrid communities that developed when British, Americans, and Inuit lived closely together. As a nonindigenous scholar attempting to account for how the loss of the Franklin expedition was understood in British, American, and Inuit cultures by examining the archived traces of "ephemeral" performances, it is necessary that I proceed with caution in developing the critical reading practice Dening calls for. Despite these challenges, meticulously picking through the archive and carefully reading nonindigenous archives for signs of lingering indigenous presence, can allow one to both consider the disappearance of the Franklin expedition as an intercultural crisis and develop ways to critically unpack performance remains to reveal how cultures of the past communicated through embodied acts.

David Woodman and Dorothy Eber have each, in works that privilege Inuit oral history, implicitly argued that the story of what happened to the Franklin expedition is a narrative of intercultural contact. In this book, I attempt to take their assertions further, arguing that the story is not only one of intercultural contact but specifically one of intercultural performance. Intercultural performance—a term I use broadly to include not only performances incorporating performers from different cultures but also performances by one culture for another, performances in a monocultural environment that incorporate another culture's conventions, and performances explicitly about intercultural contact—was critical to how the loss of the expedition was understood. Embodied performance was not only a way to work across linguistic and cultural differences, although this certainly made it an effective tool when translation was impossible, but was absolutely appropriate to the content of what was being communicated. The experiences being communicated were ambiguous and ambivalent: while words and linear narratives would "fix" these experiences, erasing the ambiguity that characterized them, gestural and embodied performances were capable of expressing and preserving these very qualities.

While the chapters that follow focus on performances that responded to the loss of the Franklin expedition, they also trace how intercultural relations operated between 1845 and 1870. When Inuit met Franklin survivors as they traveled south, the British—who had dismissed indigenous knowledge, choosing to retain their own cultural practices—found themselves dependent on Inuit to pass on information and to provide food: Inuit were ultimately unable to help the large detachment survive. The first and second chapters consider how British search parties initially attempted to transform the Arctic—as Franklin's men might have—into an extension of domestic space but quickly realized their reliance upon Inuit knowledge and presence. British and Inuit adopted one another's cultural practices, adapting to new situations by learning from one another. Charles Francis Hall, who plays a role in the third, fourth, and fifth chapters, went further than any earlier explorer in adapting to Inuit culture by living among them; his close contact with Inuit gave him access to oral histories of encounters with Franklin's men, which he recorded for American and British readers. At the same time, British and American search parties brought discursive constructions of Inuit as "other"—as savages to be exterminated, as children to be civilized, or as noble savages to be emulated—to the Arctic with them. Ideological debates concerning race and culture reached a crisis point when John Rae's 1854 report of cannibalism, mixed with consternation that the British had failed to find Franklin's men and Inuit had succeeded, reached the British public. Popular constructions of the "friendly Eskimo" gave way to racist fantasies, epitomized in Charles Dickens's responses to Rae in *Household Words*, which overwrote Inuit oral history with rhetorical fervor. During the search for Franklin, space seemed to open up for intercultural understanding; ultimately, however, Dickens's views prevailed and Inuit were all but erased from the narrative of what happened to Franklin and his men. Indigenous accounts disappeared from the "official" record, overwritten by narratives that reiterated British cultural superiority over indigenous others.

The book begins by examining shipboard theater on the British search vessels, arguing that it not only maintained morale but also prepared men for the specific demands of the search for the missing men. In "Disciplining Nostalgia in the Navy; or, Harlequin in the Arctic," I argue that shipboard theater practices helped sailors internalize discipline, contained nostalgia for home by encouraging men to see their fellow sailors as family, and demonstrated that although the Arctic appeared to be a forbidding, dangerous, foreign territory, it could be transformed into a friendly, familiar space through theatrical interventions. The next chapter, "'The Sly Fox': Reading Indigenous Presence," focuses on a specific stage direction included in the pantomime *Zero, or Harlequin Light*, which was performed on a British search ship in 1851. The play contains a stage direction in which a fox is transformed into the ship's Inuk translator Qalasirssuaq. This chapter argues that the stage direction functions as a symptomatic point, revealing how British attitudes about racial difference were shaped by contact with Inuit and suggesting that Qalasirssuaq emerges as a liminal subject, negotiating the boundaries between indigenous and European modes of knowledge and behavior. This chapter complicates the argument that shipboard theater fulfilled a disciplinary function by exploring how theater ruptured the boundary between "civilized" and "savage" cultures, revealing that this distinction was constructed upon unstable and contradictory assumptions about racial and cultural difference.

The next three chapters draw on the mass of material produced by Charles Francis Hall during the decade he spent living among Inuit.

"Going Native: 'Playing Inuit,' 'Becoming Savage,' and Acting Out Franklin" consider how Hall carefully navigated how he "went native," eating and dressing like an Inuk but refusing to take part in Inuit spiritual practices or to engage in interracial sexual relationships with Inuit women. By doing this, Hall attempted to demonstrate that one could "go native" without "becoming a savage," implying through his acts of surrogation that Franklin and his men also could have survived by living among Inuit and that their imagined survival did not imply that they had transgressed cultural norms by committing cannibalism. "Aglooka's Ghost: Performing Embodied Memory" focuses on Hall's account of watching an Inuk man, Owwer, explain his encounter with a group of Franklin survivors at Washington Bay by reproducing the gestural performance of the group's leader Aglooka. Hall's account forces a critical analysis of the cultural, historical, and ethical implications of questions about archive and affect, allowing a close consideration of how gestural performance functions as a form of memory and how performance is transformed when it is documented in the archive.

The next chapter, "The Last Resource: Witnessing the Cannibal Scene," links Hall to another figure deeply invested in the effort to respond to the loss of the Franklin expedition through performance: Charles Dickens. This chapter begins by considering Dr. John Rae's report, based on Inuit testimony, that Franklin's men resorted to cannibalism in their final days. Dickens responded by publishing a series of articles in *Household Words* that condemned Inuit witnesses and located cannibalism as a phenomenon that occurred among debased, uncivilized others. Examining the debate reveals a deep anxiety concerning the relationship between print rhetoric and oral transmission: this anxiety becomes apparent when one contrasts Dickens's responses with an Inuk woman's story, recorded by Hall, of stealing a watch from the body of an officer (who likely committed cannibalism) and the impact that replicating the officer's desecration of a body had on the woman. The woman's story preserved the experiences of Franklin's men that Dickens's articles attempted to erase. The final chapter, "The Designated Mourner: Charles Dickens Stands in for Franklin," argues that the melodrama *The Frozen Deep*, performed in 1857, responded to the impossibility of conclusively determining what happened to the Franklin expedition by staging a coherent, though fictional, account of what happened. This chapter argues that Dickens, performing the lead role, offered himself up as a surrogate for the missing men, overwriting their real but invisible deaths with a highly affective death scene that provided spectators with an event to witness and an emotionally comprehensible loss to mourn. Taken together, the chapters trace one trajectory of how the loss of the Franklin expedition was experienced, moving from the optimistic search efforts to the realization the expedition was lost, from nostalgia for the navy's glorious past, to melancholic longing for the missing men, to mourning and closure.

1. Disciplining Nostalgia in the Navy; or, Harlequin in the Arctic ❧

Officers and sailors crowd anxiously onto the upper deck of HMS *Assistance*, a British vessel in search of Franklin. It is January 9, 1851, and the ship is frozen in pack ice off the coast of Griffith Island. Two months have passed since the men saw daylight. The thick awning covering the ship's deck provides some protection from the weather, but when the wind picks up, it is almost impossible to hear what's happening. Condensation rising from the men's mouths and bodies makes it difficult to see what's happening as well. Despite these annoyances, the men and officers of the *Assistance*, *Resolute*, *Intrepid*, and *Pioneer*—the four ships under Horatio Austin's command—have gathered on the *Assistance* for an evening of theater. During winter 1850–51, plays were put on biweekly, performed on a stage framed by a canvas proscenium arch, decorated with a painted crown and faux Doric columns, and flanked by snow statues (Markham 76–77; *Arctic Miscellanies* 120–22). While the men eagerly anticipated any event that broke the monotony of shipboard life, the evening of January 9 was special because it marked the premiere performance of *Zero, or Harlequin Light*, an original pantomime written by Charles Ede, the *Assistance*'s assistant surgeon.

Zero, or Harlequin Light opened with a magnificent but all-too-familiar image: a drop scene depicted HMS *Assistance* "moored to a land floe, and sustaining severe pressure from the heavy masses of pack ice, which [...] flow[ed] past with fearful rapidity" (*Arctic Miscellanies* 206). Strong blue light "*thrown across the stage*" added eeriness to the image of ice crushing the fictional *Assistance*; discordant music played on drums and whistles aurally evoked the ominous sound of drifting ice colliding with a ship (Ede 132). The title character Zero entered first, wearing a "full frosted wig, surmounted by a fanciful crown; long flowing beard; loose white robes with large sleeves, icicles hanging from different parts" and walk-ing "*majestically up and down the stage*" (Ede 131).[1] Zero's opening speech told audience members of British sailors who threatened to upset his icy dominion: "With papers, plays, and soirees they defy,/Up to this moment my supremacy;/With magic lantern and the bal masque,/They think to cheat me" (Ede 132). One can imagine the delight of audience members when they heard Zero describe "boisterous Tars" wintering at the same location and entertaining themselves in the same way as themselves.

The surviving script indicates that the pantomime followed the three-part structure that was conventional at the time—opening, transformation sequence, and harlequinade. The opening revolves around the adventures of an ostensibly fictional search party seeking missing countrymen in the Arctic. They are opposed by Zero and his servants, who attempt to foil their search attempts, and are protected by the benevolent spirit Daylight, who counters Zero's machinations. The opening reaches its crisis point when Zero enters the sailors' tent, planning to freeze them to death. At this moment, Harlequin appears and transforms Daylight into Columbine and Zero and his Bear into Pantaloon and Clowns. The harlequinade that follows appears loosely structured, including a pas de deux danced by Harlequin and Columbine, pranks and one-liners delivered by Pantaloon and the Clowns, and a sentimental song sung by the North Polar Star. The pantomime concludes with one of the Clowns encouraging audience members to do their duty during the spring sledge searches.

Although *Zero, or Harlequin Light* is the only surviving example of a play written aboard a Franklin search ship, amateur theater was very popular on search vessels.[2] Theater played a central role in shipboard life: printed advertisements, play reviews in shipboard newspapers,[3] and per-sonal diaries testify to the time and attention devoted to producing, watch-ing, and responding to plays. Reviews indicate that audience members were delighted by *Zero*'s grand scenery, inventive transformation sequences, and the "fun and frolic" of the harlequinade (*Arctic Miscellanies* 204–06). One anonymous reviewer commented, in a lighthearted piece of puffery, "We only wish that one of the critics [...] had been present to glance his eye over the brilliant *ensemble*, he would have penned such a graphic and glow-ing description of it as would have immortalized the Arctic Theatre [...] and generations yet unborn would read in the pages of history of the flour-ishing state of the drama at Griffith's Island in the winter of 1851" (*Arctic Miscellanies* 207).[4] While many documents reporting on shipboard theat-ricals convey a strong sense of playfulness, the Royal Arctic Theatre—as it was dubbed—was also very serious business, intervening in shipboard life in surprising ways. Examining the performance practices of the Royal Arctic Theatre with a specific focus on *Zero, or Harlequin Light* demonstrates that these amateur theater practitioners recognized the potential threats to the success of their expedition—boredom, breakdown of discipline, homesickness, fear of the unknown—and used performance as a disciplinary mechanism to contain and transform these threats.

To understand how shipboard theatricals functioned as both "fun and frolic" and a form of Foucauldian discipline, it is helpful to situate these performances in relation to theories of the carnivalesque. Mikhail Bakhtin argues that carnival "celebrated the temporary liberation from the prevailing truth and from the established order [marking] [. . .] the suspension of all hierarchical ranks, privileges, norms and prohibitions" (218). Shipboard theater—because it was separated from ordinary shipboard life, because it allowed sailors and officers to act in silly or inappropriate ways, because it appeared to sanction such transgressions as cross-dressing—provided a time and place for men to safely "let loose" and vent frustrations. As a genre, pantomime also displays specific traits of the carnivalesque, as Millie Taylor explains:

> The ritual and participation of pantomime involve the audience in seemingly subversive activity, while the laughter at physical comedy and the grotesque body as well as at topical and political humour allows the audience to laugh at the joke while becoming aware of its own subjectivity and complicity. Carnival is also the opportunity for symbolic disruption and subversion of authority, but the license for subversion for the period of carnival is granted by the authorities, thus reinforcing the social containment in the seemingly anarchic. (17–18)

Taylor's description of carnival elements in pantomime highlights two points that are central to the argument I propose in this chapter: first, shipboard theater, because it was sanctioned by shipboard authorities, appeared to license transgression but actually subtly regulated behavior; and second, *Zero, or Harlequin Light*, through its representation of audience members' lived experiences, encouraged men to recognize their own subjective agency in making correct choices in daily life. Although theater in general and pantomime in particular appeared to allow an opportunity for misrule to take over, shipboard performances actually supported the structures of authority that governed the ship.

Shipboard theater, as Patrick O'Neill and Mike Pearson have suggested, was encouraged because it maintained morale and prevented cabin fever while ships wintered in the Arctic. I contend that during the search for the Franklin expedition, theater also functioned as what W.T. Lhamon, drawing on Foucault, terms "anticipatory discipline," a form of discipline that "preempt[s] transgression before it might be *thought*" (128). Spring sledge expeditions required men to internalize discipline and behave responsibly with minimal supervision. At the same time, they needed to cooperate with one another, think creatively, and stay motivated: working on plays provided an opportunity to "rehearse" these beneficial behaviors. Furthermore, by providing positive characterizations of sailors involved in a fictional search, *Zero* staged an extended example of how sailors should conduct themselves while away on overland expeditions.

Not only did shipboard theater promote good behavior, it also encouraged appropriate structures of feeling among sailors, disciplining affect. It mitigated homesickness by framing men's attachments to one another, to the Navy, and to the missing men in sentimental, domestic terms. Men were encouraged to imagine themselves as part of two families—the homosocial naval family and the heteronormative domestic family—and to think of their naval family as a temporary replacement for the domestic family.[5] At the same time, homosocial desire had to be carefully contained lest it manifest itself inappropriately: men were simultaneously encouraged to dream of returning to the women they had left behind. The feminine characters in *Zero* demonstrate the tension between these two objectives: they are abstracted and asexual, discouraging men from indulging in longing fantasies, but they also entice men to remember the actual women waiting for them at home.

To recognize the scope of *Zero, or Harlequin Light*'s intervention as anticipatory discipline, one must finally consider the implications of Ede's decision to write a pantomime, a genre characterized by elaborate transformations. The opening's close relationship to off-stage reality situates the play in the liminal and metatheatrical world of Pantoland. Millie Taylor describes Pantoland as the "performance frame within which the story is told by performers who become characters in a story, but who also exist as comic or anarchic personas who comment on the story, the performance, the perceived world of the performers and the audience's lived reality" (91–92). In Pantoland, characters' references to performance conventions, to their own role-playing, and to off-stage reality allow a production to acknowledge that the play is "make-believe" and simultaneously assert its reality for the characters.

In *Zero, or Harlequin Light*, Ede maps shipboard realities onto the dramaturgical conventions of pantomime and the phenomenological matrix of Pantoland in an effort to assuage real anxieties about exploration by relocating them to, then vanquishing them from, the theatrical world. The incursions of the real into the theatrical—the backdrop that represented the ship's actual location, Zero's references to the men's real actions, theatrical reminders of the threats the Arctic posed—emphasize the extent to which the pantomime served as a fantastic mirror of the audience's reality. Through pantomime's generic reliance on transformations, *Zero* demonstrated that sailors could reimagine the actual threats of the Arctic as familiar and harmless figures then imaginatively overcome these threats with perseverance and positive thinking.

REHEARSING DISCIPLINE

Shipboard newspapers and diaries indicate that theater was one of many activities available to men serving in the Arctic. Austin's men could choose from a range of pastimes that provided mental stimulation: they had access to the ship's library, and officers organized classes in navigation, steam technology, seamanship, arithmetic, music, and languages (*Arctic Miscellanies* ix–x). Men in the squadron also hunted bears and captured foxes, setting up trap lines and going on overnight hunting trips. When weather permitted, officers and crew would play sports on the ice. Hobbies like carpentry and even "drawing room occupations, such as fine needlework, knitting, crochet," also filled men's time (Armstrong 492). Crew and petty officers put on improvised theatricals and sketches; these informal productions were often performed below decks for peers, although officers were occasionally invited (O'Neill, "North" 363).

This range of entertainment options begs the question of why formal, rehearsed theater was popular among men and sanctioned and supported by officers. Obviously, putting on plays occupied men's time and this was no minor thing. After ships settled in for winter, chores and work routines were drastically scaled back. This lack of activity could lead to boredom and depression, causing relationships between individuals and ranks to deteriorate. Richard Collinson, commander of HMS *Enterprise*, noted that although tensions arose on every ship, problems were much worse during the northern winter: "There appears to be something in that particular service—either the intense cold, or the poor feeding, or the close confinement between decks for several months without regular employment, or in all these together—that stirs up the bile and promotes bitter feelings comparatively unknown under the ordinary conditions of sea service" (402).[6] Clements Markham makes the link between entertainment, preventing boredom, and shipboard harmony explicit in the following comment: "Such were the amusements which were considered absolutely necessary, and a part of every individual's duty to promote, to drive away the *ennui* that might otherwise have seriously injured both the bodily and mental health of the Expedition" (79). Theater also provided an enjoyable respite from winter monotony, improving morale. This effect is noted by Patrick O'Neill, who calls theater a "morale booster" for audience members and theater producers alike ("North" 356), and by Mike Pearson, who comments that polar theater was "an acknowledged means of maintaining morale [...] provid[ing] those rare occasions when the whole crew could come together" (53). One can argue, however, that although theater kept the men busy and maintained morale, other pastimes did the same. Furthermore, one might play devil's advocate and argue that theater was less productive than other activities, consuming precious materials and time without producing any tangible benefits (unlike, for example, hunting), and debasing men by promoting cross-dressing and drunkenness.

To address shipboard theater's somewhat surprising popularity among both the men and officers, one must consider the possibility that it made a unique contribution to the search for Franklin's missing men. Sherard Osborn makes a comment that supports this contention: "These were our amusements; but the main object of our coming to the North was kept constantly in view, and nothing that labor or ingenuity could devise toward the successful accomplishment of our mission was wanting" (139). Osborn's semicolon creates a physical link between theatrical amusements and the object of the expedition, subtly suggesting that shipboard theater contributed to the "main object" of finding traces of Franklin. To explore this possibility further, one must address two questions: What did the search require of men and officers? How did the production methods and repertoire of the Royal Arctic Theatre prepare men for the search?

The Admiralty did not expect search expeditions to find traces of Franklin by observing shorelines from the safety of their ships, but by conducting overland sledge searches. In the fall and spring, men and officers were divided into parties of six to ten and assigned regions to search. Travel was arduous: the crew man-hauled loads averaging 250 pounds per man, through wet snow and slush, up and down hummocks and across gaping cracks in the ice. On a good day, they kept up a painfully slow pace of one mile an hour; a successful detachment would cover four to five hundred miles of coastline in forty to fifty days (Collinson 374). Sledge travel was physically and psychologically draining, as Osborn indicates in his description of how the landscape taunted his men: "No pen can tell of the unredeemed loneliness of an October evening in this part of the polar world [...]. The very wind scorned courtesy to such a repulsive landscape, and as the stones, before the blast, rattled down the slope of a ravine, it only recalled dead men's bones and motion in a catacomb" (117). Conditions didn't improve when the men were encamped. Markham illuminates just how miserable things were when the "shivering inmates of the tent" awoke in the morning: "the frightful agony of forcing the feet into boots frozen hard as iron was to be undergone, while the breath, which had condensed on the roof of the tent, fell in thick showers over its half-frozen inmates" (84). Markham also describes discovering that bears had destroyed depots, eating food frozen solid day in and day out, constantly watching out for frostbite, and suffering with the pain of snow blindness. Fun and frolic indeed.

The discipline required during overland sledge searches was different than that required when men were aboard the ship: men and officers had to internalize their obligations to the expedition and conduct themselves appropriately with little supervision; cooperation, always important when a ship was at sea, became a matter of life and death; traveling for extended periods of time in changing weather conditions and over uncharted terrain meant that men had to adapt to new circumstances quickly and intelligently. Disciplinary models based on a chain of surveillance, with a commander watching his officers and officers closely watching the crew, could not be sustained when small groups traveled for months at a time under the command of only one or two officers. One can imagine discipline collapsing if, for example, a resentful officer was paired with lazy sailors: once away from the regimentation of the ship, a sledge party could simply refuse to work. To get up each morning and continue the search—despite the conditions, despite knowing that success was unlikely and that failure would probably go undiscovered and thus unpunished—men and officers had to internalize their obligations to their commanders, the Admiralty, and the missing men. They had to identify with their superiors and peers to such an extent that they could not imagine failing to fulfill their duties. For discipline to become internalized, the men had to implicitly condone shipboard authority structures and to trust that obedience served both the greater and their individual good. Shipboard theater acted as a mirror of shipboard authority in much the same way as Pantoland mirrored reality, replicating and reinforcing structures of authority but always situating them as a natural and beneficial part of theatrical production. This can be seen in the organization of theater committees and in the physical layout of shipboard theaters.

Once a ship was in winter quarters, its captain would recruit commissioned officers to form a theater committee. The committee delegated one member, usually a senior officer, to act as theater manager. On the *Assistance* in 1850–51, Captain Ommanney filled this role. Even when the captain was not manager, he usually participated in the committee.[7] Encouraging theatrical productions was good public relations for a captain, creating the impression that he was accessible and caring, but the configuration of the theater committee also legitimated shipboard authority by replicating its hierarchy, particularly when the captain also acted as manager. This was, however, replication with a difference: while the captain and his officers normally doled out orders, work assignments, and punishments, as members of the theater committee they also provided the opportunity for entertainment and fun, showing that power could be exercised to benefit its subjects.

Theater also provided a way to regulate relationships between the ranks. The officers who made up the committee supported the manager by organizing rehearsals and overseeing the construction of set pieces, props, and costumes. When committee members appeared to cooperate with one another, it provided the impression that the ship's leadership was united. This both deterred sailors from mutiny and provided a model of how to work together to achieve a common goal. While theatrical productions facilitated cooperation between officers, they also reinforced distinctions between crew and officers, preventing inappropriate "fraternization." The practice of preparing two plays to be performed on the same evening—one to be performed by officers and one by the crew—ensured that officers spent their leisure time with their fellow officers or in positions of authority over the men. This limited the camaraderie between actors to bonds between men of comparable ranks.

Although the theater committee's control over productions replicated shipboard authority structures, its disciplinary power was subtly enacted. When a ship was at sea or in winter quarters, men were obviously punished if they failed to follow orders, with severity depending on the infraction. In contrast, there is no record of a theater manager punishing men for being late to rehearsal or failing to learn lines. This may indicate that actors were well disciplined, but it is more likely that managers did not need to overtly punish minor transgressions: if, for example, an actor didn't learn his lines and couldn't improvise his way through a scene, he would be rebuked through audience mocking and his fellow actors' frustration during the performance. Conversely, actors were publicly rewarded when they did their jobs well—by learning their parts and making strong choices in characterization, for example—with applause and positive reviews. This equation of disobedience with public embarrassment and obedience with public appreciation naturalized authority, reinforcing the necessity of following directions without requiring the theater manager to exercise his power directly.

Zero, or Harlequin Light provided a model of benevolent authority in its depiction of an officer. The officer who accompanies the three sailors is a bit gruff, but his orders are reasonable.[8] For example, he tells them: "Look smart with the things—don't be all night!" (136), ordering them to hurry to avoid setting up camp in the dark. His role is to take care of his men, ensuring they stay on task and remain healthy. It is he, not a sailor, who notices that one man has developed frostbite: "By Jove! you've got a frostbite on your face;/Rub, rub it well! Lucky it is but slight" (136), suggesting that officers were more vigilant and observant than men when it came to these matters. In the play, the officer's authority is limited by necessity: he messes and sleeps in a tent with his men, reflecting actual practices intended to reduce the amount of weight men dragged. The fictional officer demonstrates that it is less important to rigorously respect rank divisions than to ease the burdens of travel; in so doing, he demonstrates that he can be flexible in applying regulations.[9] The play's paternal officer both provided a model for officers in the audience and reinforced the idea that officers' authority was legitimated by their fundamental care for crew and the expedition.

The spatial arrangement and appearance of shipboard theaters provided a material representation of authority structures, suggesting another way that theater practices were complicit in the necessary process of internalizing discipline. Officers serving in the search for Franklin resurrected staging traditions that had originated thirty years earlier, when Captain Edward Parry's ships became the first British vessels to intentionally winter in the Arctic. Parry, concerned with preventing boredom and flagging morale, organized performances to keep his men occupied during the long winters of 1819–20, 1821–23, and 1824–25. Many commissioned officers involved in the Franklin search, including Horatio Austin, began their careers serving under Parry, and on their own ships revived the production and performance conventions he had developed.

Wintering practices did not evolve much between 1820 and 1850. Parry's staging methods remained practical, and their retention also signified respect for the much-revered commander. Like many naval traditions, theater practices were transmitted orally and experientially; performance records tend to be anecdotal rather than comprehensive, meaning that attempts to describe performances always require some speculation. That said, there were three potential locations for shipboard productions—the upper deck, the lower deck, or outside on the ice—and the upper deck was, by far, the most popular choice. Outdoor performances were only feasible when the weather cooperated. The lower deck was warm, but was spatially divided according to rank: there was no common space where plays could be staged.[10] The upper deck could be cold, but was not connotatively linked to a specific naval rank and offered more space than the lower deck, particularly after spare supplies were moved offshore when the ship was in its winter quarters.[11] On the upper deck, the stage was generally positioned ahead of the foremast, with the audience seated between the fore and mainmasts (O'Neill, "North" 360).

The configuration of the theater was not only the result of practical necessities but also reflected the theater's role as a site of discipline. Because performances did not take place in purpose-built theaters, decorations and audience organization were significant conditions of production, providing glimpses of how theater practitioners manipulated their surroundings. Seating arrangements "reinforced the social hierarchy on board": men sat on trunks while the captain and his guests (usually captains or senior officers from ships wintering nearby) sat in chairs that "form[ed] a royal box" (O'Neill, "North" 360). Decorations also visually signified authority. The upper deck was often adorned, as on the *Assistance*, with patriotic and naval emblems and flags. Captain Ommanney, for example, had his men remove the royal coat of arms from the *Intrepid* and mount it on the proscenium arch above the stage as decoration (O'Neill, "North" 375). Printed playbills also bore the royal coat of arms, bearing the mottos "*honi soit y mal pense*" and "*dieu et mon droit*" ("Shamed be he who thinks ill of it" and "God and my right"). On the *Assistance*, snow sculptures of the Prince of Wales and the Princess Royal were carved to grace the sides of the proscenium arch (Markham 76–77). Although the theater's location in a communal space communicated that men and officers were "in it together," the placement of the captain and the decorations reminded the men on the *Assistance* of the local and colonial authorities to whom they reported.

It is critical to recognize that sledge searches required men not only to internalize discipline but also to cooperate with one another: shipboard theater reinforced the power of authority structures, but it also, perhaps more importantly, provided extended opportunities for men to work in teams. The perceived ability of theater to promote cooperation is explicit in Collinson's remark that of all the amusements offered aboard his ship, none told "so well on the tone of the men, or rouses their co-operation so much, as the theatricals" (394). Theater, unlike many pastimes, required cooperation: men did not work in parallel, as they might in classes, or independently, as they might while hunting, or competitively, as in sports and games; they worked together. Rehearsals, though undemanding by today's standards, began ten days to two weeks before a scheduled performance and included a read-through, two or three dramatic rehearsals, a musical rehearsal if necessary, and a dress rehearsal (O'Neill, "North" 368). A glance at surviving cast lists indicates that productions tended to involve the same actors over and over again. Shipboard theater practitioners worked closely together regularly during rehearsal periods and repeatedly throughout the winter, developing—one can imagine—a kind of shorthand communication, friendly physical comfort with one another, and an intense camaraderie. Shipboard theater, in this way, was very similar to sledge travel: spring journeys required a small group of men to work closely together for weeks, and the physical task of hauling the sledge required men to, quite literally, "keep step" with one another, to move as a single unit. The bonds created in rehearsals resembled those required by sledge expeditions: men had to work together for a sustained period of time and to think of their cast as a single performing unit. The metaphoric and metonymic link between theater and sledge travel allows one to see theatrical rehearsals as potential preparation for the demands of spring travel.

Sledge journeys also required men to think independently, adapting training and policies to meet changing circumstances. Blindly following orders could be counterproductive and potentially deadly. This is seen in Markham's proud statement that after nineteen days of travel, no one in his party suffered from frostbite and his attribution of this success to the fact that his men replaced their navy-issued canvas boots with loose-fitting ones made out of sleeping rugs (89–90). Markham understood that circumstances sometimes required men to ignore orders, even creatively replacing components of their uniforms that proved unserviceable in adverse conditions, and to have the ability to judge when these derelictions of duty were necessary. This was precisely the kind of thinking that theater production encouraged.

Search ships went north prepared to stage plays. Not only were the ships supplied with libraries that included a selection of scripts, supplemented by officers' private collections (O'Neill, "North" 363), but they also transported materials that could be used as costume and set pieces. Commissioned officers generally brought costumes to wear to masquerade balls, which were held every season, and most ships also carried communal costume pieces, although the quantity and quality of these items varied drastically.[12] The 1852–54 experiences of George McDougall, master of HMS *Resolute* and a member of its theater committee, seem fairly representative. Describing the "hurry and bustle" of acting as both scene-painter and dressmaker, he remarks that dressmaking was "puzzling [...] particularly in the ladies' department" and describes how he adapted available costume pieces: "The skirts and polka jackets had been brought from England. A stiff duck petticoat made a capital substitute for a hair ditto; this, with the addition of a comforter stuffed with oakum, made the after part of the dress resemble a miniature St. Paul's dome" (159). McDougall had some basic costume pieces—skirts and jackets—at his disposal and used materials available in the ship's stores—oakum,[13] for example—to create the pieces a particular play required.

Although a few ships carried set pieces north (O'Neill, "North" 373–74), set design, like costume design, often required a creative eye for repurposing materials. Ships usually carried spare sail canvas, which was appropriated to make drop scenes, but materials like paint were sometimes hard to come by. McDougall, for example, was challenged by "the want of proper materials" and used soot, blacking, and chalk to decorate scenery (158). Similarly, in preparing sets for *Zero*, Lieutenant Browne used what he could find, "'Day and Martin,' black ink, black-lead, whitening, washing blue, glue, and other unusual ingredients, consisting of chimney-soot and lamp-black, to complete his picture" because of a "scarcity of paint" on the ship (*Arctic Miscellanies* 204–05).[14] His ingenuity was rewarded with high praise in *Aurora Borealis*, which noted that the scenery "redounded to the credit of the artist, more particularly when it is generally known that there having been a scarcity of paint on board" (204). One can see a parallel between looking at supplies and seeing painting materials and looking, as Markham's men did, at a sleeping bag and seeing a way to prevent frostbite: both involved repurposing official supplies and being confident this would be rewarded, not seen as a misappropriation of goods. Although theater reinforced and legitimated authority structures, it also allowed men to decide when following orders was necessary and when solving problems in unconventional ways was more beneficial. This flexible approach to regulation was necessary when men traveled independently in sledge parties.

The success of shipboard theater practices relied upon men respecting the disciplinary regimentation of rehearsal and production and promised, in exchange for this obedience, hours of entertainment. Obeying orders, shipboard performance suggested, could be fun. Similarly, the opening scenes of *Zero, or Harlequin Light* suggested that sledge searches, like

shipboard winters, could be enjoyable if approached with the right attitude. In these scenes, Ede uses humor to downplay the hardships of sledge
travel, providing an example of how to cope with frustration. The characters joke about the Admiralty: "if those were here as plann'd these cruises/
How jolly hard they'd rub their ancient noses" (136). They also poke fun
at ongoing debates between ships' surgeons about how to best ventilate a
ship: "What do you think of our Ventilation?/Does it meet your learned
approbation?/We have no theories when in a tent,/Nor care which way the
foul air finds a vent" (138). Ede carefully directs characters' frustration
at two "appropriate" targets: the Admiralty, which was, unlike officers,
perceived as out of touch with the realities of the search, and surgeons, a
self-deprecating move that showed Ede, as assistant surgeon, was willing
to mock himself.

The opening scenes also demonstrate that men could choose how to
understand the challenges of Arctic travel. Ede has the sailors speak almost
exclusively in rhyming couplets, which makes their complaints sound
lighthearted and humorous. For example, the lines "I'm very thirsty, when
the rum I sip/The pannikin sticks fast unto my lip" (137) make the conflict over whether to drink and risk food sticking to the lips or whether
to go thirsty sound comic, rather than suggesting the miserable conditions Osborn's and Markham's accounts describe. The pain of frostbite,
likewise, is addressed in verse: "Confound it all, I'm bitten in the thumb/
How soon your flesh becomes cold, white, and numb" (137), reducing the
real danger to a verbal trick. The men, because of the rhyming language
and constant joking, show that one could remain cheerful and look for the
humor in a harsh situation. The beginning of the play proposes a formula
for success: a reasonable respect for rank combined with camaraderie with
one's fellow men, a dash of perspective, and a strong sense of humor could
remedy the psychological and physical hardships of sledge expeditions.

AUSTIN'S HAPPY FAMILY

Shipboard theater not only disciplined men on a mimetic level but also on
an affective one, cultivating fraternal affiliations between men and filial
respect for officers, replacing devotion to family in Britain with affection
for naval peers, and transforming women at home from absent objects of
desire into rewards that would be bestowed for service. The Royal Arctic
Theatre was part of an attempt to regulate not only men's behavior but
also their feelings, carefully balancing attachments to the military and to

biological families by restaging the ship's space as domestic rather than martial; *Zero* participating in this attempt by suggesting one way to reconcile temporary homosocial bonds with lasting heterosexual desire. By examining how theater—and exploration—were constructed as nostalgic pursuits, how the ship's complement were imagined as members of a "family," and how feminine characters were deployed in *Zero*, one can see the delicate balancing acts at play in the attempt to discipline affect.

It was essential to maintain good mental health on a wintering ship: homesickness could jeopardize this. George McDougall noted that "of all the discomfort attendant on wintering within the Arctic Circle, none perhaps is so much felt as the absence of light, which [...] [is] injurious to the mind; the temper becomes irritable, the mental energies impaired, and the habits of some gloomy and solitary" (168). Claiming the solution lay in balancing the "sweet and soothing influence of memory" with "bright hopes for the future" (168), McDougall addressed the importance of balancing the longing for home against ambitions for a successful voyage and a safe return home. Osborn concurred with McDougall, noting that "it was not alone love for our own kith and kin which reminded us of where our sure and certain hope should rest, but the feeling that we carried with us the sympathies of all the great and good of our countrymen and countrywomen" (Osborn 122). Imagining home retroactively, as a place left behind, led to homesickness; imagining home as a promised future, as a place to which one could return, could motivate men to work harder.

Nostalgia for home was contained by expanding the idea of the family. Sailors were encouraged to imagine themselves as part of both their own families and the naval family, which included shipmates, Franklin's men, and British explorers of the past. The resurrection of the Royal Arctic Theatre's performance traditions suggest one way that Arctic explorers practiced a form of ancestor worship. In the mid-nineteenth century, Admiral Nelson remained the most celebrated British naval hero, but Sir Edward Parry was firmly established as the *paterfamilias* of the Arctic "family." Parry was famous for his accomplishments in exploration—he held the records for the farthest western longitude and northern latitudes reached by a modern European expedition—and for introducing a morally guided approach to naval discipline. Pierre Berton argues that Parry was part of a "new generation of explorers [...] He had an unquestioning faith in the British ability to surmount any obstacle [...] Devout, steadfast, and loyal, he believed in hard work and team spirit [...] and saw the absolute necessity of keeping the lower orders occupied" (*Grail* 35). Francis Spufford expands on Berton's assessment, noting that Parry was remembered as an "activist reformer [. . .] of naval manners; a captain dedicated to effecting the shift away from drink, sodomy, and the lash" (99). Parry imagined his role as "paternal, almost pastoral. He was supposed [. . .] to exercise moral supervision over the men, and to deliver a fatherly blend of advice and reassurance to them" (Spufford 99). Many officers who oversaw the Franklin search expeditions, including Horatio Austin, had served under Parry and, like Parry, understood their authority as paternal and Christian rather than strictly martial.

The officers serving under Austin recognized and emphasized links between their expedition and Parry's: for example, in the January edition of *Aurora Borealis*, an editorial commented: "Thirty-one years have now elapsed since the gallant Parry [. . .] had the glory of planting his country's flag in lands never visited before. Although less fortunate in penetrating the Arctic wilds, we ought in gratitude to thank a Divine Providence for what we have already performed, for having run through dangers unscathed, and for having reached a longitude never attained since that successful Arctic navigator" (147–48). The editorial reminded readers that they were the first since Parry to reach Griffith Island. It also implied that reaching their goal—finding Franklin—would continue Parry's glorious legacy. Officers made an explicit effort to educate the crew about Parry's accomplishments: Osborn relates how Lieutenant Aldrich sat with "Parry's glorious pages open by his side" and told his audience about "the sufferings, the enterprise, the courage, and the reward of imperishable renown exhibited and won by others." Hearing about Parry's accomplishments transformed the crew from "stern men with tender hearts" into a "tier of attentive, upturned faces, listening like children to some nursery tale." This "education" was affectively successful: the "glistening eye and compressed lip showed how the good seed was taking root in the listeners around, and every evening saw that sailor audience gather around him whom they knew to be the 'gallant and true'" (Osborn 125). The men's emotional responses and their desire to hear the same stories repeated demonstrated the positive impact of these stories on the rough sailors.

Parry's influence extended to the transformation of the wintering ship into a domestic space. Richard Collinson wrote that in the winter, he and his men transformed their ship from a "solitary little house of life into a veritable English home," noting, "It was the kind and thoughtful disposition of Captain Parry [. . .] which gave the tone to all the subsequent arrangements. The work of keeping the ship sweet and clean, always so methodically carried out on board ship, occupies a good part of every dark day" (394). Parry, according to Collinson, imagined and organized his ship as an extension of the middle-class home: cleaning duties, always part of shipboard routines, were refigured as domestic tasks that created pride in the home. Discourses of the domestic also shaped how relations between men and officers were imagined: Osborn's account of Aldrich reading to the crew discursively infantilizes the "rough" men, suggesting they became childlike by listening to "family" stories, and feminizes Aldrich by transforming him into a nursemaid educating his juvenile charges. The space of the ship is domesticated in Collinson's remarks and becomes a nursery in Osborn's, a place where the children of the navy—enlisted men—learned to be good citizens. Alexander Armstrong notes that men also practiced "feminine" hobbies: reading—a contemplative pastime—was the most common activity; men also "indulged" in "drawing-room occupations" like needlework (492). Armstrong's description of domestic hobbies as "indulgences" suggests that these were unusual activities for the boisterous and rambunctious men. While theater was not as explicitly feminine as needlework, amateur theatricals were often put on by middle-class families as a private, domestic pastime. On Arctic ships, amateur theater linked participants to Parry's traditions and to domestic practices that epitomized the mid-Victorian ideal of the peaceful middle-class family. The threat of the maudlins was channeled, through the figure of Parry and the ideals of middle-class domesticity, into nostalgic attachments to the navy and the ship as family and home.[15]

Officers recognized the familial figurations at work. The editors of *Aurora Borealis* referred to the paper as "a reflection of the harmony and good-fellowship, the order and the Christian union, which prevailed in the Expedition" then expressed the fear that "the time is far distant before 'the peoples' of Europe will feel any of the brotherly spirit which animated 'the Austin Happy Family'" (xviii). An article titled the "Arctic Happy Family," may have motivated this assessment; its author remarked that "there is, towards the close of 1850, far removed from scenes of other happiness, a family still more wonderful for its harmony" (94). In this multigenerational home, crew were brothers, Austin was father, officers were nursemaids, and Parry, overseeing the expedition from his retirement at home, was patriarch. Men looked up to authorities with wide-eyed adoration; they spent winter evenings learning and practicing civilized hobbies, such as reading and needlepoint; the family even put on amateur theatricals together. The economies of the military and the family came together, apparently seamlessly, in the "Austin Happy Family."

This homosocial world was, however pleasant, an incomplete and fleeting substitute for heterosexual family life. It was limited and defined by the pervasive absence of actual women: though the family could gain new members, it could not reproduce them. Furthermore, erotic desire arising within the naval family had to be firmly contained: while the men could bond with one another as fathers, sons, or brothers, sexual bonds were strictly prohibited. When the voyage ended, men were expected to give up their attachments to fellow sailors and return to their wives and sweethearts, at least until their next voyage. The surviving text of *Zero* suggests that Ede recognized that the shipboard family was a temporary, though necessary, construction. The play prevented men from expressing bonds to one another into inappropriate ways by including two feminine figures who reminded them of the women who awaited them at home; at the same time, the female characters were desexualized and unlikely to arouse, suggesting that erotic desire had to be relocated from the Arctic present to the domestic future.

To address how Daylight and the North Polar Star contributed to the play, it is important to first consider how Ede modified the conventions of mid-century pantomime.[16] Michael Booth characterizes pantomime's traditional structure: the opening, drawn from mythology or fairy tale, introduces a father figure and his servant, a marriageable young woman, and her preferred suitor, disapproved of by the father. The patriarch attempts to keep the couple apart, but as he verges on success, a "benevolent spirit, usually female, brings the opening to an end by [...] transforming [the lovers] into Harlequin and Columbine, while father and servant become Pantaloon and Clown" (198). The intervention and transformation mark the beginning of the harlequinade, in which Pantaloon pursues Harlequin and Columbine through a parade of shifting locales. The pantomime concludes with the characters' reconciliation and a celebration of the "triumph of true love" (Booth 198). By mid-century, the two-part structure was evolving. Openings were longer, functioning as stand-alone entertainment and were "elastic enough to permit slight variations." Despite this evolution, the young lovers and father remained "easy to identify or characterize [as] the pair who [would] be transformed into Harlequin and Columbine" (Mayer, *Harlequin* 37).

Ede modified the conventional opening in establishing a conflict between Zero and the cheerful sailors, choosing a topical over an archetypal plot. Although Zero's tyrannical behavior resembles that of the father figure, he is opposed to homosocial affiliation and geographic exploration, not heterosexual romance. This modification, clearly a response to shipboard conditions, suggests that sailors and officers were meant to understand their familial relationships to one another, like the modifications to pantomime's conventions, as a necessary and temporary substitution of homosocial for heterosexual relationships. The play limits its depiction of homosociability, representing only the ideal world in which men were bonded to one another by respect for authority and a common purpose. Extremes of homosociability—mutiny or sodomy, for example—are outside the representational and expressive economies of the play. This was arguably prescriptive: by staging only one model of homosocial relations, the play excludes "dysfunctional" relations from shipboard life.

The imagined impossibility of shipboard homosexuality is underlined by the changes Ede made to conventional before-after pairings in the transformation sequence. Rather than transform the opening's protagonists into Harlequin and Columbine, Ede has Harlequin appear by jumping through an oiled silk sun, then has Harlequin transform the peripheral character Daylight into Columbine. Pantomimic transformations relied upon audience members recognizing a figurative relationship between "before" and "after": young lovers could be transformed into Harlequin and Columbine because each pair was bonded through desire. Transforming male sailors into the harlequinade's lovers would have implied that sexual desire existed between the men. Ede's decisions about the transformation sequence suggest that he strategically adapted pantomime's conventions to respond to specific shipboard anxieties.

The line dividing permissible from forbidden gender transgressions becomes visible when homosocial desire and cross-dressed performance intersect in performance. Plays involving heterosexual romances were certainly staged on Arctic ships, although no record survives describing precisely how all-male casts represented heterosexual love on stage. It seems likely that scenarios staging a man in love with a woman (played by a man) were presented with a wink, acknowledging the dissonance between the actor's female role and his male body. Advertisements and reviews in shipboard newspapers demonstrate that a sense of playfulness generally surrounded theatrical representations of gender. For example, an advertisement for *Bombastes Furioso* lured spectators by claiming: "The only Lady in this piece has been engaged at an Enormous Sacrifice it being her first appearance on any Stage" (*Illustrated Arctic News* 31). Similarly, a review of *Charles the Twelfth* commented: "Where the young ladies could possibly have acquired the subtle knowledge they displayed in the wooful intricacy of female attire we know not, suffice it to say, that not a point was missing" (56). These winking references to gender call attention to the illusion produced by men dressing up as women, highlighting the camaraderie that developed between men in the absence of women and supporting Marjorie

Garber's contention that cross-dressing in all-male environments often asserts "the common privilege of maleness" (60), functioning as part of normative homosociability.

Laurence Senelick, however, complicates matters by pointing out that gender play and cross-dressing also function as escape valves allowing "so-called feminine feelings and intra-gender affection" to be expressed in "neither threatening nor suspect" ways (350). Cross-dressing allowed problematic desires to be expressed in socially sanctioned performances, theoretically preventing desire from emerging inappropriately, but also making prohibited desires visible. Marjorie Garber concurs, noting that the "fantasies expressed in cross-dressing are simultaneously erotic and misogynistic" (60). On wintering ships, cross-dressing was acceptable and even funny when it was required by a play and supported male bonding, but it became immediately troubling when it seemed to signal homosexual desire or effeminacy.

Recognizing this sheds light on Ede's modifications of pantomime conventions and the apparent lack of attention paid to these changes. The central conflict in conventional pantomime revolved around forbidden romantic love and was resolved when lovers were united in marriage. Ede not only changed the conflict to meet the necessities of an all-male environment, replacing heterosexual desire with homosocial affection, he—and those watching the play—also sidestepped virtually all questions of gender and sexuality. The female characters, played by cross-dressed men, are excluded from romantic relationships with male characters. Ede's dramaturgical changes were made silently: although the play includes several metatheatrical comments, none were made concerning these modifications. Reviews made no jokes about the "skills" of the "actresses" or about their "femininity." This silence seems at odds with jokes made about cross-dressing in other performances, unless one notes that *Zero* had a much closer relationship to shipboard reality than other plays. It appears that it was fine to play with gender and sexuality when theater bore little resemblance to real life, but that it was problematic to raise these questions in a performance that, through the theatrical framing device of Pantoland, represented shipboard reality.

Recognizing this contradiction permits a more nuanced understanding of the female characters in *Zero*. Refusing to broach questions of normative heterosexuality and homosocial desire, the play carefully contains femininity in a pair of abstract figures aligned with domesticity and sentimentality, locating desire as something to be deferred until the return home. The primary function of Daylight/Columbine and the North Polar Star is to provide emotional commentary on the performance; this is achieved through songs that sentimentally propose that the missing men are kin to the audience and promise that if audience members search for the missing members of their naval families, both the missing and the searchers will return home to their heteronormative families.

Daylight appears early in the play, dressed in white, wearing a wreath around her head and carrying a wand (Ede 131). Her white robes visually associate her with the landscape, but she is a protective Arctic spirit: her clothing signifies the purity, not the danger, of the snowy world. She hovers over the tracking party, then descends to address the audience (134): "I dream'd, when slumber hung over mine eyes,/ Of love, of hope, and Arctic enterprise,/When a soft voice broke through my troubled dreams,/ [...] I rose, for well the music charm'd my watchful ear,/Turn'd and beheld a pensive maiden near" (134–35). Daylight's speech entices the audience to imagine her sleeping, dreaming of them and their Arctic adventures, then picture her awoken by the singing Maiden, allowing men who had not had female company in months to insert themselves into the two-woman scene voyeuristically. But if conflicting desires were aroused by the scene— for example, if audience members imagined themselves awakening the Maiden—the hyperawareness that Daylight was played by a man quickly mitigated that pleasure.[17] The song that follows the speech, furthermore, contains any desire aroused by reminding the men of the higher purpose they were serving and the women who worried about them at home.

The song begins with an appeal to Daylight to help searchers find Franklin: "Bright spirit of light, grant thy powerful aid,/Guide England's bold sons where the missing have stray'd" (135). The second verse describes women waiting at home: "pale are our faces with love's silly fears;/Asleep or awake, we still mutter a prayer,/That success may soon give them again to our care" (135). Conflating the missing and the searching men, the Maiden suggests that the hopes of the audience's wives and sweethearts and of the women left behind by Franklin's men rest upon the men in the audience, creating a link between the audience and Franklin's men through the image of the women awaiting their safe return. Recognizing homesickness but preventing the maudlins, the song reminds the men of the women they long for, but urges them to remember that their nostalgia is shared by the women and Franklin's men and encourages them to assuage sad feelings by moving forward with the search.

When Daylight finishes her song, she tells the audience that she will watch out for the British sailors: "Knowing that lovers' songs ne'er have an end,/My help at once I promised her to lend;/Then hither came, I hope to find you well,/But don't expect I've any news to tell" (135). These final lines, which may have mocked the long-winded Maiden's song or the men's constant desire for news from home, describe Daylight's role for the remainder of the opening: she will look out for the search party and "counteract [Zero's] evil deeds" (135). As the sledge party enters, Daylight is ready to help, but her intervention is somewhat limited: the stage directions indicate that she waved her wand over one of the sailor's frostbitten hands to heal it, and then fades from view until she is transformed into Columbine. As Columbine, the character plays little role in the action, suggesting that she appeared because pantomime conventions dictated it, not because she contributed to the harlequinade in a meaningful way. Daylight/Columbine's significance is limited to her speech and song and lies in the song's contribution to the emotional economy of the play, encouraging audience members to identify with the missing men and sentimentalize their mission.

The North Polar Star plays a similar role to Daylight, promoting patriotic and nostalgic sentiments while making a minor contribution to the harlequinade. The character appears late in the play in "*rough dress*" (Ede 142) that underscores her lack of feminine charms. She advances to center stage, perhaps echoing Daylight's blocking, and sings directly to the audience. Her song reminded audience members of what they left behind,[18] but also glorified their role in the Arctic. In the first lines, she flatters listeners, complimenting their courage: "A noble soul has that man, I ween,/Who braveth these regions cold:/No dangers that threaten his life are seen/When he seeketh the brave and bold" (142). The second verse reminds audience members of the scope of British exploration: "Through ages long past, the British name/Has been known in every clime,/And all must trust that the well-earn'd fame/Will endure to the end of time" (142). Bravery and a common relationship to the navy's historical glory join all members of the expedition: rank and class are less important than the courage and self-sacrifice they inherited from past heroes and will carry into the future through action. After evoking nostalgic attachments—to the past, to fellow sailors, to Franklin's men—the song tells the men, unambiguously and urgently, what they must do: "To rescue from death the friend, or foe,/Was ever the sailor's boast;/And now, 'mid the terrors of frost and snow,/His courage is needed most" (142). The final verse specifies what is expected in the spring: "Soon night will be past, and spring draweth nigh,/To gladden us all again,/When we'll seek around, with a watchful eye,/Nor at any toil complain" (143). The final reminder—to never complain—links the song with the example set by the cheerful sailors in the opening. Finally, the song concludes by promising a private, domestic reward for success: "They await us in England, the beauteous, the fair,/When our dangerous task is o'er" (143). The ultimate reward, the song suggests, is the return home to one's proper place in society, as a heterosexual partner.

The female characters' songs sentimentalize Arctic exploration, transforming duty from drudgery into a noble pursuit. By embedding these messages in songs sung by feminine characters, the play encouraged men to acknowledge—but contain—feminine feelings of homesickness, nostalgia, and sentiment by channeling them into the search ahead. Daylight's song, which reminded audience members that they were searching for men who had left families behind, and the North Polar Star's song, which cemented the identification between searchers and the missing, are physically and stylistically bracketed off from the pantomime, allowing the affective messages offered to be communicated without detracting from the fun.

Ede made a strange choice in concluding the pantomime, rejecting reconciliation or dramaturgical closure. In the final moments, immediately following North Polar Star's song, the 1st Clown is swept up by a balloon and descends, a moment later, with a paper in his hands. After reading fictional news from home, he gives the audience some "advice":

A fool may sometimes wisdom speak,
    Though wanting youth and beauty;
        So let me say,
        In Nelson's way,
England expects that every man
    This spring will do his duty. (143)

While anxiety concerning homosocial desire explains why the play does not end in marriage, its refusal of narrative closure is significant. The Clown's paraphrase of Nelson's famous signal command reiterates the North Polar Star's evocation of the navy's glorious past by citing arguably the most famous example of naval morale building.[19] Both the song's encouragement of search efforts and the Clown's final lines function as calls for further action: together they suggest that it will only be after penetrating the Arctic and locating the missing men that the sailors in the play—and the men in the audience—will receive their promised rewards. The final moments, by suggesting that closure depends on action, demonstrate that the play's cultural work extended beyond Pantoland: closure could only happen outside the world of the pantomime. The ending situates action as a military and patriotic duty, as a way of affectively engaging with those absent, and as a requirement for a safe return home. In this way, the domestic and the military, the past and the present, and the absent and the present are metatheatrically linked through the play's deployment of nostalgia and sentiment.

HARLEQUIN TRANSFORMS THE TUNDRA

David Eng and David Kazanjian's observation that nostalgia constitutes one of the "discourses and practices" that respond to loss (2) suggests that the play's nostalgia and sentimentality had purchase precisely because the men in the audience, consciously or not, shouldered the burden of loss. While *Zero* and the Royal Arctic Theatre's practices trained men for their work in the Arctic and forged a series of affective connections—to the past, to peers, to Franklin and his men—to help overcome homesickness, neither anticipatory nor affective discipline could erase the fact that something real was indeed lost. Only months before *Zero* was produced, the squadron was part of a convoy of ships that located the remains of Franklin's first winter site on Beechey Island and discovered the graves of three men. This discovery must have caused some men enormous anxiety, demonstrating that discipline and cheerful attitudes were not a panacea and reminding them that the dangerous world outside the ship could mysteriously take lives. To overcome these anxieties, the Arctic had to be imaginatively transformed into a familiar, safe space: pantomime, a genre that both relied upon transformation as a dramaturgical principle and thematized mobility and change, had the potential to theatrically resolve the crisis. By personifying the threats of the Arctic and transforming them into familiar pantomime characters, *Zero, or Harlequin Light* suggested that the environment could be conquered through imagination, superior character, and good humor. This is demonstrated in the transformation sequence that divides opening and harlequinade, which stages the dangers facing the fictional sailors as domestic transpositions that the arch-British Harlequin could outsmart.

Arctic expeditions always carried a measure of danger, but the British navy, which had never experienced a "fatal catastrophe," was initially optimistic in assessing what might have befallen Franklin's expedition (McClure 10). The Admiralty was so confident in Franklin's abilities and so painfully bureaucratic that it was not until 1848, when the expedition had been in the north for three full winters, that search efforts began; this, despite the fact that the longest any British expedition had spent in the Arctic was four winters.[20] By 1850–51, public opinion remained optimistic, but privately, hopes were not as high. Clements Markham wrote: "It would be mere trifling in one who has seen those barren frozen regions to hold out a hope that, without provisions or ammunitions, and with the cold of that rigorous climate undermining and weakening their constitutions for seven years, any of those gallant men [...] can still survive" (125). Markham's editor, tempering his comments for publication, argued that "it is neither rash, wanton, nor ill-judged, to foster hopes which, however doomed to be disappointed, are still fairly within the bounds of reasonable probability" (vii).

The ambivalent discovery of Franklin's first winter site prompted both Markham's pessimism and his editor's guarded optimism; it provoked a similar range of reactions from search parties. Markham was relieved that Franklin and his men had reached Beechey Island, announcing: "Here fell to the ground all the evil forebodings of those who had, in England, consigned his expedition to the depths of Baffin's Bay on its outward voyage. Our first prayer had been granted by a beneficent Providence; and we had now risen, from doubt and hope, to a certain assurance of Franklin having reached thus far without shipwreck or disaster" (104). The more experienced Osborn, however, was disturbed when searches failed to turn up written records: "every one felt that there was something so inexplicable in the non-discovery of any record, some written evidence of the intentions of Franklin and Crozier on leaving this spot, that each of us kept returning to search over the ground, in the hope that it had been merely overlooked in the feverish discovery of the cairns by Captain Ommanney and Captain Penny" (96–97).

The relief of knowing that *Terror* and *Erebus* had reached Beechey Island was also short-lived due to the discovery of the graves. Three fatalities in the first winter was a high number, suggesting that something had gone wrong. The lack of written records exacerbated this; an observer commented that it was "very singular—that no memento was left regarding the cause of their deaths, or any as to the period of the arrival and departure of the ships, or of the course which they intended to pursue. There is much mystery in all that" (White 5). Markham found the ambiguity troubling, commenting: "There stood the graves, and the recent vestiges of his crews having laboured on those very spots [...] but they were gone, nor was there anything to tell the anxious searcher whither they had sailed. It was with feelings of mortification and regret that, in the beginning of September, the vessels left Beechey Island" (64). Strange epitaphs on two headstones added to the mystery: William Braine's, from *Joshua* 24.15, read, "Choose ye this day whom ye will serve"; and John Hartnell's, from

Haggai 1.7, was "Thus saith the Lord of Hosts, consider your ways" (Beattie 93). The strange choices of verse prompted later historians "to believe foul play or mishap had marred that first winter" (Beattie 93), but were, oddly, ignored in most contemporary public responses to the discovery. A piece printed in the *Illustrated Arctic News* remarked: "What a tale of regret and kindly feeling, was told by the neatly furnished head board!—all replete with interest. [...] Yet apart from regret, for the departed, and anxiety for the missing, there was nothing unusually terrible in such a last resting place from the fevered labours of this life—here at any rate, the cairn, which marks one's resting place, stands a monument of human enterprise! of British perseverance! (2–3). Sherard Osborn echoed the anonymous journalist in his refusal to see anything but evidence of heroism in the headstones: "I thought I traced in the epitaphs over the graves of the men from the 'Erebus,' the manly and Christian spirit of Franklin. In the true spirit of chivalry, he, their captain and leader, led them amidst dangers and unknown difficulties with iron will stamped upon his brow, but the words of meekness, gentleness, and truth were his device" (112). Considering the peculiar epitaphs, Osborn's words feel like overcompensation, an attempt to ignore what he actually saw in order to focus on the headstones' function as signifiers of Franklin's lingering presence and, by extension, his continued existence.

Although later exhumations revealed that the three men died of natural causes—pneumonia stemming from tuberculosis and lead exposure (Beattie 124, 161), in 1850 there was no way to determine whether disease, accident, or foul play had caused the deaths. For the search parties, the specific causes of death were less significant than the fact that three men died so early: the deaths were a bad omen for both Franklin's and the 1850 expeditions. Austin's men, attempting to follow in Franklin's footsteps, were trained and outfitted in the same way as the missing expedition: if there was a problem with practices, stores, or health on Franklin's ships, it was possible the same dangers lay dormant on the search ships. The men were searching uncharted lands, with limited knowledge of the animals or peoples they would encounter and, while they understood the danger of vitamin deficiencies like scurvy, they didn't know how to prevent them. There was good reason for Austin's squadron to be nervous. But for search parties to succeed, the men had to believe that searching the Arctic was not a fatal mistake and that they would survive where Franklin's three men had not.

Charles Ede personified Arctic threats—hunger, scurvy, cold, wild animals—as characters in his play's opening and then demonstrated how pantomimic transformations could eradicate these threats. Reviews and the script provide little detail about costuming, set, or acting styles; furthermore, advertisements suggest that changes occurred between the first performance on January 9 and the second on March 14.[21] Despite these archival omissions, one can speculate about what the transformation and performance looked like. First, iconic and symbolic costuming allowed audience members to recognize figural relationships between characters and the threats they signified. The script indicates that Scorbutus, for instance, wore a "tight white dress, covered with purple and reddish-brown spots; mask pale, with bluish-red and blotched mouth" (131), suggesting the physical changes scurvy inflicted on the body. Hunger's "Long thin mask face, pale dress, loose and scanty" (131) signified the drawn facial features and shrinking body of someone who had spent too long on short rations. The *Illustrated Arctic News* included an image of Zero, Bear, and Clown; this picture must be taken with a grain of salt as this group of characters never, according to the script, appear on stage together, but it provides a

Image 1.1   Scene from the Pantomime of *Zero*. Library Archives Canada. *Illustrated Arctic News*, R11555–0-4-E. Reproduction copy number C-028289.

sense of what Zero and the Bear might have looked like. The script refers to the Bear as "Dean's model bear," noting that Mr. Dean, the ship's carpenter, constructed it (138). Knowing that the Bear had to be transformed into Pantaloon and 2nd Clown, it is likely that two actors played the Bear in the opening. The artist's rendering of the scene suggests that Bear was three-dimensional and that the costume fit over the actors. It is likely the costume was made of real bear fur as the men caught several bears before *Zero* was staged: again, one can see the incursion of the outside world in Pantoland. In contrast to the servants and the Bear, Zero represented not a specific threat but an amalgam of the dangers of the Arctic; costuming signified his role symbolically, rather than iconically. Ede's directions indicate that Zero wore "loose white robes" and a "fanciful crown" draped with icicles (131); the illustration depicts him with a heavy beard but does not indicate whether he, like his servants, was masked. His crown, robes, and the thermometer-scepter he carried symbolized his authority over the territory.

After the opening introduced the insidious and often invisible threats of Arctic exploration, Ede used pantomimic conventions to demonstrate how these threats could be neutralized. Hunger, Scorbutus, and Frostbite are "destroyed by the appearance of the more puissant good spirits, Sun and Daylight" (*Aurora Borealis* 204). Neither the script nor reviews describe how this was staged, but the indication that the characters wore masks suggests that the sequence was performed using "big heads." David Mayer describes how characters in a pantomime's opening typically wore papier-mâché masks—big heads—that concealed their second (harlequinade) identities: "at each wave of the benevolent agent's wand [...] the big heads are snatched away by stagehands, and the costumes, loosely held, are stripped away to reveal the comic types that populate the 'harlequinade'" (*Harlequin* 28). The script does not indicate precisely when this transformation occurred, but because the review relates that Daylight and the Sun—rather than Harlequin—performed it, one can assume that it occurred before Harlequin's first appearance.

The sailors reach what Millie Taylor terms pantomime's "point of desperation"—the moment when the antagonist is on the verge of overcoming the young lovers—when Zero enters their tent; the point of desperation, according to Taylor, sets the transformation sequence in motion by motivating the good spirit to act (13). In Ede's play, Zero entering the tent prompts Harlequin to leap through the oilskin Sun, changing "*(the Good Spirit)* DAYLIGHT *into* COLUMBINE" (138). Following this, the Bear enters and prowls around the tent and Harlequin slaps the ground near the tent with his bat, causing the tent to disappear, "*leaving the* CLOWN *grinning and making faces; he sees the* BEAR, *becomes dreadfully alarmed, and makes off for a gun; returns, snaps the gun, which refuses to go off; the* BEAR *approaches, when he succeeds at firing it;* BEAR *falls, and out roll* 2nd CLOWN *and* PANTALOON, HARLEQUIN *slapping the ground near the* BEAR" (138–39). While the stage direction is, for a pantomime, extensive, one is still left wondering exactly how this sequence was performed. First, Harlequin "jumps" through the Sun, suggesting that the Sun "becomes" Harlequin. The Sun that Harlequin jumps through, though described as a "good spirit," was a set piece, not a character played by an actor, and was likely a rudimentary star trap, a trick set piece consisting of "an aperture covered with leather slit to resemble the radiating points of a star" (Mayer, *Harlequin* 116). On the *Assistance*, the traditional leather may have been replaced by canvas, which was more readily available. The script does not reveal how Daylight was transformed into Columbine: it is possible that her transformation, as with Zero's helpers, was achieved by dropping her white robes to reveal a second costume. After Columbine's transformation, Harlequin slaps the ground near the tent, causing it to disappear and revealing 1st Clown. Again, Ede's text does not indicate how this was performed: although the ship carried a supply of large tents, it seems likely that such a tent would have had to be modified to collapse quickly on stage. Zero's transformation into 1st Clown occurred in the tent, so the actor likely just shed his costume while he was hidden from the audience. Ede's script explains that the 2nd Clown and Pantaloon "roll" out of the Bear when it falls, suggesting that the costume was open at the bottom for the characters to emerge.

The transformation sequence departed from strict conventions of pantomime, as described by Booth and Mayer, not only because a minor set piece and the "benevolent spirit"—rather than a pair of young lovers—become Harlequin and Columbine, but also because the before-after pairings of Zero/Bear and Clowns/Pantaloon are remarkable. One would expect Zero, the play's "patriarch," to become Pantaloon and Bear (or another secondary character) to become Clown (Mayer, *Harlequin* 28). Instead, Zero becomes 1st Clown and Bear becomes both Pantaloon and 2nd Clown. The decision to double the Clown role also marked a departure from generic conventions: while doubling a role was not unheard of, it was unusual.[22] Shipboard reviewers apparently found these modifications unremarkable and accepted the transformation as operating within generic limits: one reviewer noted that "the good spirits become Harlequin and Columbine, and frosty old Zero, who has all along been the leader of the evil spirits, is changed into First Clown; a Bear, which has been for some time prowling about, was then fired at, and falling to pieces, discovers Pantaloon and Second Clown" (*Arctic Miscellanies* 204). While Ede's changes were silently accepted, they reveal how the play's tacit argument for transforming the threats of the Arctic through imaginative acts operated.

Harlequin's ability to transform the world around him through magical intervention was a central component of the worldview underlying pantomime. David Mayer uses the term "visual simile" to describe Harlequin's transformations, arguing that when he slapped his bat to transform objects, characters, or settings, he changed them into "something which, in some hitherto unnoticed way, [they] resemble[d] [...] disclosing that one thing has a hidden likeness to another" (*Harlequin* 39). A reviewer recognized the similarity between the characters of Hunger, Scorbutus, and Frostbite and the real threats they represented, noting, "Turning all the dangers and inconveniences to which we are exposed in these inhospitable climes into evil spirits that are leagued against us, [the pantomime] supposes them continually watching every opportunity to surprise an unfortunate traveling party" (*Arctic Miscellanies* 204). Although Harlequin himself does not transform Hunger, Scorbutus, and Frostbite, the way they are destroyed—by Daylight's magic wand—is significant for its reliance on audience members recognizing a simile at work. Just as Daylight destroyed the characters, the actual dangers disappeared when winter ended: hunger and scurvy disappeared when game returned; cold and frostbite were no longer hazards when the weather got warmer. The theatrical solution to the fictional threat reminded audience members of how to overcome several real threats: patiently wait until spring.

The visual simile provides a potent way to explain the transformations of Zero and the Bear that follow, suggesting that if these deadly threats were reimagined, they could be overcome. Zero represents the danger of the Arctic, overseeing and coordinating its specific threats and using all the "weapons" in his arsenal to stop them: an Iceberg pinches the ships; Frostbite "bites" the men; his Fox steals their food; he attempts to freeze the men in their tent. In contrast to the script's detailed characterization of Zero, it is relatively silent about the Bear's actions; a review only indicates that Bear is transformed after having "been for some time prowling about" (*Arctic Miscellanies* 204). It is possible that the script provided less detail because Bear, an iconic figure, was one that actors and audience were already very familiar with. Sherard Osborn notes that the men saw no less than eight bears that winter; these sightings broke the monotony of winter, and the men developed into enthusiastic and competitive hunters (129–30). Because of the men's previous experiences with real bears and because of the playful conventions of pantomime, the opening suggests that Bear is a lurking, lumbering beast rather than a real danger; likewise, Zero, though an obstacle, is already partially contained in the opening because he was far more theatrical and playful than the actual dangers men faced.

Zero and Bear's transformations emphasize that although the dangers of the Arctic appeared threatening, the men should see them as quite harmless. In the early nineteenth century, Clown was "a figure of anarchy and criminality, but also of naiveté; he could not be held accountable for his actions because his cruelty to other characters seemed more the effect of carelessness than malice" (O'Brien 112). Transforming Zero into Clown suggests that the Arctic's harsh characteristics were, like Clown, easily foiled with wit and invention. Likewise, the stock character of Pantaloon, based on Commedia dell'arte's Pantalone, was an elderly man who attempted to separate Harlequin and Columbine through "wily"—and always unsuccessful—plots and who always ended up the butt of Clown's jokes (Mayer, *Harlequin* 43). The transformation suggests that polar bears, like the post-transformation Bear, had a dual nature. Real bears were like Pantaloon because they attempted to threaten the expedition's success, and like Clown because they failed to obey "rules"; at the same time, bears, always only animals, could be outsmarted by the British, mirroring how both Pantaloon and Clown function as ultimately naïve, silly characters.

Furthermore, the transformation sequence suggests that the threats of the Arctic appeared to be foreign but were actually as familiar and domestic as a holiday pantomime: the Arctic, in other words, could be reimagined as an extension of British territory. The figural relationship between Zero, Bear, Pantaloon, and the Clowns operates on a second level, if one thinks of the before-after transformation in a holistic way, with Zero and Bear as "before" and Pantaloon and Clowns as "after." As John O'Brien argues, pantomime was an intensely nationalistic genre that allowed Britons to understand their cultural identity within the empire: "the expansion of the range of places to which pantomime took its spectators maps the imaginative spread of British culture [...] its expansion outward to embrace a world and an empire" (113). Considering pantomime as a fundamentally British cultural production suggests that Zero and Bear, linked to the familiar Clowns and Pantaloon through visual simile, were essentially British figures. The transformation implied that the Arctic, as metonymically represented by its threatening inhabitants, only appeared to be a foreign land but could become, through the slap of the imperial bat, as familiar and domestic as the archetypically British characters of Clown and Pantaloon.

The figure of the carnivalesque Clown allows one to link the theatrical and disciplinary operations of the shipboard pantomime. Clown, who "mocked conventions" and "rebelled against stuffiness and tradition" (Mayer, *Harlequin* 44), exemplifies Millie Taylor's description of how pantomime implicated the audience in "seemingly subversive activity," encouraging "laughter at physical comedy and the grotesque body as well as at topical and political humour" (17). The Clown, an anarchic figure who acted outside social norms, could poke fun at established authorities; similarly, the pantomime, a historically illegitimate and thus unregulated genre, could deploy social satire that would be unacceptable in other situations. While the structures of shipboard theater and the content of *Zero, or Harlequin Light* provided a model and rehearsal for "good" behavior and regulated affective attachments, they also indicate the potential for the carnivalesque to erupt in and briefly disrupt shipboard life. Far from being problematic, the carnivalesque contributed to naval theater's function as a disciplinary practice because, by providing a temporary space for transgression, it allowed and contained disruptions of order.

This raises the question of whether *Zero* actually contributed to the development of anticipatory discipline aboard ship: did the play, for example, ensure that men were well-disciplined during spring searches? Did it convince men that the dangers of the Arctic could be overcome by overlaying British culture on the "blank" landscape? Proving a causal relationship is impossible, but anecdotal evidence suggests that the men in Austin's squadron approached their work with remarkably positive attitudes, even compared to their contemporaries. Francis McClintock wrote that despite their failure to find traces of Franklin, his men's conduct was exemplary: "I cannot conclude this account of a journey of eighty days without expressing the satisfaction their conduct has afforded me. Their ever cheerful behaviour, untiring perseverance, and patient enduring spirit, under many severe trials and privations, excited my warmest admiration" (qtd. in Markham 99–100). Sherard Osborn, similarly, describes his men's optimism about finding Franklin:

Hope, thank God, rode high in every breast, and already did the men begin to talk of what they would do with their new shipmates from the "Erebus" and "Terror" when they had them on board their respective ships; and I have no doubt they would have done as one gallant fellow replied, when I asked him if he thought himself equal to dragging 200 lbs. "O yes, sir, and Sir John Franklin too, when we find him." (189–90)

Another of Osborn's anecdotes indicates that the men personified the dangers of the Arctic and imagined they could be overcome with imagination and willpower, precisely as the play suggested: "they spoke of cold as 'Jack Frost,' a real tangible foe, with whom they could combat and master. Hunger was met with a laugh, and a chuckle at some future feast or jolly recollection told, in rough terms, of bygone fear" (217). Osborn does not directly link the play to the men's attitudes, and one must acknowledge the possibility that he overemphasized their happiness to put a positive spin on the expedition for readers. On the other hand, one cannot ignore that the personification of cold as "Jack Frost" and the claim that he was a tangible foe to be mastered rather than a natural force to be tolerated, replicate the play's discursive construction of Zero as a character who could be reimagined and overcome. McClintock's and Osborn's stories suggest that *Zero, or Harlequin Light*, in its fluffy treatment of Arctic life, its model for how to overcome obstacles, and its assertion that the Arctic was a familiar place just like home, made a lasting impression on audience members, furthering our understanding of theater's potential to operate as anticipatory discipline aboard search ships.

2. "The Sly Fox": Reading Indigenous Presence ❧

S hipboard theater participated in the work of the carnivalesque by
providing a time and place for men to "act out," to briefly ignore
the boundaries dictated by naval rank, and to temporarily challenge shipboard authority.[1] Minor transgressions provided the experience
of rebellion but ultimately—because they occurred in contained circumstances and were officially sanctioned—reaffirmed and reinforced order.
Phil Deloria, building on Bakhtin's work, argues that carnival traditions
are fundamentally characterized not only by their relationship to order but
also by the confusion of boundaries, "demonstrating the commonalities
between upper and lower classes, law and custom, food and flesh, past
and present, civilized and savage" (16). While some performances con-
fused boundaries precisely to validate them, the surviving script of *Zero, or
Harlequin Light* includes a stage direction that goes further than Bakhtin
or Deloria suggests, not confusing but rupturing the boundary between
"civilized" and "savage" cultures, revealing that the distinction between
"civilization" and "savagery" was constructed upon unstable, often contradictory assumptions about racial and cultural difference.

In August 1850, HMS *Assistance* stopped at Cape York on the north-
west coast of Greenland, and when it continued west, it had an additional
person on board: a young Inuk man named Qalasirssuaq joined the ship's
company to act as navigator and interpreter. Qalasirssuaq, who was given
the English name Erasmus York, became a favorite of the crew and the
officers, who delighted in teaching him English, watching him imitate
British customs, and seeing him participate in shipboard life. Ede's script
indicates that Qalasirssuaq made a brief appearance in the pantomime:
during the harlequinade, the "1st CLOWN *fetches in a fox trap, and places
it at back of stage. All run off and watch it. White fox enters, and the fox
trap falls. Enter* CLOWNS, *who open the trap.* HARLEQUIN *slaps the
trap, and out comes E. York*" (141). The stage direction sends up red flags

when one recalls David Mayer's description of how Harlequin's transformations relied on the visual simile, on audience members recognizing that the "before" and "after" of a transformation bore a hidden resemblance to one another. One must ask what similarity between Fox and Qalasirssuaq audience members may have perceived.

The script provides no additional information about Qalasirssuaq's performance, and surviving reviews make no mention of his appearance at all; this leaves one in the uncomfortable—and familiar—position of glimpsing the fragmented remains of a performance in the archive and being left with pressing but unanswerable questions about what actually happened. Some of these questions, like those raised in relation to Jane Franklin's dresses, are deceptively simple: one doesn't know if Qalasirssuaq played the Fox prowling about in the opening, or if he changed places with another actor while the trapdoor was closed; it is unclear whether the trap was based on something a theater committee member saw on stage in England, whether it was Mr. Dean's own design, or whether Qalasirssuaq, perhaps, had some input into its construction;[2] one cannot ascertain whether Qalasirssuaq volunteered to act in the play or whether he was asked to appear; one doesn't know when the transformation was added to the production.[3] Questions about the details of Qalasirssuaq's performance are also impossible to answer: did Qalasirssuaq wear fur and skin clothing or did he wear British clothes, as he usually did on board? Did he appear surprised when he was revealed in the trap, as if he had been tricked by the Clowns, or did he acknowledge that he was "in" on the gag? Did Qalasirssuaq play up stereotypes of how the British thought Inuit acted? Considering reception produces still more questions: Was his performance funny? How did audience members react to seeing him on stage? Why didn't anyone comment on his performance in reviews?

The impossibility of answering material questions about the transformation sequence is mirrored by the difficulty of establishing the precise similarity suggested by the transformation as visual simile. Reading the transformation as visual simile requires one to consider how Inuit, as a race, and Qalasirssuaq, as a member of that race, were understood by British seamen; the implications of the transformation concerning contemporary attitudes toward racial and cultural differences obviously go far beyond the boundaries of "Pantoland." Furthermore, while the transformation provides a rare opportunity to examine how race was staged and performed, this opportunity is limited because the moment survives only in a lone textual trace that provides no indication of how men watching the play understood what they saw. With no records of response, one is left to consider what the transformation implied in terms of racial difference by examining the broader collection of documents—particularly personal accounts of the expedition and articles printed in shipboard newspapers—produced on search vessels. Interrogating these documents reveals contradictory discourses on racial difference, unstable formulations of the difference between "civilized" and "savage" peoples, and confusion over how to reconcile Qalasirssuaq as an individual with popular constructions of Inuit.

The transformation of Fox into Qalasirssuaq is a symptomatic point, a moment that undermines the regulatory and disciplinary aims of the performance by revealing the volatility of the system of differences that justified these aims. Terry Eagleton describes the symptomatic point in Derridean deconstructive criticism as an "apparently peripheral fragment in the work—a footnote, a recurrent minor term or image, a casual allusion," which one may work "tenaciously through to the point where it threatens to dismantle the oppositions which govern the text as a whole" (133). Gayatri Chakravorty Spivak, in her introduction to *Of Grammatology*, explains the process of deconstructive reading in another way:

> If in the process of deciphering a text in the traditional way we come across a word that seems to harbor an unresolvable contradiction, and by virtue of being *one* word is made sometimes to work in one way and sometimes in another and thus is made to point away from the absence of a unified meaning, we shall catch at that word. If a metaphor seems to suppress its implications, we shall catch at that metaphor. We shall follow its adventures through the text and see the text coming undone as a structure of concealment, revealing its self-transgression, its undecidability. (lxxv)

Eagleton and Spivak focus on literary texts, but the method they describe applies to performance as well, particularly to performance as it survives in the archive. The transformation is precisely what Eagleton and Spivak describe: a minor moment that, if one works it "tenaciously through" and "follow[s] its adventures through the text," reveals crucial instabilities in the play's representation of the Arctic and its inhabitants. If one reads the transformation alongside other documents related to Qalasirssuaq, Inuit, and race, its impact spreads, creating significant cracks in discursive constructions of racial and cultural difference circulating among those participating in the Franklin search.

Looking at the stage direction in its broadest terms, it suggests a similarity between animals and Inuit, affirming racializing discourses that presumed members of "savage races"—both socially and genealogically—resembled animals more than civilized humans. Narrowing one's critical gaze, the visual simile suggests that Fox resembles Qalasirssuaq, implying that Qalasirssuaq, like Fox, was a thieving character who appropriated what he could from the British. Yet another reading emerges if one adds temporality to Mayer's formulation: the transformation *from* animal *to* human suggested that Inuit could also go from being *like* animals ("savages") to being *like* humans ("civilized") through exposure to British culture and religion, thus affirming the ideological foundations of missionary efforts. If we shift perspective again to focus on what is known about Qalasirssuaq, the stage direction suggests that Qalasirssuaq, like Fox, could strategically adapt in order to thrive, emerging not as animal/savage/Inuit or as human/civilized/ British but as a hybrid subject who could integrate himself into shipboard life while retaining indigenous skills and knowledge. Finally, by shifting attention from the stage to the audience, the transformation reflects not a change that occurred in Qalasirssuaq at all but a change of perspective among the men on the ship as they became familiar with him: the British went from seeing Qalasirssuaq as animal-like to seeing him as a fellow human. The conclusion of the chapter imagines how Qalasirssuaq might have understood his performance and argues that his archival survival constitutes an early and partial example of what Gerald Vizenor terms indigenous "survivance," acknowledging that the lack of archival evidence makes any such reading highly speculative. Working through these readings reveals that the ideologies on which they depend conflict with one another, demonstrating that the transformation sequence, as it survives in the archive, emerges as a symptomatic point that allows one to see the irreconcilable conflicts that underlay contemporary perspectives on racial difference.

INTO THE HANDS OF STRANGERS

British attitudes toward Inuit varied widely in the years immediately preceding John Rae's allegations of cannibalism and Dickens's vitriolic responses in *Household Words*. This instability is evidenced by popular representations that ranged from depictions of Inuit as fat, smiling "children of nature" to lurid descriptions of Inuit devouring raw meat in filthy igloos. Despite this range of opinions, one can observe that Arctic explorers generally believed Inuit could—and would—provide crucial assistance if an expedition got into trouble. Franklin's orders, for example, instructed him to find local Inuit and "prevail on them to carry to any of the settlements of the Hudson's Bay Company, an account of [his] situation and proceedings, with an urgent request that it may be forwarded to England"

("Instructions" 5). John McLean, a partner in the Hudson's Bay Company, explained the benefits of Inuit cooperation to Jane Franklin: "In the first place, the services of Esquimaux would be indispensable, for the twofold reason, that no reliable information can be obtained from the natives without their aid, and that they alone properly understand the art of preparing snow-houses, or 'igloes,' for winter encampment, the only lodging which the desolate wastes of the arctic regions afford" (qtd. in Simmonds 191). It was widely believed not only that Inuit could help British explorers survive if things went badly by providing food, helping with communication, and making shelters, but also that Inuit, if anyone, would know what happened to Franklin and his men.

But if the British saw Inuit as potentially helpful, they also approached them with caution. While at Cape York, Austin and other officers[4] heard a convoluted story that initially seemed to concern Franklin and his men. Although this story was later refuted, it illustrated the need to exercise caution toward Inuit and justified the Admiralty's directions that both encouraged officers to "cultivate a friendly feeling" toward Inuit, and warned them to be wary of "treacherous attack" (Collinson 25–26). Adam Beck, an Inuk Greenlander, told officers that Inuit on shore had told him "that in 1846 [...] two vessels with officers having gold bands on their caps and other insignia of the naval uniform, had been in some way or another destroyed at some place to the northward of us; that the crews were ultimately much enfeebled; and after great hardship and suffering, encamping by themselves in tents, and not communicating much with the natives, who were not friendly to them, were all brutally massacred" (Snow, *Voyage* 207).[5] This story generated mixed reactions: John Ross, who used Beck as a translator, believed him implicitly, while Ommanney thought only "some importance ought to be attached to" his story (Snow, *Voyage* 214), and Austin "could not believe that two ships like the 'Erebus' and 'Terror' and their fine crews, every way well equipped, could have been so destroyed; and though the ice might have done the chief work before the natives, yet it was still hardly credible" (Snow, *Voyage* 214–15). After Beck's story was discredited, Sherard Osborn expressed the popular opinion, claiming the "hobgoblin story [...] [was] cunningly devised to keep [...] his own ship on a coast whither he could escape to the neighbourhood of his home in South Greenland" (85–86).[6] The story apparently illustrated the need for wariness: if true, as many initially thought, it suggested that "friendly Inuit" could become violent upon meeting weakened Europeans; if false, as most came to believe, it proved that Inuit lied when it served their purposes.

Qalasirssuaq was asked to join the *Assistance* because the British hoped he would help them locate the *North Star*, a supply ship that had spent the previous winter near Cape York. His appointment indicates that Beck's story did not deter the British from seeking Inuit help. When Qalasirssuaq joined the crew, he was a young man of approximately sixteen who was with his family and two other families at their "spring" camp (Murray 8–13).[7] In contrast to Adam Beck, British and American officers believed that Qalasirssuaq fit positive stereotypes of Inuit as friendly, humorous, and inquisitive. Qalasirssuaq, described as "the life of the party," was immediately curious about the ship, "descending unbidden into the cabin" and "diving into the very bowels of the steamer among the machinery" (Snow, *Voyage* 201). He was "lost in amazement" at the fires, although "the heat was too much for him," and was awed by the steam engine's power: "the lever was placed in his hand, by which he was made to put the whole engine in sudden motion, he let the handle go, and hastily remounted on deck, with that sort of half comic look which represents both fear and laughter" (Snow, *Voyage* 202). Snow reports that when Captain Ommanney asked Qalasirssuaq to guide his ship to Wolstoneholme Sound, "the poor fellow was made to clearly comprehend what he was about to do [...] and both himself and his friends not only agreed to it, but seemed to be much pleased there at, stating that he was a young man without father or mother, and having no wife. He was therefore, at once shipped for the cruise, and he parted from his friends with the most stoical indifference" (Snow, *Voyage* 225–26). Qalasirssuaq's apparent willingness to serve is corroborated by T. B. Murray, who writes that he "threw himself into the hands of strangers in perfect confidence. Having arrived on board the 'Assistance,' he put off his rough native costume, submitted to the process of a good washing, and, being soon clad in ordinary European clothing, which was cheerfully contributed by the officers, the young Esquimaux with much intelligence performed the duty of pilot to the place where the 'North Star' had wintered" (10).

Qalasirssuaq received the English name Erasmus York, to commemorate Captain Erasmus Ommanney and Cape York, but was often called "Kalli" by his shipmates. The men took him under their wings, teaching him English and British customs, likely for their own amusement as much as his "education." Snow, who spent only a few days with Qalasirssuaq but extensively detailed his encounters with the young man, relates how Qalasirssuaq imitated the English phrases he heard:

> 'How d'ye do?' said I, in English, to him, while he was surrounded by his new master, – probably the first he ever had, – and several other persons; and, to our great astonishment, he answered in precisely the same words, and with as clear

an articulation. To try him again, I said, 'Very well, thank you;' but though he endeavoured to effect this, he was unable to get beyond 'Wer-well-you,' or something like it; and then, perceiving he did not speak it aright, he laughed aloud, and ran forward. (*Voyage* 226)

Qalasirssuaq also attempted to imitate his new companions' gestures, as Snow reports:

I happened to take off my cap and remove some of the loose hair from my fore-head; he instantly did the same; and as I purposely continued the movement, so I found he did, parting his shaggy locks, if so they could be called, exactly as my hair was parted. I perceived that whatever was done before him, as related to the person, he attempted in the same manner; and this proved to me, that what has before been said of their excellent powers of mimicry is not in the least exaggerated. (*Voyage* 227)

These attempts at imitation amused the men, as Snow's story of Qalasirssuaq looking at himself in a mirror demonstrates: "A looking-glass was presented to him; when, upon seeing his own features therein, his laugh suddenly vanished, but as instantly came again as his eye caught mine [...] Some of us arranged our hair before the glass, and he immediately, with exquisite mimicry, and with all the attention and little arts of a lady at her toilet, attempted the same with his own, all the time laughing at himself for his awkwardness" (*Voyage* 227–28). Snow's story also implies that Qalasirssuaq was self-conscious of his performance, "putting on a show" for the other men, and emphasizes Qalasirssuaq's ability to mimic the actions of those around him: Snow's opinion that Qalasirssuaq was a "natural" actor may provide a clue about why Qalasirssuaq performed in the theatrical.

Although Murray's biography of Qalasirssuaq relates that he was quick to don British-style clothing, he did not do this immediately: Snow describes how Qalasirssuaq repulsed some officers when he "came rather too close to them with his greasy skin dress and wild appearance" (*Voyage* 228). He wore his own clothing to the officers' mess, where he tried European food for the first time:

[W]hen he motioned to sit down and partake of some food that was put before him, he began to eat most voraciously. Some of the things he appeared to like very well, but others he discarded, after tasting, in a very unceremonious and nauseous manner. His fingers, of course, were used by him in preference to the fork, but upon the latter being shown to him and explained how he had to use it, he made efforts to do so in a creditable manner. A jack-knife had been given to him prior to his coming on board, and he made great show of it, as if proud thereof. At dinner he used it once or twice in the manner we pointed out. In the midst of rapidly eating, however, he suddenly left off; I presume he had had enough; and, rising from his seat, made one or two of the officers shrink away[.] (*Voyage* 228)

e002291387

Image 2.1   "Portrait of Qalasirssuaq." Library Archives Canada. *Kalli, The Esquimaux Christian*, by Thomas Boyles Murray, CIHM Microfiche series no. 62894. Reproduction copy number E002291387.

While officers were fascinated by Qalasirssuaq, some found his "wildness" a bit too real: he ate too "voraciously;" he preferred his fingers to forks; he played with his knife. Snow's description plays out the tension between interest and repulsion that recurs in responses to Qalasirssuaq's actions.

Once the *Assistance* left Cape York, Qalasirssuaq was apparently accepted as a member of the ship's company and was involved in many aspects of shipboard life, including not only the play but also entertainments such as a masked ball. He was "under the care of the serjeant [sic] of Marines, who instructed [him] in the rudiments of reading and writing" (Murray 12). In 1851, the *Assistance* returned to England with Qalasirssuaq; in London, he became a minor celebrity, making public appearances at the British Museum and the Great Exhibition of 1851. In November of that year, he was placed at the Missionary College at Canterbury to receive a Christian education; two years later he was baptized in a ceremony attended by Franklin's daughter Eleanor and her husband, among others (Murray 36). In 1855, Qalasirssuaq returned to North America, arriving in Newfoundland to assist Moravian missionaries in their work with Labrador Inuit; he died in Newfoundland four months later (Murray 46–68).

OUT COMES E. YORK

Claiming that Qalasirssuaq learned much about British culture and was accepted as a member of the ship's company does not mean that his peers didn't recognize his differences. This perception of difference is, no matter how one interprets the Fox's transformation into Qalasirssuaq, central to any reading of the stage direction. It is useful to recall David Mayer's argument that pantomimic transformations relied on "visual similes" based on the assumption "that one object shared a hidden kinship with another, and that it was the job of the pantomimist to reveal this relationship" (*Harlequin* 49). Viewing the transformation as visual simile suggests that Qalasirssuaq resembled—shared a hidden kinship with—the Fox. Mayer's phrase "hidden kinship" is suggestive, implying that the transformation indicated that Fox and Qalasirssuaq were part of the same family. The broadest application of Mayer's concept suggests that audience members first saw the Fox, then saw Harlequin transform the Fox into Qalasirssuaq, and understood that Qalasirssuaq was like the Fox because both were animals. The resemblance suggested here situates the transformation as complicit in the discursive construction of nonwhite races as animal-like, one of several competing theories of race popular during the Victorian era.

The validity of this reading of the transformation, oversimplified as it may seem, is supported by contemporary theories of racial difference, by circulating representations of Inuit, and by textual evidence within the play.

Mid-nineteenth century theories of race were fluid, changing with developments in archaeology, proto-anthropology, and early evolutionary theory; when examined as a body of thought, they appear contradictory and even incoherent. The debate between monogenists and polygenists in the years immediately preceding the 1859 publication of *On the Origin of Species* is indicative of both the tone and scope of Victorian ethnographic and anthropological thinking. To summarize complex and evolving positions, monogenists believed that members of different races constituted a single human species, whereas polygenists believed that different races were distinct species. Although the debate first emerged in the eighteenth century,[8] in the mid-nineteenth century it was rejuvenated by developments in archaeology and physical anthropology, as ancient sites and previously unknown peoples were discovered and categorized. Both theories had considerable implications for how the difference between "civilized" and "savage" races was understood and how "savage" races were placed in taxonomies. For example, polygenists, drawing on work in physical anthropology, argued that there was little potential for races to either degenerate or improve: "On the basis of skeletal and cranial evidence, polygenists insisted that blacks were physically distinct and mentally inferior [...] on the basis of the mortality of whites in tropical areas, they hypothesized that different races were aboriginal products of different 'centers of creation' and could never fully 'acclimate' elsewhere" (Stocking 67). Each race occupied a relatively stable position in a hierarchy: neither degeneration nor improvement was possible. In contrast, monogenists attempted to reconcile biblical history and developments in archaeology with the diversity of humanity, arguing that varying levels of "civilization" between races were the result of degeneration over time. Archaeological discoveries left "little time" for "civilized" peoples "to have raised themselves from savagery, but there was plenty of time available for nineteenth-century savages to have fallen from an originally higher state" (Stocking 71). Monogenist thought allowed for races to move up and down a ladder of civilization, supporting missionary ideologies by implying that "savage" races could return to an original, higher state of civility through education and conversion.

Arctic exploration generated specific theorizations of racial difference. By mid-century, the Arctic was one of the last "uncharted" regions on earth. Lisa Bloom and Francis Spufford examine Victorian representations of Inuit to argue that exploration was legitimated by the fantasy that the remote and forbidding landscapes being explored and mapped were unpeopled: there was little glory in "discovering" lands that already supported sophisticated cultures. Francis Spufford claims that explorers imagined polar travel as "wholly separate—in mood and technique, aims and expertise—from the Inuit experiences of inhabiting the Arctic" because "the spectacle of the Inuit, living their domestic lives in a place Europeans were considered heroic for reaching, aroused a degree of tension"; Inuit presence "complicate[d] the vision of exploring bravery predicated on the idea of an empty Arctic" (189).[9] Bloom points out that the strategy of textually erasing indigenous inhabitants was one the British rehearsed in Africa and Australia: marking spaces as "empty" was a "discursive strategy that produced the rationale to justify the process of filling them in by the West" (2). To imagine the Arctic as uninhabited when confronted with the reality of its Inuit inhabitants, exploration narratives reduced "the vital participation of Inuit men and women to subordinate 'native bearers' imagined as either 'primitive' or 'unspoiled' figures" (Bloom 3). Claiming that the Arctic was imagined as unpeopled is not to say that Inuit were invisible in representations: they were extensively described and documented. Their position, however, was "in descriptions of the region, in accounts of its natural history, studies of its folklore, word-paintings of its scenery. They did not belong in the stories of discovery and achievement" (Spufford 188). By mythologizing Inuit as natural inhabitants who survived, as foxes or geese might, through instinct and habit rather than through technological innovation or intelligence, British exploration could continue without ideological disruption.

One can observe this pattern of thinking in Clements Markham's nostalgic editorial in *Aurora Borealis*:

> No human foot will probably, for ages, tread their dreary shores. Our remains will lay unnoticed along the snowy beach; and our proud architectural monuments will rear their lofty heads in solitude, with no admiring eyes to gaze upon them; while with no bright protecting abodes to defy his might, the despotic Zero will exercise his life-destroying power, and spread bleak desolation along the deserted floe. Winter after winter will follow each other, the bears and foxes will roam unmolested over the ground where once the vocal and theatrical arts were brought to such perfection[.] (318–19)

While the region was not part of Inuit annual migrations, Qalasirssuaq's knowledge of the area indicated that Inuit had visited it. Markham, knowing Inuit were familiar with the land, excludes Inuit from the category of the human by remarking that only animals will visit the region again. This is a concrete example of precisely what Bloom describes: the tendency to group Inuit and animals as natural inhabitants of the region.

The suggestion that the transformation relied upon audience members recognizing a resemblance between animals and Inuit is supported not only by theories of polygenesis and Bloom's comments but is underlined by Ede's script. Immediately after the transformation occurs, the 1st Clown asks, referring to Qalasirssuaq, "Why is he like a man with a bad cold?" When the 2nd Clown fails to respond, 1st Clown delivers his punch line: "Isn't he a little H(uskey)?" (141). The joke is ostensibly a pun based on two meanings of the word husky: it referred to the scratchy voice of a person with a cold and was whaler's slang for Inuit derived from mispronouncing "Eskimo." The O.E.D. notes that by 1852, a third meaning had entered usage: the word also referred to the dog breed. The ability to use the word husky, without modifier, to refer to both Inuit people and their dogs suggests that the transformation signaled the philosophical, anthropological, and linguistic conflation of Inuit and animals.

A second reading of the stage direction as visual simile emerges if one considers that the transformation suggested that Fox and Qalasirssuaq were similar because they were both thieving and mischievous: audience members recognized that Fox, a tricky character who stole from the sailors, was similar to Qalasirssuaq, the Inuk helping them navigate the eastern and central Arctic. The script characterizes the Fox as a thief and a threat, albeit a playful threat that is more benign than Zero or his servants, like Scurvy. When the Fox "stealthily" enters and steals pork from the sailors, one of the men chases him, calling, "Bring me the gun! Oh! Here's a precious joke:/A fox has stolen a piece of this day's pork" (137). The theft is not serious and the men treat it lightly. Since all one knows, retroactively, about the Fox is that he is a stealthy thief, reading the transformation as based on a simile suggests these traits as the grounds of the resemblance. Inuit were frequently accused of committing petty thefts while on British ships; some officers tolerated these misdemeanors, others saw them as symptomatic of Inuit's debased character. Dr. Alexander Armstrong, for instance, wrote that Alaskan Inuit "are a thieving, cunning race [...] and they would be equally treacherous and deceitful, were their cupidity excited by anything in the hands of a weaker party" (110). The audience would have been familiar with the characterization of Inuit as thieving and may have understood the transformation as suggesting this similarity. But if the relationship suggested is a simile, rather than a metonym, one would expect the comparison to be between equivalent terms: either Qalasirssuaq represents all Inuit and Fox represents all animals or Qalasirssuaq and

Fox represent only themselves as individuals. If the second is the case, it suggests that Qalasirssuaq was like the Fox because he was stealthy and thieving.

The suggestion that audience members recognized this resemblance is immediately troubling. There were no reports of Qalasirssuaq stealing from his fellow sailors or from the ship's stores. In contrast, the men liked Qalasirssuaq and thought highly of him. Murray's memoir reprints a poem entitled "Kalli in the Ship," attributed to a sailor on the *Assistance*, which recounts Qalasirssuaq's sadness at missing his mother, and claims, "We cheer'd him up, and soon he grew/So useful and so kind,/The crew were glad, and Kalli too,/He was not left behind" (13–14). Even midshipman Clements Markham, who thought little of Inuit, remarked that Qalasirssuaq, "though slow to learn the English language, has yet by his constant cheerfulness and good humour, and willingness to make himself useful, become a general favourite, and the remarkable accuracy of York's chart [...] has invariably proven perfectly correct" (*Arctic Miscellanies* 327). Markham's comment appears to dispel the possibility of reading Qalasirssuaq as a thief, yet the two abilities he highlights—Qalasirssuaq's growing proficiency in English and his ability as a cartographer—are skills only a "civilized" citizen could possess: "savages" did not speak English or possess navigational skills superior to those of a British seaman. Is it possible that Qalasirssuaq's ability to adapt to British life might have been construed—consciously or not—as cultural appropriation?

To claim that the transformation reflected latent anxiety that Qalasirssuaq not only might become civilized but could become *more* civilized than the British seems like a stretch. If one keeps in mind, however, the possibility that the transformation suggested that Qalasirssuaq resembled Fox, the menacing implications of Arctic exploration flash into view in a joke told by the 2nd Clown shortly before the transformation, making the idea of latent anxiety more convincing. Shortly before Fox is trapped, 2nd Clown asks, "What foxes are easiest to shoot?" After Pantaloon suggests several incorrect answers to the Clown's riddle, the Clown responds, "Tame ones to be sure" (140). The punch line is innocuous unless one considers it in relation to the transformation as visual simile: if the transformation relied upon audience members recognizing a figural relationship between Fox and Qalasirssuaq, the joke has ominous undertones. The 2nd Clown states that taming a fox makes it easier to shoot: taming is a means to a violent end. Recalling the presumed resemblance between Fox and Qalasirssuaq, the joke implies that taming Inuit—converting them to Christianity and British ways—is similarly a means to an end: either cultural or literal genocide. There is no evidence that the squadron pursued assimilation or extermination in any calculated or coordinated way; however, early in the expedition Clements Markham suggested that the native population of Greenland could be improved and ultimately eliminated through miscegenation: "These settlements are inhabited in a great measure by a mongrel population; for there can be little doubt that the pure Danes, who established themselves there from time to time, have in many instances intermarried with the natives, and greatly improved their physical condition [...] it is to be hoped that eventually by the admixture of European blood the original stock will disappear and be replaced by a finer race of men" (15–16). I am not suggesting that Markham wrote out of malice, but the alignment of "civilization" with racial disappearance is certainly apparent in his comment; furthermore, it is unclear how many men shared Markham's opinion that strategic miscegenation was potentially beneficial.

The framework of the visual simile suggests a figural equivalence between Fox and Qalasirssuaq; since Fox was characterized as a thief, Qalasirssuaq was, according to this logic, also a thief. Qalasirssuaq never literally stole from his shipmates, but his quick adaptation to British life might be understood as cultural appropriation. Cultural appropriation emerges as the threatening flipside of assimilation: the threat implicit in "taming" Inuit to be more British could be resolved, by pantomime's logic, through extermination. The Clown's "harmless joke" makes visible—only for a moment—the threat of imperial force that lay beneath professed intentions of benevolent conquest of the Arctic.

TIME AND TRANSFORMATION

Although both interpretations—that audience members understood the transformation to mean that Qalasirssuaq, because he was an Inuk, was like an animal or that, because he was learning English and had excellent navigational skills, was thieving like the Fox—emerge from surviving documents, they are insufficient to capture the complex relationships that developed between Qalasirssuaq and his shipmates or the matrix of desire and anxiety that underlay British attitudes toward Inuit. It may be that Mayer's formulation of the simile is inadequate when one leaves "Pantoland" to consider the range of cultural understandings audience members brought to the theater. Taking the spirit of Mayer's visual simile—the idea that transformation sequences relied upon audience members perceiving a relationship between the "before" and "after—and considering the temporal element of the transformation—that is, that something changes into another thing as time progresses on stage—one can further complicate the transformation sequence's implications for Qalasirssuaq and the men of the ship.

The simplest possibility that emerges when one considers temporality is that the transformation sequence suggested that Qalasirssuaq became more "human" than "animal" as the winter went on. While he initially was "like an animal"—uncivilized and indigenous—he became "like a human," civilized and anglicized. In other words, both the Fox and the character Qalasirssuaq are Qalasirssuaq, representing *his* before and after states, separated by his exposure to British culture, signified by the figure of Harlequin.

The desire to improve Inuit by exposing them to European or American culture was common among officers serving in the Arctic. William Parker Snow, the man who wrote such detailed descriptions of Qalasirssuaq's first days aboard ship, confessed that he yearned to take an Inuk boy with him when his ship left Cape York. His desire, as expressed in his published account of his expedition, was to bring the boy home to America, because the boy was

> a fine specimen of the Esquimaux race—one, too, that would, no doubt, greatly improve, and with due teaching might become, if not a useful member among civilised society, at least serviceable to his own people; and be the means of doing much good [...] Could I but bring this poor creature within the *good*, and withhold from him the *bad*, results of civilisation—give to that animate piece of clay intelligence, knowledge, and a right understanding,—teach him the knowledge of his Maker, his God, and Saviour!—I felt that it would afford me intense delight. I would keep him as my own; and, while I could work, neither his proper education nor his improvement in all things, spiritual as well as temporal, should be neglected. (*Voyage* 196–97)

Snow's belief in the inherent value in improving even one Inuk by teaching him about Christianity and civilization also runs through Murray's biography of Qalasirssuaq, which suggested that sailors and officers hoped to convert Qalasirssuaq. The sailor's poem Murray reprinted describes how Qalasirssuaq "learn'd to make the best of it,/And now, by time and care,/They tell us he can read a bit,/And say an easy prayer" (14). After linking literacy and conversion, the poem addresses "Kalli" directly: "O Kalli, fail not, day by day,/To kneel to God above" (14) and promises that he "will pass, in wisdom's race,/The idle English boy" (15). The poem concludes by promising Qalasirssuaq that he will rise from student to teacher, from new convert to missionary: "if you learn and practise too/The lessons of your youth,/Some heathen tribes may gain from you/The light of gospel truth" (15). Murray—a man of the church himself—may overstate the case slightly—although many of Austin's men were devout Christians, the project of educating Qalasirssuaq was likely an extension of the activities of the shipboard school, a fun distraction, as much as it was an explicit effort at conversion—however, it points to the ways that missionary ideologies underwrote the transformation sequence.

The stage direction suggests not only Qalasirssuaq's "improvement" from animal to human in religious terms but also his general assimilation into British life. While Qalasirssuaq lived on the ship, he acted like his fellow sailors, trading his clothing for British-issued garments donated by the sailors, participating in shipboard events, and learning rudimentary English. The poem Murray cites is not the only example of a shipboard author representing Qalasirssuaq's impressions of British culture: the December 1850 edition of *Aurora Borealis* included a letter to the editor attributed to Qalasirssuaq, providing a fascinating example of an attempt to ventriloquize the young man in order to imagine how he understood British material culture. The copy of the newspaper held by the Scott Polar Research Institute includes penciled-in initials beside articles to designate authorship; the initials "JJD" appear beside Qalasirssuaq's letter, indicating that James John Donnet, the editor of the published collection of papers and the surgeon on the ship, probably wrote it. It is unclear how much input, if any, Qalasirssuaq had into the content of the letter: because he spoke limited English, even when he arrived in England (Murray 22), the letter might have been Donnet's attempt to help him put his thoughts to paper; it is also possible that Donnet took considerable liberties with the letter's content, imagining not only the language Qalasirssuaq might use to express himself but also his thoughts.

The letter, taken at face value, suggests the extent to which Qalasirssuaq participated in British culture, but also underlines that his cultural comprehension was incomplete. He understood that the British were in the Arctic "to save a great chief, who, with his companions, has been wandering about these terrific seas for the last six winters" but wondered "what could have induced them to come to our land of snows and everlasting snows?" (*Arctic Miscellanies* 90). The letter has Qalasirssuaq list the ways he is like a British sailor—"I have eaten of the same biscuit, drank of the same drink; slept under the same roof, and acted the part allotted to me, with yourselves"—but emphasizes his difference from the British: despite living like a British sailor, Qalasirssuaq says, "yet I cannot understand you" (89–90). Qalasirssuaq's appearance in the play does the same thing as the letter: it both includes him in British cultural practices and marks him as different. The recognition of his difference from the pantomime's stock characters can be seen in the textual conventions at work in the script: while character names appear in nonitalicized capitals (e.g. HARLEQUIN), "E. York" and the Fox are both written in italic lower case (*E. York, White fox*). The difference in notation suggests that while the stock pantomime characters were implicitly recognized as "characters" and the actors playing them as "actors" separate from their characters, Qalasirssuaq was not acting but just "being himself" when he appeared in the play.

A closer look at the letter, however, reveals a rhetorical complexity that suggests that Donnet recognized that Qalasirssuaq possessed a fairly sophisticated understanding of British culture and was capable of translating unfamiliar British ideas and objects into familiar cultural terms. This is seen not only in his interpretation of Franklin as a "great chief" (a fairly common description in Inuit culture during the early stages of contact) but also in how the letter addresses his understanding of British technology: Qalasirssuaq compares the sailing ships to birds "propelled by wings" and recognizes that the smaller steam-powered ships were propelled by "a greater Augerkok [shaman] [...] than the genius of the winds, for when the former tires, the latter pulls him along with a leading string, as our dogs do our sleighs" (*Arctic Miscellanies* 90–91). The author suggests that Qalasirssuaq understood not only the difference between sail and steam powered ships but also that steam ships towed sailing ships in the same way as dogs pulled sleds. At the end of the letter, Qalasirssuaq's "confusion" about British culture belies a similarly sophisticated understanding of British religion: Qalasirssuaq claims that "all these things have puzzled me strangely; much of my curiosity has been satisfied by my friend the serjeant, who has been very kind to me, and who is now teaching me to talk through leaves with the good Augerkoks" (93). Here Donnet suggests that Qalasirssuaq understood precisely how Christianity appeared to someone from a culture without printed books: one read the Bible and prayed aloud (talking through the leaf-like pages) in order to communicate with God (the "Augerkok").

Far from implying that Qalasirssuaq went from being completely indigenous to being completely anglicized, or that this kind of cultural transformation was even possible, Donnet's inclusion of Inuktitut terms and Inuit ideas recognizes that Qalasirssuaq actively moved between cultures, incorporating elements of each in his worldview. While colonizing and missionary projects often sought to convert and assimilate indigenous populations, this would not have been beneficial on the *Assistance*. While one can theorize that Qalasirssuaq's knowledge of the landscape and his ability to draw accurate maps following British conventions was appropriative, in practical terms it was an essential retention of indigenous cultural knowledge. Qalasirssuaq's understanding of Arctic geography was based on both oral transmission of indigenous knowledge and his ability to adapt to British conventions, not on his ability to abandon one form of knowledge in favor of the other.

This is not insignificant when one considers the stage direction. It raises the possibility that the relationship between the Fox and Qalasirssuaq might not have been based on either a one-to-one similarity or on a linear transformation but on parallel abilities that arose in specific contexts. The Fox steals food from the British in order to survive, taking advantage of the situation that presents itself: the Fox survives by cleverly adapting to changing circumstances. Similarly, Qalasirssuaq adapted to British life on the ship, wearing British clothing and learning English, but retained his indigenous worldview, viewing British life through this gaze. Qalasirssuaq's value lay not his ability to *become* British but in his ability to live between cultures, adapting to life on the British ship and retaining indigenous knowledge of navigation and language.[10] He was valuable not because he could assimilate but because he—like the Fox—could adapt, bridging cultures, adapting to shipboard discipline and retaining aboriginal qualities.

Qalasirssuaq's importance to the ship's company becomes clear when one remembers that only months before *Zero* was performed, Austin's squadron found Franklin's first winter site and the graves of three of his men. Confronted by evidence that something had gone wrong, Austin's men must have worried that a similar fate might befall them. If disaster struck—if ships were irreparably damaged or food supplies ran out—one of the only ways the men and officers could survive was by finding Inuit to provide fresh food and warm clothing, carry messages, and guide them through uncharted lands.[11] With Qalasirssuaq aboard, the men of the *Assistance* were better prepared than other British expeditions: Qalasirssuaq knew how to survive on the tundra, where to find game to hunt, and how to get back to Greenland.

Considering both the temporality implicit in the stage direction and the importance of Qalasirssuaq to the ship's company allows one to consider a final interpretation of the transformation sequence: it metaphorically represented how perceptions of Inuit changed as the men and officers got to know Qalasirssuaq. This change is apparent in Clements Markham, for whom familiarity bred some degree of racial tolerance. Soon after leaving England, Markham compared Greenland Inuit to the Danish inhabitants of Greenland, proposing that the races differed not because of increased opportunities or time to become 'civilized' but because of fundamentally incomparable intellectual abilities:

> To say that the one was in a higher state of civilization than the other would be equally inadmissible, for in the ninth century, the Norman in his frail bark, crossing a vast and stormy ocean, had no greater conveniences than the Esquimaux in his kayak [...] but the one great advantage which the Norman possessed was the superiority of his mental powers; powers which enabled him as easily to form a republic on the shores of Greenland and Iceland, as to found monarchies in England and Italy [...] and this advantage alone will suffice to account for the difference between the Caucasians who inhabited Iceland and Greenland in the fourteenth, and the Mongolians who grad out a miserable existence in Greenland and Labrador in the nineteenth. (184–85)

According to Markham, the difference between Europeans and Inuit lay in their respective mental capabilities. He frequently reiterated his belief that Inuit were stupid, commenting that their "powers of thought are so small" (*Arctic Miscellanies* 243) and that "with no method of improving the mind, and no words in their language to express abstract ideas, the stupid and insensate state of the Esquimaux's mind forms a striking contrast to the unobscured clear horizon" (54). But by the end of the winter, Markham's opinion had subtly shifted. He wondered, for example, "whether the Arctic Highlanders in their isolated position are destined to increase, to obtain the blessings of Christianity, and to render their condition as tolerable as the climate will admit; or whether they are fated to die off and disappear from the face of the earth" (*Arctic Miscellanies* 327). While Markham does not problematize the binary distinction between "savage" and "civilized" races, his comment indicates that while he initially thought there was no way to improve the Inuk mind, he later allowed for the possibility of racial improvement through exposure to Christianity and civilized practices. Inuit were transformed—for Markham—from savages akin to animals to primitives who could be improved and civilized: this is a more progressive—although still disturbing—perception. The final reading of the transformation—as a metaphor for a process happening aboard ship—is supported by Markham's changing opinion. It suggests a change that occurred not in Qalasirssuaq but in British perceptions of Qalasirssuaq. The stage direction illustrates how the Arctic and its inhabitants became more familiar: Fox, representing the perception of Inuit as animal-like, becomes Qalasirssuaq, representing the perception that Inuit were fully human.

THE NATIVE INFORMANT

The transformation sequence, read in the context of supporting documents, produces multiple hypotheses concerning reception: it reaffirmed theories of polygenesis that understood Inuit and British as separate species; it made visible latent signs of anxiety concerning appropriation and assimilation; it echoed missionary claims that exposure to British culture "improved" "savages"; it represented Qalasirssuaq as a hybrid subject and situated this cultural hybridity as beneficial to the men on the ship; it demonstrated how perceptions of Qalasirssuaq changed over the winter. Although some of these interpretations appear more palatable or plausible today, each is supported by the surviving archive. These contradictory readings demonstrate that ideologies of racial difference were ambivalent and flexible: Inuit and non-Inuit did not occupy stable, discrete positions in binary opposition to one another. The archive also preserves the sense that Qalasirssuaq himself occupied an unstable position, moving between cultures, adopting the practices that made sense, living in and between two worlds. I conclude this chapter by shifting perspective, considering Qalasirssuaq not as a sign or symbol manipulated by the conventions of the performance and coded by receptive possibilities but as a subject in his own right, an actor with agency in the performance.

From the outset, it should be clear that this is a "mistaken" reading. Qalasirssuaq's performance is barely documented. His voice is silent in the archive. His "perspective" on shipboard life survives only in second-hand documents: the ventriloquizing letter to the editor, poetic representations of his process of assimilation, newspaper reports of his participation in shipboard life. Seeking Qalasirssuaq in the archive is tricky: one gets a sense of him emerging as subject, only to have him disappear moments later. Gayatri Chakravorty Spivak's description of the imaginary but theoretically useful "native informant" provides a starting point for interpreting the flickering signs of Qalasirssuaq's archival presence and illuminates the critical potential of a careful "misreading" of the archive. The "native informant" is "the implausible, if often unacknowledged, contemporary reader" (*Critique* 50), a figure who "in ethnography, can only provide data" to inform texts of colonization (*Critique* 49). Imagining the perspective of the native reader of a colonial text—for example, imagining Qalasirssuaq's understanding of his role in a play that demonstrated how the Arctic could be imaginatively colonized—is "of course mistaken [...] because it attempts to engage the (im)possible perspective of the 'native informant' [...] it attempts to transform into a reading-position the site of the 'native informant' in anthropology, a site that can only *be* read, by definition, for the production of definitive descriptions" (*Critique* 49). Acknowledging that imagining the perspective of the "native informant" is "mistaken" does not mean it is an unproductive exercise, particularly because this practice allows one to explicitly locate the "native informant" as a reading subject, not as a subject to be read.

Simon Gikandi's comments on colonized writers working between cultures resonate with Spivak's explanation of the "native informant," allowing one to consider what happens when the "native informant" is—like Qalasirssuaq—uprooted, relocated, and positioned between cultures. Gikandi describes writers who "seemed to position themselves squarely within colonial Englishness and to affiliate themselves with a set of identities and values that were considered to be the very condition of existence of colonialism itself—civilization, progress, literacy, and civility" but also "took their local histories and traditions for granted and assumed that whatever Englishness had brought to the colonized had not supplanted such histories and traditions; indeed they assumed that what made their cultural moments and identities unique was the simple act of social hybridity" (xiii–xiv). Qalasirssuaq, acting in not just a play but a pantomime (a particularly British genre), participated in the project of making the Arctic familiar to the British, arguably a first step toward colonization of the region. But his presence—his native body interrupting the British performance—suggests that his participation was more than just a sign of his complicity. Furthermore, one must consider whether the performance allowed moments when Qalasirssuaq's worldview could emerge to challenge the play's construction of the Arctic as an extension of British territory. This possibility arises when we note that Qalasirssuaq's role in the play was as the subject of a transformation. Transformation was central to the dramaturgy and the philosophical vision of British pantomime, but was also a central feature of Inuit religion and culture: Qalasirssuaq might have recognized *Zero*'s reliance on transformation not as an example of the imposition of foreign artistic practices but as an example of how British and Inuit cultures existed in conversation with one another.

Eurocentric interpretations of the transformation sequence rely upon the perception of a difference in value between animals and humans and the belief that humans occupied a higher position in the hierarchy of beings. From this perspective, the transformation of Fox into Qalasirssuaq (of an animal into a human) suggests improvement, whether in a religious sense or in the sense of cultural adaptation. Qalasirssuaq, however, might have understood the implications of the transformation very differently because he conceptualized the difference between animals and humans differently. While Christianity assumes that only humans have fully developed souls and that this is one reason animals are inferior to humans, Inuit understood the difference between the two in a substantially different way. Inuit held the foundational belief that "all objects, animate and inanimate, contained an *inua* or inner soul. These *inuat* had a human form, a reminder of the distant past when animals transformed into human beings at will" (Bennett and Rowley 43). The belief that animals, like humans, possessed *inuat* underlay hunting and consumption practices, instilling a fear of offending animals in Inuit who relied upon healthy and available animal stocks for survival. This belief also emerges in Inuit stories concerning the difference between animals and humans, which was more fluid than in European culture. We can see this difference by comparing British and Inuit stories of transformation.

Aurora Borealis included a story that relied on the recognition of a resemblance between Inuit and animals for comic effect and which reaffirmed the difference between animals and civilized humans. In the story, Mr. Muff goes bear hunting and "discovers a native of a rough exterior, who on approaching, extends his arms, as a sign of amity, and welcomes the stranger" (29).[12] Unsure of whether this native is friendly or not, reflecting the same caution advised by the Admiralty, Mr. Muff tries to get away but the native "playfully follows him on all fours" (30). Growing worried, Mr. Muff takes off his hat and "leaves it for the native, who now bears a strong resemblance to a bear. The native having inspected the cap with savage curiosity, appears greatly annoyed at not having found a head in it. Mr. Muff is now convinced that his follower is a bear" (30). Mr. Muff finally tries to shoot the bear/native and, when his gun fails to fire, he runs away. Hearing the defective gun discharge, he turns to see "the bear mortally wounded, having fallen victim to an ill-timed piece of curiosity" (32). The illustrations accompanying the story depict the character as a bear, suggesting that the transformation occurs in the eyes of Mr. Muff and is not an actual change of state. The story reverses the transformation in *Zero*, suggesting that Inuit and animals are so similar that one can mistake one for the other, but by staging degeneration not progress. At the same time, as the native becomes more animal-like, he becomes more aggressive, and the story's tension is only resolved when he is mortally wounded. The story suggests anxieties concerning the difference between animals and indigenous peoples, but quickly contains them using the comic conventions of mistaken identity: the story and its illustrations hint that low light causes Mr. Muff to mistake a bear for a person. Though animals and indigenous peoples appear to exist in a flexible continuum, the story implies that transformation from a human into an animal involves degeneration and that this degeneration must be contained or revealed as a mistake.

The story resembles Inuit stories of human-animal transformations; indeed, one cannot be certain that the author had not heard a similar story from Inuit. Peter Freuchen and Alex Spalding both record versions of a Greenland Inuit story about a hunter who is helped by a fox, then marries a beautiful woman, only to discover, upon attempting to exchange his wife with one of his friends, that his wife was actually the fox who helped him (Freuchen 265–71; Spalding 64–66). In the story, the fox becomes a woman and then returns to being a fox: it is unclear and unimportant whether the character is essentially a fox or human. In the Inuit story, the value of the fox/woman does not change: the woman punishes the man by becoming an animal (rejecting her role as wife), but the story doesn't convey the sense that this is a degeneration. Both the Mr. Muff and the Greenland Inuit story express the difference between animals and humans in ambiguous terms, however, the Inuit story does not associate the shift with a change in civility or with aggression. The Inuit story conveys the sense that transformations emerge in response to circumstances and are performed *by* the individual being transformed, for his or her own advantage, not by another (Harlequin) or the viewer (Mr. Muff). The Mr. Muff story is about figuring out the Arctic, about Mr. Muff trying and failing to understand the difference between bears and Inuit. Through its illustrations, it infers that transformations didn't really occur. In contrast, the Inuit story assumes that transformations were real and an essential component of the animal-human continuum.

Inuit, furthermore, had specific ideas about what foxes and fox hunting signified in daily life. Freuchen's and Spalding's stories provide the sense that the fox is clever and helpful, assisting the man in his hunt; it is tempting to bring this perception to interpreting what the Fox in the play meant to Qalasirssuaq. At the same time, in Greenland Inuit culture, trapping foxes was traditionally women's work; while a "husband is at the blowholes, the wife borrows the dogsled and goes out to set and tend her traps" (Freuchen 68). Freuchen notes that until white men arrived at Thule, fox trapping fell to women because foxes "didn't fight or run away, the cowardly animals, and therefore were not worthy of a man's attention" (68). Aligning Qalasirssuaq with a fox—an animal that didn't run away— has a certain resonance with his role on the ship: he probably didn't see himself as cowardly, but he also didn't try to escape. At the same time, one can imagine Qalasirssuaq finding the Clowns' (and the real sailors') attempts to trap foxes funny: if trapping foxes was "women's work," what did trapping them imply about the Clowns and sailors? I suggest these possibilities not to claim they represent how Qalasirssuaq understood the play, only to suggest that even a brief consideration of Inuit worldviews produces a range of interpretive possibilities.

Gerald Vizenor points out the complex roles that animals play in indigenous literature: "Native metaphors, then, may not be easily understood outside the 'background knowledge' of the native, visionary world. Clearly, the metaphors of native creation, totems, natural reason, transmotion, the tease of names, and the mighty stories of animals, have been translated, more often than not, by social scientists, as evidence or romantic revisions, and with minimal comprehension of native intentions and meaning" (*Fugitive* 134). While one cannot reconstruct precisely what Qalasirssuaq thought the transformation meant, a nuanced consideration of the performance moment must take cultural differences in views of animals and transformations into account. Reading the performance with this in mind disrupts the division between actor/spectator and subject/object of performance, suggesting one must view Qalasirssuaq not only as an object to be interpreted but also as a subject with agency over self-representation, an actor producing meaning, and a spectator interpreting the transformation sequence according to cultural codes different from those inscribed in the script.

Surviving documents suggest that at least a few men on the ship recognized and, in at least one case, attempted to represent Qalasirssuaq's agency as a subject. This is evident in Donnet's letter to the editor, which recognizes even as it ventriloquizes Qalasirssuaq's indigenous worldview. In the letter, Donnet has Qalasirssuaq criticize the British tendency to call the land bleak, writing, "You speak of a country, which you always call 'our beautiful England;' you say it abounds in pussis, narwhals, tuktuk, and in everything a man wants; notwithstanding its beauty and abundance, you leave that country for these bleak, and, as you are pleased to term them, desolate regions; (I think that politeness might have spared this insult to my native land)" (90). Whether the criticism is Donnet's or Qalasirssuaq's, one gets the sense that the letter recognizes Qalasirssuaq's ability to talk back to the explorers. The inclusion of Inuktitut terms for animals (*pussi*, *tuktuk*) indicates Donnet's attempt to attribute authorship, or partial authorship, to Qalasirssuaq, suggesting that even though the letter ventriloquizes Qalasirssuaq, it also incorporated information he provided. The letter also acknowledges Qalasirssuaq's agency as a performing subject in his remark that although he had "acted the part allotted to me, with yourselves" (90), he still did not understand many aspects of British culture. The recognition that Qalasirssuaq acts a part may refer simply to his ability to perform his duties on the ship; however, the implicit assumption in this comment—that by acting British Qalasirssuaq would understand British culture—suggests a subtle acknowledgement that cultural identity was itself an act. Whether this was Donnet's intention or not, the idea that assimilation and adaptation are forms of performance remains in the archive, preserving the idea that Qalasirssuaq was both a performing object filling a role assigned by others and a performing subject with agency to control how he filled his role.

Archival documents concerning Qalasirssuaq indicate his persistent presence as indigenous subject, resonating with Gerald Vizenor's articulation of the idea of Native survivance. In the introduction to *Survivance: Narratives of Native Presence*, Vizenor defines survivance as "an active sense of presence over absence, deracination, and oblivion; survivance is the continuance of stories, not a mere reaction" (1). Distinguishing between Indians and Natives, Vizenor argues that Indians are simulations, constructions made by others, while Natives are actual subjects existing in historical moments that either precede or follow these simulations: "Natives are elusive, the traces of presence are unnameable in literature; the origins are deferred, and the acts of reading native stories are the *différance*, a *postindian* 'fragmentary insight.' The trick native, not the racialist simulation of the *Indian*, is an invitation to a 'pleasurable misreading'" (*Fugitive* 35). Examples of Qalasirssuaq's archival survival complicate Vizenor's distinction, as Qalasirssuaq survives both as a simulation created by others (an "Indian") and as an elusive trace presence (a "Native") lying behind or beneath, but informing these simulations. What is essential to notice, however, is Qalasirssuaq's mobility, fluidity, and persistence as trace presence in the archive: this combination is central to Vizenor's concept of survivance as a mode of indigenous resistance.

The simulated representations that survive and bear traces of presence also illustrate Vizenor's concept of manifest manners, "the notions and misnomers that are read as the authentic and sustained as representations of Native American Indians" (*Manifest* 6). Reading the simulations at our disposal—emerging from discursive constructions of Inuit as animals, as threatening colonized subjects, helpers, potential converts—as discrete examples produces limited subject possibilities for Qalasirssuaq, containing him as an object of analysis rather than a performing subject. Taken together, however, the interpretive possibilities produced by the transformation sequence are more illuminating, suggesting that a range of representational possibilities were available to contemporary audience members and exemplifying the complex ways that manifest manners determine and overwrite a performance moment. The ambivalence and fragmentation apparent in the body of archived simulations of Qalasirssuaq also allow one to see Qalasirssuaq himself as a complex presence in the archive: simultaneously as trickster, as colonially dominated object, as young boy, as future missionary. These perspectives—although all simulations— come together to produce a complex image of how Europeans imagined radicalized others.

It is essential to keep one eye on the political and social implications of this body of simulations, particularly when one considers that both British sailors *and* Qalasirssuaq were responsible for creating these representations. Vizenor argues that:

> The postindian warriors and the missionaries of manifest manners are both responsible for simulations; even that resemblance is a simulation that ends in silence, or the presence of an original referent to tribal survivance. The warriors of simulation are entitled to tease the absence of remembrance in the ruins of representation, and in the tribal performance of heard stories. Simulations in oral stories arise from silence, not inscriptions. The causal narratives of missionaries and ethnologists are terminal simulations of dominance, not survivance. (*Manifest* 13)

Qalasirssuaq demonstrates—as an archival presence and historical subject—a persistent and sustained indigenous presence in the archival remains of the search for the Franklin expedition. Like Vizenor's postindian warriors of survivance, Qalasirssuaq remains in archival silences, in textual fragments of live performances of the past, emerging through the words of others but slyly persisting. While the archive reveals little about how the transformation scene was understood or what Qalasirssuaq's performance was "meant" to mean, the stage direction with which we began serves as a relic of an intercultural world that briefly emerged during the search for the Franklin expedition. The stage direction is a prescient and tangible reminder that the search was neither a monocultural enterprise nor an opportunistic exploitation of Inuit assistance but was an enterprise intimately tied to the experience of figuring out and performing racial difference.

3. Going Native: "Playing Inuit," "Becoming Savage," and Acting Out Franklin ⟡

Qalasirssuaq is a fascinating example of how those involved in the search for the Franklin expedition played with, adapted, and cross-cultural boundaries. Intercultural contact worked reciprocally and mutually, shaping not only Inuit but also the Euro-Americans engaged in the search. Qalasirssuaq's experience of living among British sailors is mirrored in American Charles Francis Hall's accounts of living with Inuit in the 1860s. After McClintock's expedition returned to England in 1859 with the Victory Point record—which confirmed Franklin's death and convinced many that all 105 men who abandoned the ships in 1848 were long dead—Hall became fixated on discovering what "really" happened. Because McClintock established where Franklin's ships had been abandoned and the approximate route the retreating men took, Hall thought it was obvious that further searches of King William Island would uncover relics and records from the expedition; he criticized the British government and the Admiralty for failing to recognize that "the truth could now so easily be obtained obtained, and the ground to explore so small and comparatively so easy of access!" (*Life* 3). Furthermore, Hall was certain that previous searches failed because no one had bothered to thoroughly interview Inuit: "neither McClintock nor any other civilized person has yet been able to ascertain the facts. But, though no civilized persons knew the truth, it was clear to me that the Esquimaux were aware of it, only it required peculiar tact and much time to induce them to make it known" (*Life* 4). Finally, and most controversially, Hall was convinced that survivors lived among Inuit, citing a letter he received from Thomas Hickey claiming "some of Sir John Franklin's men are yet to be found living with the Esquimaux" (*Life* 6).[1]

Hall's plan was, to say the least, a long shot. Franklin and his men had been missing for fifteen years: it was highly unlikely survivors still lived. In addition, Hall was utterly unqualified for the expedition he planned. Pierre Berton remarks: "It would be hard to imagine a more unlikely polar explorer than Charles Francis Hall. [...] [H]e was a high-school dropout with no scientific background, no knowledge of navigation, and no training in any related skills. He was, however, obsessed with the Arctic, a quality that more and more seemed to be the prime requisite for would-be northern adventurers" (*Grail* 345). Against the odds, however, Hall secured funding from Arctic aficionado Henry Grinnell and gained free passage north on the whaler *George Henry*, acting as the self-appointed captain of the two-man "New Franklin Research Expedition."[2] Hall did not reach King William Island or uncover news of Franklin during his 1860–62 expedition, but he learned much about Arctic travel and Inuit culture and applied this knowledge during two successive expeditions to the Arctic.[3] Using the *George Henry* as a base, Hall traveled with Inuit families and lived like them: sleeping in skin tents and igloos, wearing fur clothing, and eating raw game. Hall was not the first explorer to adopt Inuit behaviors to survive in the Arctic, however, his narrative is valuable because it provides an exhaustive account of how he "went native," employing social performance strategies both—and often simultaneously—to ingratiate himself to his companions and to locate himself as an outsider among Inuit.

"Going native" is a voluminous phrase with specific connotations in particular disciplines and which encompasses diverse concepts outside the academy. Considering this, it is necessary to pause in order to contextualize the phrase's meaning in relation to Hall's actions. In *Post-Colonial Studies*, Bill Ashcroft, Gareth Griffiths, and Helen Tiffin argue that "going native" is a process fraught with anxiety, through which a "civilized" subject was contaminated "by absorption into native life and customs" (106).[4] Anxiety surrounding intercultural contact emerges from the "construction of native cultures as either primitive or degenerate in a binary discourse of colonizer/colonized"; while the threat was most commonly associated with interracial sexual desire, because "sexual liaisons with 'native' peoples were supposed to result in a contamination of the colonizers' pure stock," Ashcroft et al. point out that "'going native' could also encompass lapses from European behaviour, the participation in 'native' ceremonies, or the adoption and even enjoyment of local customs in terms of dress, food, recreation and entertainment" (106). "Going native" appears to be a function of the colonizer's agency: it is the colonizer who has sex with native women, who watches native ceremonies, who eats or dresses in a native fashion, who is "tainted" by the encounter. This process seems to render the colonized passive, erasing his or her agency. Thinking more deeply about Ashcroft, Griffiths, and Tiffin's examples of how colonizers "go native," however, reminds one that the process also required the native to provide something consensually—sex, performances, food, clothes—for nonnative consumption: it involved an exchange. When, for example, whalers or explorers entered into sexual relationships with Inuit women, Inuit women received "luxury" goods such as cotton fabric or jewelry and their families gained access to commodities such as bullets, flour, and tea as a result of the relationship. Furthermore, "going native" was not only an economic exchange but also a performance practice: one "goes native" by doing—rather than thinking or feeling—something, by watching natives perform and imitating their actions. W.T. Lhamon's explanation of the cultural exchanges at work in blackface performance illuminates how the cultural and economic aspects of "going native" are linked: "in cultural exchange, the transfer is not of one good for another, but a compounding of goods, one onto others. When I pick up a cultural gesture, it need not bump out a corresponding gesture I already practice. Rather I graft it onto who I am. Perhaps even more important, when one group passes its gestural practices onto another group, there is not a loss of those practices. Nor is there a unilateral ownership on either side. Instead, there are mutual transactions" (91). "Going native" is a cumulative practice that allows one to pick up new practices and add them to one's cultural repertoire: it is a process of addition, rather than a zero-sum game. Euro-Americans living closely with Inuit learned indigenous practices (building igloos, using Inuit musical instruments) and taught Inuit their practices (shooting guns, square dancing); this exchange did not mean Inuit gave up the ability to build igloos or that *qallunaat* (non-Inuit) stopped square dancing when practices were exchanged, but that both groups learned new things.

Hall's narrative is a firsthand account of the complications of "going native" as a cultural exchange, and it explicates precisely how he adopted some cultural practices and rejected others. Hall saw a distinction between what he did while living among Inuit and what other non-Inuit did: Hall lived like an Inuk in order to survive physically and socially, but he was outspoken in his disapproval of interracial sexual relationships, which were common between *qallunaat* whalers and Inuit women, and refused to participate in Inuit spiritual rituals, believing they were corrupted by unethical *angakkuit* (shamans). Although Hall does not explicitly distinguish between modes of "going native," a thorough reading of his narrative reveals that he saw two ways to participate in Inuit life: I term these "playing Inuit" and "becoming savage." "Playing Inuit" was what Hall did, and it was temporary, trivial, and superficial and included actions like consuming Inuit food and wearing Inuit clothing. Although Hall enjoyed "playing Inuit," he never, his narrative implies, became fully absorbed in his performance: he presents himself as always alienated from his own actions. "Playing Inuit" confirmed that Hall was absolutely not Inuit, reflecting Phil Deloria's remark that the lingering appeal of "playing Indian" lies in how "wearing a mask also makes one self-conscious of a real 'me' underneath" (7).

"Becoming savage," on the other hand, was symptomatized by losing oneself, forgetting one's cultural identity in the performance: it did not reinforce white cultural identity but denigrated it. One way *qallunaat* "became savage" was by engaging in interracial sexual relationships. These relationships, according to Hall, occurred when white men ignored their cultural obligation to improve Inuit and gave into "base" desires, corrupting themselves and their partners and contaminating the Inuit race by producing mixed-race children. In Hall's worldview, both Inuit and *qallunaat* could "become savage": through exposure to Christianity and Euro-American social practices, Inuit could become relatively "civilized." If these Inuit engaged in interracial sexual relations or returned to traditional spiritual practices, they effectively chose to "become savage." While "playing Inuit" was necessary and harmless, "becoming savage" was gratuitous and dangerous, permanently changing the subject by contaminating him physically (through interracial sex) or spiritually (through false religion).[5] Like many nineteenth-century Americans living among indigenous peoples, Hall denied the power of cultural exchanges to change his own subjectivity as a "civilized" American, instead believing that "going native" was a temporary activity through which he could, to paraphrase Shari Huhndorf, reveal what "truly" happened to the missing explorers he sought and thus redeem them (5).

In Hall's narrative, intercultural performances are always sites of anxiety: while Hall's own actions had no long-term consequences, they were culturally transgressive and had to be carefully mediated for white readers. Inuit performances of "playing white" had the potential to transform Inuit into "civilized subjects" but often ended in stagnation or degeneration, producing liminal subjects like his translator Tookoolito. Intercultural spiritual-sexual performances permanently changed Inuit subjectivity, either physically (by producing mixed-race children) or metaphysically (marking participants as spiritually corrupt). These intercultural performances exemplify the problematics of "going native," particularly the inherent anxiety concerning racial contamination: "going native" produced—temporarily or permanently—transgressive, hybridized subjects and disrupted the civilized/savage and white/native binaries upon which Hall's understanding of culture was founded. In other words, "playing Inuit" was not a safe performance in contrast to "becoming savage," which was dangerous: both were part of a spectrum of performance, a necessary cultural performance to ensure survival, but one in which permanent slippage was always a danger.

The binary Hall imagined between modes of "going native" was a false one: "playing Inuit" and "becoming savage" could not be neatly severed. On some level, Hall recognized this and it provoked intense anxiety for him: the continuum between "playing Inuit" and "becoming savage" and the anxiety generated by their interconnection is apparent in Hall's account of a theatrical performance he watched aboard the *George Henry*. The performance began as what Hall thought of as a conventional Inuit performance—men drumming on a *keeloun* (skin drum) accompanied by women singing—but was interrupted when one of the whalers entered in blackface makeup and women's clothing. The performance then incorporated both Inuit drumming and American songs and concluded with Inuit women and whalers square dancing together. Hall's account of this performance is strange: while he usually presented himself as a participant in shipboard and Inuit social performances or, if he did not actively participate, described his response to what he watched, in this case Hall depicts himself as completely passive, sitting apart from the group and refusing to interpret what he saw. Hall's spectatorial passivity and editorial silence concerning the "theatrical" occurred because the performance—by recalling Inuit spiritual rituals, by staging the possibility of interracial desire through its citation of minstrelsy, and by enacting how interracial sexual relationships might have developed at shipboard dances—made Hall's anxieties about "becoming savage" visible.

Although the distinction between the two modes of "going native" is an imaginary one, it helps explain how Hall understood his relationship with Inuit and legitimated his work in the Arctic. By proving a white man with no survival skills could thrive among Inuit by adopting their habits, Hall validated his fantasy that some of Franklin's men had survived by "playing Inuit." Hall's account of his own actions suggested it was possible to live with Inuit without engaging in interracial sex, showing that "playing Inuit" did not necessarily lead one to give into "inappropriate" desires and "become savage." This was important because, although McClintock's report exonerated Franklin from charges of cannibalism, the ghosts left by Rae's 1854 report still hung over the expedition. If some of Franklin's men survived, as Hall claimed, it would have been difficult for readers to forget the accusation that they had survived by consuming human flesh. Hall had to perform complicated magic to overwrite this possibility. By claiming he was following in Franklin's footsteps by living like an Inuk, then showing by example that a white man could live among Inuit without transgressing the boundary between civilization and savagery—in Hall's case, by engaging in interracial sex—Hall demonstrated that Franklin's men could have survived by adopting Inuit habits and without crossing the line between civilization and savagery—in their case by refusing to consume human flesh.

"PLAYING INUIT"

Hall was convinced he "had been called" to rescue Franklin survivors (*Life* 3) but was, Pierre Berton suggests, utterly unqualified for polar exploration (*Grail* 345). His expedition was poorly provisioned. He had none of the skills—snowshoeing, navigation, hunting—that overland explorers like John Rae possessed.[6] He prepared for his expedition by camping on a hill behind Cincinnati's observatory, devouring narratives of Arctic exploration, and meeting with every whaler or explorer who would talk to him. Hall's naiveté is reflected in his initial plans for the expedition: Hall believed that once the *George Henry* reached Northumberland Inlet in late summer, he would find Inuit to accompany him by boat to Igloolik, and then overland to King William Island—a trip of at least 1500 kilometers, depending on the route—before winter set in.[7] Despite receiving warnings that his plan was impossible, it was only after his small boat was wrecked that Hall decided to delay his trip to King William Island and use the *George Henry* as a base for visits to Inuit encampments.

During his first winter in the Arctic, Hall adopted a number of indigenous behaviors, including sleeping in igloos and wearing fur and skin clothing, but he identified eating Inuit food as the primary activity that ensured his physical and cultural survival in the Arctic. Eating Inuit food meant overcoming culturally ingrained taboos about consuming raw meat and physically learning how to eat Inuit food. Hall's accounts of eating with Inuit can be contextualized in relation to structural anthropologist Claude Levi-Strauss's argument that the difference between "raw" and "cooked" is analogous to the division between nature and culture. Levi-Strauss uses the term "culinary triangle" to describe a semantically empty field that reveals how specific societies understand the relation between ideas of "raw," "cooked," and "rotten":

> We will start from the hypothesis that this activity [cooking] supposes a system which is located [...] within a triangular semantic field whose three points correspond respectively to the categories of the raw, the cooked and the rotted [...] No doubt these notions constitute empty forms: they teach us nothing about the cooking of any specific society, since only observation can tell us what one means by "raw," "cooked," and "rotted" and we can suppose that it will not be the same for all. (587)

Hall intuitively recognizes Levi-Strauss's argument that attitudes toward food are culturally determined in his description of watching Inuit eat whale meat:

> To one educated otherwise, as we whites are, the Esquimaux custom of feasting on uncooked meats is highly repulsive; but eating meats raw or cooked is entirely a matter of education [...] When I saw the natives actually feasting on the raw flesh of the whale, I thought to myself, "Why cannot I do the same?" and the response to my question came rushing through my brain, independent of prejudice, "Because of my education—because of the customs of my people." (*Life* 110)

While Hall's attitude toward Inuit life and customs appears objectionable today, in the 1860s his cultural relativism, which developed during the first few months he spent in the Arctic, was progressive.[8]

In early September 1860, Hall recorded his shock at Inuit "gluttony" while feasting on whale meat: "the quantity taken in one day—enough to last for several days—is what astonishes me!" (*Life* 100). As Hall observed the meal, his perspective changed and he quickly decided to overcome his "education" in order to join the feast:

> I peeled off a delicate slice of this spinal ligament, closed my eyes, and cried out "Turkey!" But it would not go down so easy. Not because the stomach had posted up its sentinel to say "no whale can come down here!" but because it was tougher than any bull beef of Christendom! For half an hour I tried to masticate it, and then found it was even tougher than when I began. At length I discovered I had been making a mistake in the way to eat it. The Esquimaux custom is to get as vast a piece into their distended mouths as they can cram, and then, boa constrictor-like, first lubricate it over, and so swallow it quite whole! (*Life* 110–11)

Hall suggests that he participated enthusiastically but that his observation skills left something to be desired: though he wanted to eat the whale, he didn't watch Inuit carefully enough to learn *how* to eat it. This is typical of Hall's behavior, particularly early in his expedition, when he did not know quite how to interact with Inuit. It is also significant that Hall does not indicate whether he asked if he could join the feast or how he thought Inuit understood his participation: this silence suggests that he did not yet perceive his actions as a social performance produced for an Inuit audience. Hall quickly learned that to participate in Inuit life, he had to become more skilled at reading and imitating Inuit actions: he had to become a better spectator and actor.

By October 30, 1860, Hall believed he was becoming better at imitating Inuit and that this was leading Inuit to accept him socially. He describes attending a seal feast and sampling seal blood for the first time:

> On first receiving the dish containing this Esquimaux stew, I hesitated. It had gone the round several times, being replenished as occasion required; but its external appearance was not at all inviting [...] But I screwed up courage to try it, and finally, when the dish came again to those by my side, I asked Koojesse, "Pe-e-uke?" (Is it good?) "Armelarng, armelarng" (Yes, yes), was the reply. All eyes were fixed upon me as I prepared to join with them in drinking some of their favourite soup.

> Now the custom of the Esquimaux in drinking seal-blood is to take one long s-o-o-o-p—one mouthful, and then pass the dish on to the rest till the round is made. I followed suit, and, to my astonishment, found the mixture not only good, but really excellent. (*Life* 140)

Hall intended to merely participate in the feast but actually became the center of attention. Unlike when he ate whale, this time he watched what others did before joining in and imitated what they did. He also recognized the importance of demonstrating his enjoyment of the dish because everyone in the tent was watching him. Hall tells readers that his display of pleasure ingratiated him to his hostess:

> Seeing I was pleased with it, she who presided at the feast instantly made ready a pretty little cup [...] and filled it with the hot seal-blood. This I sipped down with as much satisfaction as any food I had eaten in my life; and, in return for the friendly act of my Innuit hostess, I gave her a highly-coloured cotton handkerchief. She was in ecstasies with it, and the whole company joined with her in expression of kindness and goodwill toward me. Clearly I had ingratiated myself with one party of the natives here, and this I was determined to do in like manner elsewhere. (*Life* 140)

The reception of the special, personal cup and the gift of the hand-kerchief mark the moment as a complex intercultural exchange. Hall's enjoyment of the blood and the woman's "ecstasies" over the handker-chief indicate that the exchange made both happy, but the woman's gift also set Hall apart by recognizing him for doing what Inuit did normally. Hall hoped that drinking seal blood would make him appear to be like his companions and would thus ensure his inclusion in the group; how-ever, the act both included Hall in the group and reinforced his status as an outsider.

Eating Inuit food was a physical and social necessity for Hall. Even with Inuit help, he could not have carried sufficient food for his planned journey to King William Island: he had to eat food obtained on the land. Furthermore, Hall believed (correctly) that fresh meat prevented scurvy: when he returned to the *George Henry* following his first extended trip in February 1861, he found that some of the whalemen suffered from scurvy and commented that "the best cure for them" was "forty-three days in an igloo among Innuits" (*Life* 190). Because Hall had no survival skills, he could not take care of himself on the tundra: he was well aware that he was completely reliant on Inuit for food and navigation.[9] Hall also knew that upsetting his guides would jeopardize his chances of success. In September 1861, Hall's friend Koojesse made this point clear to him. While travel-ing by boat in Frobisher Bay, searching for relics of the sixteenth-century Frobisher expedition,[10] Koojesse refused to stop to allow Hall to examine the shoreline. Hall does not explain Koojesse's refusal to stop, but he was upset by it, recording that when Koojesse "curtly and even savagely replied, 'You stop; I go,'" he was "forced to smother [his] anger, and submit to the mortification of being obliged to yield before these untamed children of the icy north" (*Life* 383). Recognizing that Koojesse had publicly under-mined his fragile authority, Hall wrote, "I was completely at the mercy of Koojesse and his companions, [...] if I attempted to show opposition or express a determination to do as I might wish, ominous looks and sharp words met me. Several times I felt obliged to submit, for I knew my life was wholly in their hands" (*Life* 382–83). Hall's frustration emerges in his implicit comparison between himself, a "civilized" explorer hoping to find valuable historical evidence, and the "untamed children of the icy north" and his recognition that his supposed cultural superiority did not give him any real authority over Inuit.[11] Koojesse's behavior demonstrated that while imitating Inuit gave Hall limited access to what Stephen Greenblatt terms "mimetic capital" (6),[12] these actions did not necessarily give him any actual power.

Hall was well aware that he was performing for two audiences: the Inuit he was with and his imagined readers. While he behaved deferentially to Inuit, he ensured that readers would recognize that this was necessary. This negotiation between audiences emerges in his account of attending a seal feast in April 1861:

> This was served to every one but me in pieces from two to three feet long. I saw at once that it was supposed I would not like to eat this *delicacy*; but, having partaken of it before, I signified my wish to do so now; for, be it remembered, *there is no part of a seal but is good*. I drew the ribbon-like food through my teeth Innuit fashion; finished it, and then asked for more. This immensely pleased the old dames. They were in ecstasies. It seemed as if they thought me the best of the group. They laughed—they bestowed upon me all the most pleasant epithets their language would permit. I was one of them—one of the honoured few! (*Life* 235–36)

Hall assumed he was excluded because his companions did not think he would like the seal entrails. Hall not only ate them, but surprised his audience by eating them in "Innuit fashion." The women responded by laughing and praising him. Hall tells readers that the laughter was a sign of inclusion: his performance made him "the best of the group." At the same time, Hall's italicization of "delicacy" and his description of the Inuit elders as "old dames" suggest that he was being ironic. Few readers would think of raw seal entrails as a delicacy or of elderly Inuit women as "dames" deserving respect.[13] While readers may have been fascinated by the scene, they would have been scandalized to join the "honoured few" included in the feast. Through satirical gestures, Hall indicates that even as he suggests the feast facilitated intercultural sociability, he also recognized that his readers would see the scene as evidence of Inuit's lack of civility.

Michael Taussig's description of intercultural mimesis illuminates the ambivalence with which one must read both Hall's imitations and Inuit responses to his performances. Mimesis, which Taussig broadly defines as "the faculty to copy, imitate, make models, explore difference, yield into and become Other" (xiii) is always reciprocal and always raises the question of "Who is mimicking whom [. . .]?" (76–77). In the colonial encounter, mimesis "becomes an enactment not merely of an original but by an 'original'" (Taussig 79), it dances "between the very same and the very different," registering "both sameness and difference, of being like, and of being Other" (Taussig 129). Taussig implores one to consider how imitations are reciprocal, foregrounding questions of how Inuit understood Hall's performance. For example, if Inuit recognized that Hall was attempting to fit in by mimicking how they ate and that his enthusiasm was, in a sense, put on for them, one must consider that Inuit responses—"ecstasies," laughter, "pleasant epithets"—might have been a deliberate imitation of Hall's own enthusiastic demonstrations of pleasure.

When the seal feast occurred, Hall had been in the Arctic for almost a year and had gained some understanding of Inuit customs, but he may have misread the women's laughter as a sign of acceptance. When Hall parted company with these Inuit shortly after the feast, he had forgotten his own clothing and borrowed some from a man named Seko. The reindeer trousers Seko gave him were so small that a woman had to slit them with her knife so he could wear them; even so, Hall "could only *waddle* and tumble down!" (*Life* 237). Hall described the "ringing, side-splitting laughter" of Inuit "at the grotesque figure I cut in old Seko's skin-tight breeches" and noted that "long after our departure, on my looking back, I could see the merry lot still watching, and apparently enjoying the fun I had created" (*Life* 237). Hall's attempt to dress like an Inuk became a comic performance that underlined, by emphasizing Hall's "abnormal" size, his physical difference from Inuit.

Considering the laughter at Hall's pants in the context of Homi Bhabha's theorization of colonial mimicry allows one to imagine that the women's laughter at the seal feast was both mocking and inclusive, marking Hall as both in and out of the community. Bhabha uses the phrase "almost the same, *but not quite*" (123) to explain how colonial mimicry acts as a "complex strategy of reform, regulation and discipline, which 'appropriates' the Other as it visualizes power" (122). By linking the disciplinary function of mimicry with the appropriation of the Other and with the ability to make colonial power dynamics visible, Bhabha implies that colonial mimicry is enacted along a linear axis of power. In Hall's case, however, the unidirectional power associated with the binary of colonizer/colonized is disrupted: Hall, an explorer with missionary impulses, *should* act as colonizer, yet he, not Inuit, had to engage in complex acts of social mimicry to ensure his survival. Hall's situation resembles what Mary Louise Pratt terms "mutual appropriation," a phenomenon which occurs in encounters that render the colonizer passive, in which "his own agency and desire play little part": Pratt describes these events as "not conquest, but anti-conquest" (80).

The disruption of expected colonial power differences occurs in moments of slippage, when the impossibility of complete mimesis becomes visible. Slippage, a phenomenon complicit with the deployment of power, allows a counter-reading of the women's laughter to emerge: the elders may have laughed at Hall eating seal entrails not because his imitation was successful but because it highlighted the difference between him and them, underlining the naiveté of his attempt to fit in through mimesis. Considering Hall as a (reversed) rendition of Bhabha's "mimic man" suggests that successfully "acting Inuit"—having the performance conventions disappear into the guise of natural action—was impossible. Anne McClintock describes the problem: "The mimic men are obliged to inhabit an uninhabitable zone of ambivalence that grants them neither identity nor difference; they must mimic an image that they cannot fully assume [...] in the slippage between identity and difference the 'normalizing' authority of colonial discourse is thrown into question [...] Mimicry becomes 'at once resemblance and menace'" (63). If colonial mimicry is always a failure, if it is impossible to "authentically" perform, one must consider that laughter recognized this failure: the Inuit women might have laughed not because Hall was one of them but because his performance affirmed that he was absolutely not, and would never be, one of them.

If one considers Hall's performances in relation to his imagined readers at home, his goal shifts from disappearance to proximity: Hall situated himself in a fantasy of "almost the same, but not quite," straddling a fine line between collapsing racial difference—telling his readers that if they saw him, they would not be able to differentiate him from an Inuk—and reinforcing his difference from and his readers' assumptions about "savages." This is clear in Hall's description of how he imagined readers would react to entering an Inuit home:

> When a white man for the first time enters one of their tupics or igloos, he is nauseated with everything he sees and smells—even disgusted with the looks of the innocent natives, who extend to him the best hospitality their means afford [...] Any one fresh from civilization [...] would see a company of what he would call a dirty set of human beings, mixed up among masses of nasty, uneatable flesh, skins, blood, and bones, scattered all about the igloo. He would see, hanging over a long, low flame, the *oo-koo-sin* (stone kettle), black with soot and oil of great age, and filled to its utmost capacity with black meat, swimming in a thick, dark, smoking fluid, as if made by boiling down the dirty scrapings of a butcher's stall. He would see men, women, and children—my humble self included—engaged in devouring the contents of that kettle, and he would pity the human beings who could be reduced to such necessity as to eat the horrid stuff. The dishes out of which the soup is taken would turn his stomach, especially when he should see dogs wash them out with their long pliant tongues previous to our using them. (*Life* 476–77)

Hall invites readers to imaginatively enter the igloo and interprets the scene for them. His emphasis on the novelty of the situation for readers "fresh from civilization" implies that as *qallunaat* grow accustomed to Inuit life, the scene will become less shocking. Yet Hall's description does nothing to convince readers that their initial disgust will disappear: in fact, he reinforced discourses of racial difference, particularly by collapsing the difference between Inuit and animals. Not only is the Inuit home unrecognizable as human habitation, it is shared with dogs who take part in the meal by cleaning the bowls with their tongues before Inuit eat. Hall's extensive description of the "remains"—unidentifiable flesh, skin, bones, and blood—around the igloo and in the filthy pot reiterated that Inuit could not distinguish between raw, cooked, and rotten foods: they are "uncivilized" because they do not understand the difference between appropriate and inappropriate consumption.

Contemporary readers would have been familiar with John Rae's report: the passage, particularly Hall's use of the word "kettle" to describe the serving vessel, would have reminded readers of Rae's infamous description of kettles of human remains that served as evidence that Franklin's men had resorted to cannibalism. Rae's critics often asked how Inuit knew that the remains were human and not animal. By failing to identify what kind of animal remains are in the igloo, and indirectly citing Rae's report, Hall raises the possibility of accidental cannibalism, perhaps even reminding readers familiar with Arctic exploration of the alleged cannibalism during Franklin's 1819–22 expedition. Hall plays with the ambiguity explicit in Rae's report and implicit in Franklin's early expedition, encouraging readers' repulsion by providing space for them to fill the kettle with whatever they imagine.

Although Hall suggests that initial visceral reactions to the material conditions of Inuit life are groundless when he relates how he devoured the contents of the kettle alongside his companions, the passage makes the difference between Hall and Inuit clear: Hall can "play Inuit," but his ability to narrate what happened during the feast and anticipate readers' disgust marks him as a "civilized" spectator. He appears to accept what is happening around him as normal, avoiding overt expressions of repulsion, but his rhetorical strategy of gazing around the space as an outsider indicates his recognition that Inuit do not live as "civilized" people do. The same cultural relativism that allowed Hall to overcome taboos and eat raw whale ligament also allowed him to demonstrate that he could return to seeing Inuit as a "civilized" person should when he returned to "civilization." Although Hall "played Inuit," he had not "become savage."

Hall's cultural relativism was not rhetorically isolated to his descriptions of Inuit domestic life but was typical of his attitude toward Inuit customs during his time in the north. Cultural relativism underscores the pleasure Hall depicted himself gaining from imitating Inuit eating habits: his representation of his attitude about "playing native" changed depending on his surroundings and companions. While Hall was traveling with Inuit, he rhapsodized about eating venison, describing how "it was *delightful*; its flavour was a kind of sorrel acid; it had an *ambrosial* taste! it fairly melted in my mouth!" (*Life* 438). In contrast, when the *George Henry's* men's rations were reduced, men had to supplement their diets with "black skin" (whale skin), leading Hall to remark: "I do not think it can be said that any of us ate 'black skin' [...] because we really liked it. Some wise person has said that man should not live to eat but *eat to live*" (*Life* 422). When Hall is performing for an Inuit audience within his narrative, he takes great pleasure in eating Inuit food; in contrast, when he is on the ship performing for *qallunaat*, Inuit food is simply necessary for survival. "Playing Inuit," was precisely that—play—and Hall imagined that it-like a game—was partitioned off from everyday life as a self-conscious, performative response to given circumstances.

"BECOMING SAVAGE"

In contrast to "playing Inuit," "becoming savage" emerges as a haunting, lurking anxiety in Hall's text, manifested in his belief that interracial sex was immoral, in his criticisms of Inuit who chose "degeneration" over "improvement," and in his denunciations of Inuit spiritual practices as corrupt and exploitative. These concerns arise in Hall's narration of sexual, cultural, and spiritual performances enacted by and on the body. While "playing Inuit" was ephemeral, unable to permanently change the constitution of the subject, "becoming savage" breached the boundaries of the performance moment with its lasting physical or metaphysical implications. One could return to oneself after "playing Inuit," but one "became savage" forever.

Hall traveled north already convinced that miscegenation corrupted Inuit. Before he left, he wrote in his journal about "the disgraceful conduct of a well-known Commander (not unknown to history) who during a winter in the Arctic Regions turned his vessel into a – – – -!" (qtd. in Loomis 52). What the vessel became is clarified by Hall's next comment: "What was it that brought destruction upon Sodom & G? This was damnable to thus treat the untutored Esquimaux. The males were indignant at the outrages committed upon their wives and daughters by CIVILIZED (?) WHITE MAN: O, my countrymen! Instead of lifting that poor benighted people by teaching virtue and civilization, you carry devils and damnation to them" (qtd. in Loomis 52). Hall imagines Inuit men's anger at white men's sexual exploitation of women and suggests that interracial sex constituted a failure on the part of American whalers who had obligations to improve, not corrupt, indigenous populations.

Once Hall arrived in the Arctic, he supported his argument against interracial sexuality by claiming that women who became sexually involved with white men and their mixed-race children were socially disadvantaged. Hall describes Puto, a "handsome" woman with a "white" child, who "had a hard time of it alone, supporting herself and child" and "suffered more from various privations than the other women. She was often a week with hardly anything to eat, and in consequence, her poor child was nearly starved" (*Life* 154–55). Hall does not spell out the cause of Puto's privations, but implies that because she was socially ostracized for her relationship with a white man, she did not receive the informal social assistance other single women did. When Hall saw Puto later, living at a whaling depot, she "was very badly off, her husband being dead, and she had but scant means of providing for herself and offspring" (*Life* 290). It is unclear whether Puto's "husband" was dead or had simply returned south, as it was common for Inuit to refer to missing *qallunaat* fathers as dead if they left the Arctic and did not return. In any case, Puto, unable to support herself, was forced to abandon her traditional lifestyle and rely on the charity of whalers.

It is unclear whether Hall ever slept with an Inuk woman. He lived closely with Inuit, often sleeping with Inuit families under communal skin blankets in the "general bed" (*Life* 175). He was certainly aware that close quarters could encourage intimate relations. Hall recounts sleeping in an igloo with Tookoolito and Punnie, two Inuit women with whom he spent a great deal of time, and being unable to sleep because his feet were cold. When he told Tookoolito his problem, she warmed his feet by "seizing them and drawing them aslant to her side." Hall, shocked when Tookoolito placed his feet on her naked body, noted that his "modesty [...] was quieted when she exclaimed, 'Your feet are like ice, and must be warmed *Innuit* fashion!'" Hall slept with his feet intertwined with Tookoolito's and describes waking to find "no less than three pairs of warm feet all woven and interwoven, so that some difficulty was experienced to tell which were my own" (*Life* 175–76). Hall warmed his feet against a naked woman's body and awoke with his legs entwined with two women's legs: while this does not prove that Hall did anything "improper," it entices readers to imagine how one could "forget" oneself. Hall's remark that his modesty "was quieted" demonstrates his awareness that he was treading on dangerous ground by placing his feet against Tookoolito's body. Chauncey Loomis, who does not believe Hall engaged in miscegenation, claims that Hall's frankness demonstrates his innocence, argues that Hall's writing reveals "something incorrigibly asexual in his personality and mind," and concludes that "sexual intercourse with an Eskimo woman would have struck him as somehow demeaning" (97–98). Loomis' assessment demonstrates the danger of implicitly trusting Hall's narrative and journals: although Hall criticized interracial sexual relations and does not mention ever having had an Inuk lover, this is not conclusive evidence of his abstinence. The history of Inuit-*qallunaat* relations is littered with examples of white men who had children with Inuit women and whose personal papers fail to document these relationships.[14]

Hall's professed disapproval of interracial sexuality was symptomatic of the time in which he lived. The fear of miscegenation—both interracial sex and marriage—was widespread in America and Europe: "*Metissage* (interracial unions) generally and concubinage in particular, represented the paramount danger to racial purity and cultural identity in all its forms. Through sexual contact with women of color European men 'contracted' not only disease but debased sentiments, immoral proclivities and extreme susceptibility to decivilized states" (McClintock 48). In the United States, legislation to contain and eliminate these troubling relationships "provide[s] a virtual map of the changing legal definition of race and offer[s] clues to a major reformulation of the notion of racial difference that emerged in the late 1800s" (Pascoe 10).[15] Unsurprisingly, fears of miscegenation and legal prohibitions didn't limit its occurrence or influence. Interracial sexual relationships were central to how colonial governance was imagined and enacted, and questions of colonial power, according to both Anne McClintock and Ann Laura Stoler, can be linked to the immense sexual fascination displaced onto colonized bodies. McClintock identifies that "long before the era of high Victorian imperialism, Africa and the Americas had become what can be called a porno-tropics for the European imagination—a fantastic magic lantern of the mind onto which Europe projected its forbidden sexual desires and fears" and argues that "within this porno-tropic tradition, women figured as the epitome of sexual aberration and excess. Folklore saw them, even more than the men, as given to a lascivious venery so promiscuous as to border on the bestial" (22).

Stoler adds: "The tropics provided a site for European pornographic fanta-sies long before conquest was under way, with lurid descriptions of sexual license, promiscuity, gynecological aberrations, and general perversion marking the Otherness of the colonized for metropolitan consumption" (43). The conflict between desire for and fear of colonized bodies was not resolved or tidily displaced: "imperial contestations over métissage suggest nothing linear about these developments. Rather, class distinctions, gender prescriptions, cultural knowledge, and racial membership were simultane-ously invoked and strategically filled with different meanings for various projects" (Stoler 84).

Hall never discusses interracial sexual activity between Inuit women and the *George Henry's* men, but the frequency of miscegenation between whalers and Inuit women during the second half of the nineteenth cen-tury is well documented. Mid-century American whalers spent extended periods of time living closely with Inuit: Inuit men and women worked for whalers and often lived aboard ships during the winters. Both ordinary seamen and officers commonly engaged in relatively long-term relation-ships with Inuit women and these liaisons frequently produced children. L. E. Borden, a Canadian surgeon aboard DGS *Neptune* in 1903, com-mented: "It was customary [...] for these whalers, when they were tied up for the winter to take an Eskimo woman on board as a companion to while away the long winter months. [...] A goodly number of children, who at the slightest glance, gave evidence that they were not pure Eskimo led me to believe that the practice of a woman companion had been fairly general" (66–67). W. Gillies Ross's study of relations between whalers and Inuit confirms that Borden's observation was accurate: although "sexual intercourse between whalemen and Eskimo women was restricted by the severity of the climate and the lack of privacy in snow houses and ships' forecastles," the frequency of interracial sexual relationships was evidenced by the spread of venereal diseases and by high proportions of mixed-race children (119, 120–22).

Hall was most vocal about his disapproval of miscegenation, but he also took issue with other signs of racial hybridity. Hall believed Inuit could be "improved" through exposure to Christianity and was troubled when con-version stalled, resulting in Inuit occupying liminal positions between cul-tures. Anxiety concerning racial "stalling" emerges in Hall's reaction when his translator Tookoolito, who seemed on the verge of conversion, returned to Inuit spiritual practices, effectively "becoming savage" in Hall's eyes. Tookoolito (the same woman who "innocently" warmed his feet) and her husband Ebierbing had traveled to England and adopted many British habits, which they practiced upon returning to the Arctic. Hall describes the first time he saw Tookoolito:

> I heard a soft, sweet voice say, "Good morning, sir." The *tone* in which it was spoke—musical, lively, and varied—instantly told me that a lady of refinement was there greeting me. I was astonished. Could I be dreaming? [...] I raised my head: a lady was indeed before me, and extending an ungloved hand [...] The doorway in which she stood leads from the main cabin into my private room. Directly over this entrance was the skylight, admitting a flood of light, and thus revealed to me *crinoline*, heavy flounces, an attenuated toga, and an immensely expanded 'kiss-me-quick' bonnet, but the features I could not at first make out [...] But, on turning her face, who should it be but a *lady* Esquimaux! [...] She spoke my own language fluently, and there, seated at my right in the main cabin, I had a long and interesting conversation with her. (*Life* 133–34)

Hall's heightened description points to the significance of the moment: first telling readers that he was unsure whether her voice came to him from reality or a dream, then describing the light illuminating her from above, Hall situates Tookoolito as a mystical figure sent through divine intervention. The mystery is heightened by the ambiguity about her racial identity—her bonnet hides both her face and her race—and Hall cannot determine whether she is white or Inuk, "civilized" or "savage." Hall quickly clarifies that Tookoolito had become partially "civilized" through contact; her clothing and speech signify this liminality. This is reinforced when Hall mentions that Tookoolito had learned the "civilized" pastime of knitting and acquired a taste for that "soothing, cheering, invigorating emblem of civilization—T-E-A!" (*Life* 138). When she first appears in the narrative, Tookoolito is a racially hybrid subject, but Hall hoped that this hybridity was only a stage in Tookoolito becoming fully "civilized."

Hall dreamed of Tookoolito becoming a missionary among Inuit, a hope based in a conflation of domesticity, "civilized" femininity, and Christianity. Because Tookoolito spoke English and had adopted "white" behaviors associated with feminine domesticity, such as knitting, Hall hoped that she could also teach Inuit about "civilized" customs, including Christianity:

> In all the places around Northumberland Inlet she has lived, and done what she could to improve her people. A singular fact relative to dressing her hair, keeping her face and hands cleanly, and wearing civilization dresses—others of her sex, in considerable numbers, follow these fashions imported by her. This

shows to me what one person like Tookoolito could accomplish in the way of the introduction of schools and churches among this people. (*Life* 136)

Hall believed that conversion was not only feasible but also highly desirable. Combined with his own modest beginnings and efforts at self-improvement (Loomis 27–28), Hall's belief in improvement through conversion locates him as part of a larger movement among Christian missionaries. George Stocking describes how self-educated British missionaries understood their encounters with "savages":

> Although they were full of the spirit of self-abnegation and Christian love, these motives were compromised somewhat by an aggressive ethnocentrism. When confronted with peoples whose cultural values seemed at polar variance, they assumed that because they themselves had risen from ignorance and low estate by their own exertions and by embracing vital Christianity, the natives to whom they offered education and the word of God would do likewise. When these expectations were frustrated, they were quite capable of portraying fallen savage man in rather bleak terms, whether to vindicate their own disappointed efforts or to extort those at home to greater ones. (87–88)

Hall, like the missionaries Stocking describes, was motivated by Christian zeal; his frustration when Inuit "became savage" resembles Stocking's description of how missionaries chastised the "fallen savage."

Hall quickly began his efforts to convert Tookoolito and took every opportunity to teach her about Christianity. He recounts a conversation in which she explained why Inuit leave family members alone to die and he tried to convince her that Christian practices were more compassionate by reminding her: "On Christmas day I gave you a good book—the Bible. That book is the Word of God. It tells you and me—everybody—to visit the sick, the afflicted, the widow, the helpless, the poor." Hall follows this by immediately telling his readers how he proceeded "to show her wherein it was wrong thus to leave the sick—the dying" and told her "it was not to be wondered at that she and her people believed many unreasonable things, when there had been no one to teach them better—no one to tell them of the Bible. I told her that some people of America and in England believed a great many ridiculous things, but that did not make them true" (*Life* 165). Hall then told Tookoolito that "if she or her people could prove to me her or their ways were all the best, then I would be one to do as Innuits did" (*Life* 165). While Hall suggested he was open to converting to Inuit beliefs, this was never a real possibility: although he deferred to Inuit when it came to survival or hunting skills, in spiritual matters he had the ultimate authority—the Bible—on his side. Hall imagined that "acting white" would permanently change Tookoolito, making her more "civilized," but never acknowledged that Tookoolito might have "played white" in ways that mirrored how he "played Inuit": she drank tea, he ate seal; she wore a crinoline, he wore fur trousers; she read the Bible, he attended shaman ceremonies. Hall never thought that "playing Inuit" could make him permanently like an Inuk, yet his attempt to convert Tookoolito's suggests he hoped "playing white" would make Tookoolito more "civilized."

During Hall's second expedition, Tookoolito's child became very ill. According to Hall, she rejected his medical advice and instead returned to Inuit practices because the *angakkuk* (shaman, singular form) told her the *tuurngait* (spirits) were punishing her by making her son ill.[16] Hall claimed that Tookoolito and Ebierbing were "so fully under the power of their people's law" that they "gave themselves fully up to this superstition." Hall attempted to change Tookoolito's mind, but she was convinced they "would be cursed" and that "if the an-ge-ko [*angakkuk*] were not obeyed they would all desert him." Hall disapproved of the social pressure on Tookoolito and was "sincerely grieved [...] tried in spirit [...] at their degrading subjection, and yet [...] helpless [...] to afford relief" (Nourse 244). In the months that followed, Hall grew frustrated as Tookoolito "continued to live under what [he] considered to be a superstitious regimen" and "his annoyance sometimes flared into anger—at her and her culture. He did not like to be reminded that her Christianity was only a late and superficial modification of her native beliefs" (Loomis 198). Hall's lasting anger seems to emerge both from the injury Tookoolito's "rejection" caused his pride and from the challenge it posed to the worldview that justified his missionary impulses. Tookoolito's participation in *angakkuit* ceremonies demonstrated that "playing white" did not signify a step toward permanent racial "improvement" but her liminal position between cultures.

Tookoolito's return to Inuit spirituality also troubled Hall because he was convinced that *angakkuit* were corrupt, performing fraudulent and exploitative ceremonies. Hall's descriptions of these ceremonies highlight his ability to see through their conventions, illustrating his self-positioning as "skeptical observer" and his repulsion with how spiritual practices linked sexual "exploitation" and religious observance.[17] Hall's skepticism is apparent in his first description of meeting Mingumailo, an Inuk shaman, in November 1860: Hall remarks that "he was one of those who lived upon the credulity and ignorance of his race" (*Life* 142). Despite this, Hall followed Mingumailo to his tent, "desirous of witnessing some of the farther acts of this curious and important personage" (*Life* 142). Hall believed the ceremony he witnessed was intended to contact Kudlago, a man who had recently died:

> Mingumailo sat facing us. He began by rapidly clapping his hands; so rapidly, indeed, that it was impossible to count the strokes. Then he accompanied this clapping by some metaphorical expressions beyond the power of ordinary intelligences to divine [...] Of course, I demeaned myself accordingly, and was as quiet and serious a listener as any one there. Occasionally the *angeko* would cease his voice and the motion of his hands. Then all became still as death. Presently, with renewed vigour he would recommence his services, patting his hands—which were moved around during the operation—now in a circle, now before *my* face, now before Koojesse's [...] Every now and then, with his eyes staring into the farthest recesses of the tent, he would become fixed as marble, and looking quite hideous.

> At such times Koojesse was brought into active use. He was directed, as much by the angeko's signs as by the sudden and sharp words uttered, to fix his eyes upon this point of the tent, then that [...] "*Kudlago's spirit shook the skin coverings.*"

> Poor Koojesse! I could not help pitying him, though myself hardly able to control the laughter reigning within me. There he sat, large drops of perspiration streaming from his nose (Esquimaux sweat profusely only *on the nose*), and as earnest as though life and soul were the issue. (*Life* 142–43)

Hall's descriptive language in this proto-anthropological passage suggests that he saw Mingumailo's "hideous" frozen poses as grotesque and understood his performance as manipulative in its attempt to convince Koojesse that "life and soul were the issue." Hall implies that he—unlike Inuit—recognized that Mingumailo's communication with Kudlago was fake, but that he pretended to believe in order to witness the ceremony. The account suggests two ways to participate in the ceremony: as a skeptical spectator or as a naive believer. Hall—the skeptical spectator—sees the theatrical, heightened nature of Mingumailo's actions as a sign of the performance's inauthenticity and lack of "real" spiritual power. In contrast, Koojesse's "earnest" participation showed this naiveté: Koojesse could not see Mingumailo's performance for what it was.

The "climax" of the ceremony demonstrated—to Hall—that he was correct in reading the performance as theatrical manipulation. He tells readers that the finale "was done with a sprinkling of clear words in Esquimaux, just enough for Koojesse and myself to understand. The angeko spirit spoke: 'He was in want. The *kodluna* (*white man*) could relieve his wants.

Would not the kodluna give the spirit one of the double-barrelled guns in his possession?'" (*Life* 143). The shaman's "clear words" indicated that the request for the "kodluna" to give the "spirit" his gun was the point of the entire ceremony. Hall was not fooled but saw an opportunity to take advantage of the shaman's greed. After clarifying that Mingumailo was actually asking for a gun for himself, Hall asked Koojesse if Mingumailo "would be very useful in my future explorations to King William's Land?" When Koojesse told him he would, Hall made a counteroffer to the *angak-kuk*, saying: "Well, if Angeko goes with me next season, he shall have a gun—one of my best." According to Hall, "This made the wizard-man leap for joy; for he thought, as I afterward found, that I meant to give it him at once" (*Life* 143). Hall assumed that Mingumailo's intention was for both Hall and Koojesse to believe that the request for the gun came from Kudlago and that he was a mere medium. Hall, believing himself a more sophisticated spectator than Koojesse, apparently saw through Mingumailo's unskilled performance and recognized that the entire ceremony had been staged to allow Mingumailo to ask for the gun. Instead of calling Mingumailo's bluff, Hall seized the chance to secure help with his own mission, transforming Mingumailo's attempt to exploit him into a self-serving exchange.

Mingumailo's performance linked religious and economic practices; the economic motive behind the ceremony convinced Hall of its corrupt nature. Hall notes his complicity in the performance without irony: he not only witnessed the ceremony but participated in and tacitly condoned it by trading his gun for assistance. Hall tells readers that once Mingumailo got the gun, he dropped the pretense of solemnity and was thrilled that he had "accomplished a great feat in charming a kodluna into giving him a gun as recognition of his magical power" (*Life* 144). Hall recognized too late that he had misread Mingumailo's performance: the ceremony was intended, perhaps from the outset, to charm Hall into giving Mingumailo a gun. The corruption of spirituality that Hall found reprehensible then reached a crisis point when he realized that Mingumailo saw sexual acts, like spiritual practices and material goods, as exchangeable commodities. Mingumailo offered Hall a number of goods to demonstrate his joy at receiving the gun: "he told me I should have the choice of his two wives, all his *tuktoo* skins (reindeer furs) that I might need, and sealskins for making boots, and other articles in abundance. That he had great riches of this description, probably obtained from his credulous worshippers, was evident from the rolls of beautiful skins I saw around me" (*Life* 144). Hall implies that Mingumailo's wives were, like reindeer skins, obtained by manipulating "credulous worshippers" and were exchangeable commodities. When his wives entered the tent, Mingumailo repeated his offer and, although Hall tried to explain that he had a wife at home, Mingumailo and his wives persisted:

> This, however, neither satisfied his ideas about matrimony, nor, as it appeared, those of his wives; for both of them at once decked themselves out in all the smiles and blandishments that they possessed. I asked them if they really coincided in the offer their husband had made, and was immediately told they gladly did. However, I was about again declining the offer, when the angeko suddenly made a sign to Koojesse, leaving me alone with the proffered wives. I uttered a few kind words to them, and, giving each a plug of tobacco with a friendly grasp of the hand, left the tupic and went toward the boat. (*Life* 144)

Hall outlines a triangular relationship between Inuit spiritual practices, commodity exchange, and extramarital sexuality for his readers, one in which a spiritual ceremony is intended for the gain of a gun, in which a gun can be exchanged for a woman, and in which sexual rejection can be mitigated through the gift of tobacco and "kind words."[18]

Hall's account of the ceremony focuses on its performance conventions and Hall's perception of the *angakkuk*'s intentions, rather than its meaning within Inuit culture, demonstrating one of the historiographical hazards of relying upon a one-sided archive to establish what happened in a past performance. Hall makes no attempt to move beyond his initial assumption that Mingumailo was a fraud. He describes Mingumailo's gestures—rapid clapping, hand movements directed at Hall and Koojesse, motionless staring into space—and his vocal performance—metaphorical expressions, sharp tone, a limited use of Inuktitut—at length, but never contextualizes them or connects them to the ceremony's apparent purpose. Because he severs the conventions from any culturally specific meaning, the performance conventions of the *angakkuit* ceremony—its gestures, vocal qualities, spectator-performer relationships—come to signify only the spiritual corruption and the triangular relationship of spirituality, commodity exchange, and sexuality that Hall saw in the ceremony. Hall, intentionally or not, evokes this signifying chain—*angakkuit* performance conventions signify the triangular relationship, which in turn signifies spiritual and cultural degeneration—in his account of a second intercultural performance. The anxiety provoked by this performance allows one to develop a more complex understanding of what was at stake in variations on "going native."

JIM CROW AT THE SQUARE DANCE

As Hall's understanding of Inuit culture became more nuanced, he found it increasingly difficult to sever sociability from spirituality and thus to determine which activities to participate in and which to avoid. His account of one intercultural "theatrical" on the *George Henry* reveals that the binary underlying the distinction between his own cultural performances as "playing Inuit" and those of his Inuit and *qallunaat* companions as "becoming savage" was a false one and implies that ways of "going native" operated in tension and conjunction with one another. The "theatrical" relocated the performance conventions of Inuit spiritual ceremonies as entertainment, cited the range of racial meanings embedded in blackface performance practice, and ultimately enacted how interracial sexual relationships might have actually been initiated on whaling ships during shipboard square dances.

Hall claims he did not participate in the event. There are many reasons he might not have participated or might have told readers he did not: he was tired, he was bored, he didn't want readers to attach him to blackface performance—one cannot reconstruct Hall's motives. Hall's lack of participation in and his editorial silence about the performance is, however, strange: he almost always participated in shipboard entertainments and, as his description of Mingumailo's performance illustrates, when he was a spectator, he was an opinionated one. The most interesting—albeit speculative—way to read Hall's nonparticipation is symptomatically: because the performance staged Hall's precise anxieties concerning the relationships between spirituality, sexuality, intercultural sociability, and performance, there was no space for him to participate as anything but the most detached and passive of observers.

By November 1861, the *George Henry* had been in the Arctic for almost a year and a half, a year longer than planned, and "incursions of cabin fever [were already] eroding the minds of the men" (Loomis 137). As an Arctic veteran, Captain Budington was aware of the danger cabin fever posed and encouraged his men to distract and entertain themselves. Hall doesn't indicate whether Budington attended the "theatrical" in question, but he almost certainly sanctioned it: whaling captains, like their counterparts in the British Navy, believed social activities helped maintain morale. By the end of November, local Inuit were spending considerable time aboard the ship; Inuit life, like shipboard life, slowed down and became more sociable in the winter months. On November 26, the cabin of the *George Henry* was filled "to its utmost capacity with Innuits and the ship's crew" (Hall,

Life 428). With twenty-nine officers and crew on the ship and at least fifty Inuit guests, the cabin would have been crowded indeed (*Life* 430).

When Hall entered the cabin, he made his way "to the little after-cabin, and there seated [him]self so as to have a full view of what was going on" (*Life* 428). Hall's decision to position himself apart from the group, in a space that both was and was not part of the main cabin, suggests that he was immediately hesitant about participating. Walking in, he saw that "'Jim Crow,' the son of Artarkparu, occupied the centre of the cabin, and was performing on the 'keeloun,' while the other Innuits were seated all around, the female portion singing to the music" (*Life* 428). Artarkparu's son's nickname is a reference to the popular song "Jump Jim Crow," a song associated with blackface minstrelsy and whose origins, according to W. T. Lhamon, signify questions of cultural exchange and racial appropriation. Hall provides no additional information about Artarkparu's son: it is unclear whether he was always known by the nickname, whether the entire crew used the nickname, or whether he wore blackface makeup that day. Even without knowing these details, the nickname "Jim Crow" would have been familiar as a citation of blackface minstrelsy for Hall, his shipmates, and contemporary readers.

The long-accepted history of the song, which I draw from Robert C. Toll's work on blackface and minstrel performance, is that Thomas D. Rice, who was white, saw an old black man, disfigured by rheumatism, dancing an "odd-looking dance while singing: 'Weel about and turn about and do jus so;/Ebery time I weel about, I jump Jim Crow" (28). Rice learned the song and dance, added his own verses, put on burnt-cork makeup, and performed across the country in the "first clear instance of a minstrel using an Afro-American dance" (Toll 43). Toll's account aligns the song and figure of Jim Crow, because of their origins in mockery and derision, with racist appropriation. Lhamon, in contrast, argues that Toll's story is "false in fact and spirit" and that the "apocryphal" tale indicates "how distant our stories are from the way people produce culture and how starved they are for legitimating detail [...] The conventional stories tell nothing about the early meanings blackface had within its early public" (153). Lhamon questions the assumption that Jim Crow was always synonymous with American racism, arguing that he initially "represented cross-racial affiliation" and "went from fond alliance to hateful segregation" only as the Civil War approached (191). Dale Cockrell concurs with Lhamon, arguing that "the meaning of 'Jim Crow' is thus slippery—all contestation and ambiguity. The song is, in this respect, much like a carnival [...] all mingling, smudging, transgressing, fun, and blackface—all paradox and meaning" (89). One can no more determine a single signifi-cation of "Jim Crow"—the song or the figure—than reconstruct exactly why Hall referred to Artarkparu by this nickname. What is significant is Hall's indication that the performance was immediately overdetermined, overlaid with competing discourses of impersonating appropriation and, at least potentially, interracial sympathy and solidarity. Whatever it signified, Hall's use of the nickname "Jim Crow" indicates that blackface minstrelsy was already on his mind.

Despite the appearance of "Jim Crow," the performance Hall observed was actually fairly representative of Inuit entertainments, centering on a man playing the *keeloun* accompanied by women singing. The *keeloun* was a drum "made by stretching a thin deerskin, or the skin of a whale's liver, upon a wooden or whalebone hoop about thirty inches in diameter, form-ing something not very unlike the tambourine known in this country [the US]. It is held, however, by a handle, and the player strikes not the skin, but the hoop, accompanying his music by an uncouth sort of dance" (Hall, *Life* 428). Hall's reference to *keeloun* dancing as "uncouth" may shed light on his use of the nickname "Jim Crow." Hall's near contemporary Franz Boas claimed that while playing a skin drum, "the dancer remains on one spot only, stamping rhythmically with the feet, swinging the upper part of his body, and at the same time playing the kilaut. While dancing, he always strips the upper part of his body, keeping on only trousers and boots" (195). Hall also describes how a second man, Annawa, danced with the *keeloun*: he went through the "'sweating' process, playing the instru-ment and dancing the ridiculous figures that are indispensable, according to Innuit ideas, his music being accompanied by a full chorus of native female voices" (*Life* 428–29). If Artarkparu's son was, like Annawa and the dancers described by Boas, dancing wildly, sweating profusely, and stomping his feet, his performance might have reminded Hall of black-face performers vigorously dancing on their wooden shingles, creating the rhythm for the dance by stomping and slapping their own bodies, moving in a "ridiculous," because apparently unchoreographed, way. Hall might well have seen traces of familiar "Jim Crow" movements in Inuit *keeloun* dancing.

Although Hall's use of the nickname cites blackface minstrelsy, the performance did not fit into the conventions—such as they can be defined—of American minstrel shows but began as an intercultural social gathering based on Inuit practices. When Hall entered the cabin, Inuit women were singing along with the *keeloun* player's rhythm. The cabin of the ship seems to have stood in for the communal space of the *qaggiq*, a structure Inuit constructed for both spiritual and social activities in the winter.[19] Hall relates that as Artarkparu's son danced and played the drum, other men joined in with a tambourine and a triangle. Hall doesn't specify whether these men were whalers or Inuit, but the instruments added were American in origin, suggesting that whatever the race of the musicians, the performance incorporated musical traditions from both groups. The musical performance seems to have been a "jam" session, with the men improvising and passing instruments around. And as it went on, the party picked up steam: "Jim Crow" passed the *keeloun* to Annawa, who took his place at the center of the group, accompanied by a "full chorus" of "native female voices" (*Life* 428–29).

Reading Hall's passive spectatorship symptomatically, the source of his initial anxiety—the impetus for his placement apart from the rest of the audience—initially seems unclear. We know, however, that Hall was uncomfortable with Inuit spirituality when it conflated religious and sexual practices. The temporary transformation of the ship's cabin into a *qaggiq*-like space may have been disconcerting for Hall, since both entertainment and religious rituals took place in the *qaggiq*. Hall's narrative of his second expedition indicates that the *keeloun* was also associated with both social and spiritual practices: "on entering their new *igloos* the Innuits renewed their performances of the *key-low-tik* and of *an-koo-ting*" (Nourse 101). The construction of this sentence suggests the close link between the two practices: entering a new igloo was marked with both entertaining and spiritual rituals. Hall, who was disturbed by the conflation of these two domains, might have been troubled by the performance because it staged how Inuit spiritual rites refused partitioning from daily life and relied upon performative and theatrical elements for their efficacy.

Recalling that Hall found "becoming savage" troubling, one can surmise that what happened next exacerbated his spectatorial anxiety. While Annawa was playing the *keeloun*, "there came bouncing into the very midst a strapping negress, setting the whole house in a roar of laughter. It was young Smith dressed in this character" (*Life* 429). The young whaler's rambunctious entrance in burnt-cork makeup and women's clothing immediately disrupted the performance. The "whole house" Hall refers to seems to indicate the American sailors specifically, who would have recognized Smith's entrance as a citation of the figure of the cross-dressed wench that was popular in the antebellum minstrel show. Although Hall tells readers that everyone laughed, he then clarifies that "some of the Innuit women were much frightened" and that one woman, Jennie, an *angakkuk* herself, "tried to put as great a distance as possible between herself and the negress, believing the apparition to be an evil spirit" (*Life* 430). While one cannot reconstruct the women's reactions, Boas notes that a form of blackface performance was practiced by Inuit as well, in a recurring performance in which a man "writhes and makes odd grimaces" (170): the "frightened" women might well have seen grotesque performers with blackened faces before.[20] The contrast between the women's fear and the men's laughter suggests the range of receptive possibilities that emerged when blackface was performed, particularly for an intercultural audience.

The mixed reaction also signals the range of meanings one might retroactively ascribe to blackface performance. One can, as Robert Toll does, read it as synonymous with minstrelsy and cultural appropriation (43), "unequivocally brand[ing] Negroes as inferiors" (67), justifying slavery by representing "plantation Negroes [as] happy, contented, and fulfilled," and suggesting that "racial subordination did not conflict with the American Creed" (88). One might also locate blackface as Eric Lott does, arguing that blackface minstrel performances attempted to "repress through ridicule the real interest in black cultural practices they nonetheless betrayed [. . .] It was cross-racial desire that coupled a nearly insupportable fascination and a self-protective derision with respect to black people and their cultural practices" (6). Lott argues that blackface performance, as deployed in minstrel performances, enacted an intense erotic desire for miscegenation and for "black men and their culture" (57). More recent studies of antebellum blackface performance have promoted both/and readings of the practice: although by the time of the Civil War, blackface was intertwined with minstrel performance as a manifestation of racism, its conventions evolved in a "multiracial world" (Cockrell 88) in which lower-class blacks and whites lived closely together in similar social conditions.[21]

Smith's performance cited blackface conventions, particularly the stock character of the "Negro wench" popular in commercial minstrel shows, alongside Inuit and mainstream American conventions, paralleling how blackface performances blended "Afro- and Euro-American musical and dance styles" (Toll 42). Following Smith's disruptive entrance, he was quickly integrated into the performance, playing the tambourine and the *keeloun*. Hall describes how "Ooksin held the keeloun while she [Smith] performed 'Yankee Doodle,' 'Hail Columbia,' and other pieces with admirable skill and effect, using two iron spoons for drum-sticks" (*Life* 430). These songs, with their patriotic connotations, may have been an innocent demonstration of American patriotism for an Inuit audience, but they also may have signaled—instead or alongside of this naïve connotation—the threat that the United States would eventually colonize the Arctic.

It is impossible to conclusively determine what, if anything, Smith's performance reveals about interracial desire, particularly because he was not only in blackface but also cross-dressed. William Mahar argues that the wench role, because it was obviously played by a female impersonator, signaled not racial panic but a homosocial conversation about sexual anxiety: "it was the male wench's presentation of female promiscuity and the allure of sexual freedom (at least in fantasy) that attracted interest [...] the songs featuring cross-dressed characters allowed men to use the nearly exclusively male domain of the minstrel show to criticize women publicly and give broader public expression to private male conversations about gender" (311–12). Recognizing the predominance of and multiple significations of cross-dressed performances in all-male environments, such as whaling ships, suggests that young Smith's double-crossed body, in black-faced drag, was a shifting signifier, impossible to conclusively read.

Contrasting Lott's view that blackface performance signified a repressed desire for miscegenation with Toll's assertion that it signaled racist appropriation and with Lhamon's argument that minstrelsy initially expressed solidarity among the working classes and positive cross-racial identification (Lhamon 207–08) demonstrates that blackface consistently produced contradictory and inconsistent receptive possibilities. Because of this receptive complexity and Hall's reticence, it is impossible to reconstruct precisely what the performance meant. Far from being a dead end, however, this allows one to consider the performance as productive of a range of meanings: one spectator might have read young Smith's performance as an expression of interracial desire while another might have seen in it an expression of ideas of interracial community. Recognizing this range of receptive possibilities allows one to hypothesize that Hall, as Lott might suggest, read "Jim Crow's" dance as an expression of the eroticism of the nonwhite body, and young Smith's blackface act as signifying interracial sexual desire; one can then argue that the "finale" staged the enactment of this desire and that this explains Hall's anxiety and continuing refusal to participate.

The performance climaxed with "a dance by two Innuit ladies and two of the ship's crew, the music being furnished by Bailey with his 'viddle'" (Hall, *Life* 430). Hall's indication that the dance was accompanied by fiddle music and performed by pairs of men and women suggests that it was a square dance, different from those that accompanied the *keeloun* earlier. Hall participated in a square dance while the *George Henry* was in Greenland and provides an extensive description of this dance (*Life* 55–56); here, in contrast, he provides no description of the style of dance and does not indicate who joined in. This silence could be the result of many things; however, Hall's description of his participation in a cross-cultural square dance during his second expedition, combined with Lott's assertion that blackface minstrelsy represented anxiety concerning miscegenation, suggests that his reticence arose because the dancing revealed something about the enactment of interracial sexual desire. While Hall had happily danced with Inuit women in 1860, in 1866 he attended a similar dance aboard the *Ansell Gibbs* and, refusing to dance with an Inuk woman, danced with a man in drag: "when some of the crew and a few of the Innuit women were dressed like civilized ladies, Hall had to make his choice between dancing and speech-making; preferring the former, he led off with the first mate of the ship" (Nourse 289). Nourse suggests the choice was between dancing and speech-making; it is clear, however, that Hall's real choice was between dancing with a white man in women's clothing and an Inuk woman, both of whom were dressed as "civilized ladies." Hall's decision to dance with a man suggests that he became aware that square dances were not simply entertainment but performed a critical role in how interracial sexual relationships developed between whalers and Inuit.

Square dancing was the most popular pastime on Arctic whaling ships throughout the second half of the nineteenth century. L.E. Borden, the surgeon on DGS *Neptune*, noted that on whaling ships "it was the dances, held at intervals, which allowed every one to shake off any inhibitions and thus remove those hostile attitudes which were developing" (84). Dances not only diffused tension between men but also provided an outlet for heterosexual desire. While a square dance did not promise sexual liaisons, close physical contact with women would have been a hot commodity during the cold winter. One can easily imagine that dances allowed men to meet and "romance" Inuit women, initiating sexual relationships and publicly acknowledging relationships that had already been consummated.[22] Dances also allowed whalers to mitigate the threat of "going native" posed by interracial sexual encounters.[23] Square dances made Inuit women less "native" in sailors' eyes, refiguring them as appropriate sexual partners in two ways. First, women often wore "white" clothing to dances, given to them by whalers, as was the case at the 1866 dance Hall mentions: this allowed Inuit women to appear as ostensibly more "civilized" and, by highlighting their nonwhiteness, also served to fetishize them for whalers. Second, in the same way as clothing made women look "civilized," their knowledge of social dance steps made them act "civilized." Knowing how to dance temporarily marked the women as part of the same social group as the whalers since they shared embodied, socialized knowledge.[24]

While one cannot reconstruct Hall's response to the performance, one can certainly imagine what he might have seen. Hall, entering the cabin of the *George Henry* for a "theatrical," saw instead an Inuk man, possibly in blackface, dancing in a wild, uncontained, sexualized manner that reminded him of blackface minstrel performances. Hall seats himself far away from the performers, where he could observe without being incorporated into the event. The performance was kaleidoscopic, first including elements of events he had seen before: *angakkuit* rituals, sailors' entertainments, and Inuit social performances. Then the intercultural event was disrupted when Young Smith "bounced" in wearing women's clothing and burnt-cork makeup. Although some spectators were disturbed by his appearance, Smith was quickly absorbed into the music and dancing. Following this, the entertainment shifted again, and Hall's gaze focused on the spectacle of Inuit women and white men dancing together. Hall—with sex, race, and costuming already on his mind—saw these dances through new eyes. Although he had participated in square dances before, he now saw the dance as what Joseph Roach calls a "behavioral vortex," a "center of cultural self-invention" in which the "magnetic forces of commerce and pleasure suck the willing and unwilling alike" (28). Hall's editorial silence reflects his inability or unwillingness to acknowledge what was happening before him. This is an understandable response when one considers the cultural stakes of "going native." Hall's purpose in the Arctic—to live like an Inuk in order to find survivors from Franklin's expedition—relied upon a stable—though false—opposition between "playing Inuit" and "becoming savage." This distinction had real implications not only for Hall but also for the men he sought.

ACTING OUT FRANKLIN

Hall "played Inuit" by invoking not one but two mimetic relationships: he not only imitated the Inuit he lived among, but also performed precisely what he imagined Franklin's men did to survive. Like many of Franklin's men, Hall went to the Arctic with no northern experience, insufficient supplies and skills, and no firsthand knowledge of Inuit culture or language. Despite his lack of preparation, Hall survived among Inuit, on and off, for almost a decade. Hall "identified the Eskimos as [Franklin's men's] probable saviors. These 'Iron Sons of the North' [. . .] had taken in survivors of the Franklin party and taught them how to live in the Arctic. As he imagined it, the officers and crew had adapted themselves to the Eskimo way of life after they discovered that it would be impossible to escape" (Robinson 68–69). This belief was only a plausible hypothesis in 1860; by 1869 Hall had proven that Franklin survivors could have lived among Inuit if they had adapted as he did. Hall's extended performance was justified by a bizarre, circular logic: he believed Franklin's men survived by living like Inuit, so he himself lived as an Inuk, and by doing this demonstrated that his initial hypothesis—that Franklin's men survived—was viable.

Hall imagined he was completing Franklin's mission and conflated his own goals with those of the missing: "to effect the purpose I have at heart—to carry out successfully what I have undertaken to perform—to visit King William Island and lands adjacent—to continue and complete the History of Sir John Franklin and his renowned expedition, I must learn to live as Esquimaux do!" (qtd. in Loomis 87–88). Through his imaginative mimetic performance, Hall situated himself as an effigy for the missing men. The effigy, according to Joseph Roach, consists of a set of actions "that hold open a place in memory into which many different people may step according to circumstances and occasions [. . .] performed effigies—those fabricated from human bodies and the associations they evoke—provide communities with a method of perpetuating themselves through specially nominated mediums or surrogates" (36). Hall believed he had been "called" to go to the Arctic to search for the missing men; this "calling" effectively nominated him to act as their surrogate. Hall's purpose was to perpetuate and complete Franklin's mission through his own performance, which replicated the imagined survivors' actions.

Hall's fantasy may have had roots in his extensive reading of Arctic exploration narratives in which stranded sailors were saved by Inuit intervention (Loomis 42). Elisha Kent Kane's account of his second search expedition, published in 1856, was Hall's favorite. The book detailed how, after their ship was beset in the high Arctic for two winters, Kane and his men survived because of the aid of Inuit hunters from Etah.[25] For the most part, however, Hall's particular way of imagining and imitating Franklin's men was his own creation. This may be because he, unlike the explorers whose narratives he devoured, chose to live among Inuit. Hall also had the luxury, unlike Franklin's men, of safety: he had the option to return to the *George Henry* and had a reliable way to get home. Through trial and error, with relatively little at stake, Hall invented one way to "play Inuit" during his years in the north.

Hall's performance of "playing Inuit" ensured his physical and social survival, allowing him to ingratiate himself to Inuit and to ensure that they would accompany him to King William Island. It emerged from his response to the loss of the expedition and from his deep desire to locate what was lost. Although "playing Inuit" was a practical necessity, it also allowed Hall to draw the missing men into presence. Alice Rayner defines mimesis as "the very capacity to substitute one thing for another, to reconstitute a lost object in the present object, to transform the material objects of the world into imaginary objects, and the imaginary into the material, that characterizes the foundation of mimesis [...] It is [...] the point in a psychic topography where the experience of loss generates a demand for a substitute" (129). By "playing Inuit"—performing the actions he imagined the survivors performing—Hall fashioned himself as a substitute for the missing men, filling the space left by their disappearance with his own performance. His performance did not ultimately locate the missing men; however, it demonstrated that the missing men might still be alive, that those lost in the Arctic could, at least potentially, become *un*lost.

Hall's strategic refusal to "become savage" and his criticisms of those who did "degenerate" have ramifications in the context of his search. For Hall, the primary behavior that constituted "becoming savage" (for Europeans and Americans) was engaging in miscegenation. Franklin's men stood accused of having "become savage" in another way: by engaging in cannibalism. It is impossible to believe, considering his extensive reading on Arctic exploration, that Hall was unaware of these accusations. In nineteenth-century European texts, cannibalism, like miscegenation, occurred when cultural boundaries were transgressed and expressed the "opposition between civilization and savagery [...] evoked to define a threatening other that must either be assimilated or annihilated." This opposition, however, "ironically suggests the uncanny relatedness between the body of the self and the body of the other" (Guest, "Are you" 108). Cannibalism, imagined as "primitive," provoked considerable anxiety because it was perceived to lurk at the boundary between "civilization" and "savagery." If Franklin's men gave into the desire to consume human flesh in order to survive, they would have crossed this boundary, "becoming savage" and permanently contaminated by forgetting cultural taboos.

Hall recognized that discourses of cannibalism were overlaid with assumptions about class and rank: it was more problematic for a commissioned officer to engage in cannibalism than for an ordinary seaman or a warrant officer. During his second expedition, he heard Inuit testimony concerning cannibalism among Franklin survivors; Hall, convinced that senior officers would have refused to consume human flesh, was relieved when Inuit oral history supported this belief. For example, Hall records that Inuit who met *qallunaat* at Igloolik reported that: "Crozier was the only man that would not eat any of the meat of the Koblunas as the others all did. Crozier and the three men with him were very hungry, but Crozier, though nearly starved and very thin, would not eat a bit of the Koblunas,—he waited till an Innuit who was with him and the three men caught a seal" (Nourse 589). The story proved, to Hall, that an upstanding officer would refuse to give into cannibalistic desires even when the men around him did. This story was corroborated by a story told by Oeula, Shooshearknuk, and Artooa, who heard it from Tooshooarthariu, who claimed he caught seals to help Aglooka: "When he [Tooshooarthariu] first found Crozier and the three men with them, Crozier's face looked bad—his eyes all sunk in—looked so bad that their cousin could not bear to look at his face. Their cousin gave Crozier a bit of raw seal as quick as he could when he first saw him. Did not give any to the other three, for they were fat and had been eating the flesh of their companions" (Nourse 591). The two stories indicate that although Hall accepted that cannibalism could have occurred, he also relied upon Inuit stories of Aglooka's refusal to engage in the act to reconcile this evidence with his belief in the essentially "civilized" nature of senior officers.

Drawing an analogy between miscegenation and cannibalism allows one to see the relationship between Hall's deliberate mimesis of Franklin's men and his criticism of interracial sexuality. Miscegenation and cannibalism both occurred when a "civilized" person made a (usually intentional) mistake in recognizing boundaries: in miscegenation, a man mistook a native woman for an "appropriate" sexual partner; in cannibalism, one mistook human flesh for "appropriate" food. The link between sexuality and consumption is deep-rooted in early-modern depictions of "savage" cultures, as Gustav Jahoda argues: "In the writings of European moralists about the deadly sins of the flesh, lechery and gluttony have usually been coupled" (17). Cannibalism was frequently depicted with sexualized imagery in early-modern visual culture: "there can be no doubt that strong sexual elements entered into the portrayal of cannibal feasts" (102). More specifically, cannibalism was frequently represented using images and iconography that suggested "deviant" or abnormal sexual practices (127). "Deviant" sexuality, of which miscegenation was one manifestation, was—like cannibalism—the result of a cultural degeneration that allowed one to indulge inappropriate appetites and to mistake social boundaries.

Hall performed his identification with the Franklin survivors by "playing Inuit" in the same way he imagined they had and proved, through his own survival, that it was possible that Franklin's men could have survived by "playing Inuit." He also demonstrated, through his refusal to engage in interracial sex, that it was possible to live closely among Inuit without "becoming savage." Hall's ability to reject interracial sexual desire demonstrated by proxy that it was possible that Franklin's men survived in the Arctic without indulging in "deviant" appetites either for Inuit women or, more problematically, for human flesh. While Inuit stories of cannibalism could have challenged Hall's belief that survivors had not "become savage," Aglooka's apparent refusal to participate in cannibalism reinforced Hall's belief that one could avoid "becoming savage," even under extreme circumstances. By "playing Inuit," Hall created and held open an imaginative space in which Franklin's men survived and remained civilized while living among Inuit. Hall's performance repudiated both the accusations of cannibalism and the widespread belief that all of Franklin's men had died, proposing, through mimetic performance, the possibility of a different ending to the story of what happened to Franklin's expedition.

4. Aglooka's Ghost: Performing Embodied Memory ᐧᖚᐧ

Sometime between 1848 and 1850, thirty or forty Franklin survivors, marching under the command of a man called "Aglooka," met Inuit who were seal hunting. Using gestures and a few words of Inuktitut, Aglooka told the hesitant Inuit that he had friendly intentions, that he and his men were trying to reach Iwilik (Repulse Bay), and that they were hungry. Aglooka then performed gestures and sounds that Inuit believed represented his ship, or ships, being crushed by ice. The two groups camped together before the Inuit, continuing their hunt, left the white men behind. In May 1869, Charles Francis Hall interviewed Owwer and Teekeeta, two of the men present that day. Through translators and Owwer's "pantomimed" actions, Hall learned the details of the encounter. While Hall was not the first to hear the story—John Rae included it in his 1854 report—he was the first *qallunaaq* to hear it from eyewitnesses. Hall's account of how Owwer recreated Aglooka's actions is remarkable not only because of its content but also because it demonstrates precisely how Inuit, like Europeans, used performance to transmit knowledge of what happened to Franklin's men and suggests that it was often *only* through performance that these experiences of contact were preserved.

Owwer's performance serves as an example of what Joseph Roach, drawing on the work of Pierre Nora and Paul Connerton, calls the "kinesthetic imagination." Applying the term to performed social memory, Roach argues that the kinesthetic imagination "inhabits the realm of the virtual. Its truth is the truth of simulation, of fantasy, or of daydreams, but its effect on human action may have material consequences of the most tangible sort and of the widest scope. This faculty [. . .] is a way of thinking through movements—at once remembered and reinvented" (26–27). Identifying Owwer's performance in this way is both provocative and problematic: it legitimizes the performance as capable of preserving experience, justifying its inclusion in a performance history like this one. At the same time, it highlights the unanswerable historiographical questions embedded in the performance. Examining Owwer's performance as an example of the work of the kinesthetic imagination requires one to develop a methodology that acknowledges and incorporates the absences and erasures that characterize its archival remains. While the performance concerns a ship or ships being crushed, it reveals no factual details of what happened: one cannot determine whether one or both ships were affected, whether the damage occurred before or after the 1848 abandonment, or whether the ship(s) were completely destroyed. Similarly, it is unclear when Owwer met Aglooka: British and American attempts to date the meeting establish only that it occurred between 1848 and 1850. There are also questions about Aglooka's identity. Hall assumed he was Francis Crozier, who took command of the expedition following Franklin's death, but recent historians have raised doubts about this assumption. Because of these questions, Owwer's story occupies a marginal place in most histories of the Franklin expedition. Although it is generally accepted that the meeting took place and that Aglooka told the Inuit his ship had been crushed, Owwer's particular account of the meeting is generally ignored.[1]

As an archival document, Hall's journal entry is inscrutable, failing to reveal precisely what Owwer saw Aglooka do or what Owwer did when he reenacted Aglooka's gestures for Hall. The factual questions, combined with the story's complicated transmission and the inherent difficulties of transcribing gestures into words, mean that neither Owwer nor Hall provides a "reliable" account of what Aglooka did. Like the story of Jane Franklin's pink and green dresses, however, the story is compelling in its staying power: upon meeting Inuit, Aglooka needed to enact what happened; Owwer remembered Aglooka's performance so clearly that he recreated it decades later; Hall took the time, after a long day of interviews, to write pages of notes detailing Owwer's performance. I propose that one can approach a story like this—of a performance remembered but factually lost—by resisting the urge to reconstruct its details and instead interrogating its lingering affective power and its inherent mystery. By doing this, one might reconsider Hall's account, contemplating not what it fails to add to the "facts" of what happened but how it testifies to a ghostly performance in which the absent body and the unknowable experience of a Franklin survivor become temporarily present. Hall's account allows one to imagine how Aglooka's performance expressed his catastrophic experience and his failure to fulfill his responsibility to his men, allowing one to access the feelings, if not the actual events, experienced by the Franklin survivors. Working through the methodological and theoretical questions raised by the story, in turn, sheds light on Rebecca Schneider's claim that performance can be "figured as both the act of remaining and a means of disappearance" (103).

In Hall's account, Aglooka's experience of his ship(s) being crushed both remains inaccessible, forbidding the reconstruction of a coherent narrative, and erupts in the present, resurfacing in Owwer's embodied reenactment. This belated return of the past evokes Cathy Caruth's description of trauma as "the story of a wound that cries out, that addresses us in the attempt to tell us of a reality or truth that is not otherwise available. This truth, in its delayed experience and its belated address, cannot be linked only to what is known, but also to what remains unknown in our very actions and our language" (4). At the same time, Hall's account is marked by a strange doubling: the performance "jumps" from Aglooka to Owwer, resulting in Hall collapsing the two men in his account. The reemergence of past experience in a new body pushes the boundaries of trauma theory, at least insofar as Caruth applies it to individual experiences. The uncanny doubling, however, is precisely what Alice Rayner describes when she explains how ghosts "animate our connections to the dead, producing a visible, material, and affective relationship to the abstract terms of time and repetition [. . .] absence and presence [. . .] A ghost, particularly in the theater, ought to startle the audience into attention with a shiver. Doubt rationalizes the shiver, but it also signals an encounter" (xiii). Positioning theories of trauma and of the ghostly double in conversation with one another allows one to see how the unspeakable experience at the heart of Aglooka's performance took on its own (im)materiality, emerging as a ghost made visible in Owwer's performance. While Hall's account does not provide a coherent narrative of what actually happened to Aglooka, it allows one to trace how his experience survived through embodied performance, preserved by the kinesthetic imagination, moving across bodies and time, and erupting when he was no longer present to pass it on.

THE CRACK IN THE ICE

Hall's fieldnotes from May 18, 1869, provide a detailed record of his interview with Owwer and Teekeeta. Hall also spoke to Teekeeta about meeting Aglooka earlier in the month and that account appears in his posthumously published report (Nourse 406–07). While the two versions of the meeting are similar, Hall's published account of Teekeeta's testimony does not include information about Aglooka's ship's sinking. Furthermore, Hall's fieldnotes from May 18 provide details about *how* Owwer recreated Aglooka's gestures, an element lacking in the published text.

Owwer and Teekeeta began by describing an ordinary day of seal hunting on the west shore of King William Island. The sun was high and the hunters—Owwer, Teekeeta, Tooshooarthariu, and Monger—and their families were "getting ready to move." At this moment, "Tuk-ke-ta saw something in the distance on the smooth ice that looked white & thought it was a bear." He told his companions and they waited and watched, hoping to improve their day's hunting. The white object grew larger as it drew closer and "they began to see many black objects moving along with what they first espied as white in the distance." Owwer and Teekeeta realized that "[t]he object that they 1st had seen as white proved to be a sail raised on the boat & as this got nearer saw this sail shake in the wind. On seeing what they did, the object grew plainer and they thought of white men and began to be afraid" (Hall, *Fieldnotes*). Hall does not indicate whether Owwer or Teekeeta had met Europeans before, but his wording suggests that the men knew about them and believed they were potentially dangerous.

The white men approached the Inuit and, as they got closer, "2 men came on ahead [...] & were walking on the ice & were getting quite near where the Innuits were standing looking out." Tooshooarthariu and Owwer came forward to meet the *qallunaat*, stopping at a crack in the ice to wait for them. Owwer told Hall that one of the white men "had a gun which he carried in his arms. [...] The man that carried the gun stopped behind—a little back, while the other man came as close up to Ow-wer and Too-shoo-art-thar-u as the crack in the ice would allow him. The man that came up to the crack had nothing in his hands or on his shoulder." When the man stopped, he "cried out 'C'hi-mo'" to the Inuit, then spoke to the man with the gun, who laid it down and "came up at once along side the 1st man" (Hall, *Fieldnotes*). Hall's notes suggest that the encounter was initially marked by hesitation and fear. The crack in the ice was a physical boundary that prevented the white men from getting too close and promised an extra moment for retreat if the encounter grew hostile. The white men were also cautious: although the leader was empty-handed, his companion carried a gun.[2] Despite this apparent trepidation, the man called out "C'hi-mo" to indicate his friendly intentions: Europeans believed the word was a greeting Inuit used when meeting other friendly tribes (Woodman 339; Eber 43).[3]

After establishing that he meant Inuit no harm, the *qallunaaq* told them that he and his men were hungry:

The 1st man then showed that he had an oo-loo when he stooped down beside the ice crack which divided the white men from the Innuits & began cutting the ice with a peculiar kind of circling motion with the oo-loo (Civilization mincing-knife or Innuit women's knife). This peculiar motion now showed by Ow-wer with H's oo-loo on the snow floor of the igloo. At the same time, or rather right after this man had made these 'chippings' or 'scratchings' [...] on the ice, he put his hand up to his mouth and lowered it all the way down his neck and breast, as if to say he wanted to get something to eat. (Hall, *Fieldnotes*)

By specifying that Owwer demonstrated the motion using "H's" knife (H refers to Tookoolito, whom Hall often called Hannah), Hall explicitly indicates that he learned the details of the encounter not only through his translators' description but by watching a reenactment. The passage establishes the performance conventions Aglooka used to communicate: he used his knife to cut the ice on the ground, then used the ice chips as props to represent food, then pretends to eat the ice to convey his desire for food. Aglooka used a relatively straightforward representational strategy— ice chips signify food—to suggest what he wanted. At the same time, his performance was more complicated than necessary: why, if Aglooka was desperately hungry, would he bother to make props rather than simply mime eating? This performative surplus is inexplicable: perhaps Aglooka attempted a simpler action which was not understood, perhaps his other gestures were unremarkable and so did not survive in Owwer's recollection, perhaps Owwer was having fun embellishing his reenactment. These questions are important, reminding one of the need to assume that both Hall's account of Owwer's performance and Owwer's recollection of Aglooka's performance are, like all accounts of performances, incomplete and subjective.

Following the request for food, the white men crossed the ice, moving closer to the Inuit. When they reached them, "the 1st man who was Ag-loo-ka spoke to them saying Man-nik Too-me at the same time stroking 1st one & then the other down the breast & also shook hands with each repeating Man-nik-too-me several times. The other man with Ag-loo-ka did all the same in shaking hands & speaking Man-nik-too-me!" (Hall, *Fieldnotes*). Aglooka's and his companion's behavior suggests their assumption of familiarity with Inuit culture and demonstrates their attempt to communicate across cultures. Franz Boas observed that stroking another man's breast was a sign of reconciliation in many Inuit subcultures, often performed after a feud (174). Aglooka was obviously familiar with the gesture and its connotation of friendship. If Aglooka was Francis Crozier, as Hall suspected, this familiarity makes sense: Crozier participated in three Arctic expeditions under Parry's command and was, for a British officer, quite familiar with Inuit culture. Aglooka combined the breast stroking with what he believed to be its British equivalent, the handshake. He also accompanied these gestures with the Inuktitut phrase "Man-nik Too-me," which he probably thought of as a friendly Inuktitut greeting. The expression was likely passed on to Franklin's men by other officers:[4] John Ross was greeted by Inuit using this phrase during his 1829–33 expedition (Eber xiv), and British officers assumed it meant "[w]e are friends" (McClintock 261). The British misinterpreted the phrase: it actually means "do it smoothly, not aggressively," conveying a much more specific meaning as an intercultural greeting than "we are friends" (Eber xiv). One also must wonder how Inuit, after meeting Ross and his men in this way, told the story of the encounter and whether the phrase, in Inuit culture, took on new meaning as an "appropriate" way to greet white strangers, transforming its original meaning. In any case, it appears that Aglooka used the phrase to convey amiable intentions and that Owwer and Tooshooartthariu interpreted it as such.

Owwer told Hall that Aglooka then tried to speak to the Inuit, but "of all he then said they could only make out one word which was I-wil-ik," the Inuktitut name for Repulse Bay. Apparently, Owwer spent "15 to 20 minutes [...] describing in pantomimic way just how Ag-loo-ka appeared & imitating his words. Ag-loo-ka pointed with his hand to the Southward & Eastward & at the same time repeating the word I-wil-ik. The Innuits," according to Hall, "could not understand whether he wanted them to show him the way there or that he was going there" (*Fieldnotes*). Aglooka was familiar with the Inuktitut name for Repulse Bay and knew that it was a good place for the retreating men to head toward, as it promised contact with Europeans, Americans, or Inuit. Hall points out that Aglooka's intention was unclear: Inuit did not know whether he was asking for guidance or simply passing on information, but one must ask whether the question of intent is really important. If Aglooka's immediate concern was with surviving long enough to be rescued, telling Inuit his intended destination was the essential part, as this information could be passed on to other Inuit and to British search parties Inuit met.

The way Hall describes Owwer's performance is what fascinates me: first, the performance took at least fifteen minutes, which seems excessive considering the apparent content; second, Hall is explicit that Owwer told him what Aglooka did in a "pantomimic" way, with his body. One must wonder what Owwer *did* for fifteen or twenty minutes: did Aglooka actually try to communicate his intentions for this long, or was Owwer dragging out or repeating what he saw as he recreated it? One also cannot know how accurately Owwer's performance replicated what Aglooka did.

Posing this question is critical, however, as it forces one to recognize the gap between Aglooka's and Owwer's performances and highlights Hall's problematic assumption that Owwer's performance accurately reproduced Aglooka's. Hall's description of Owwer's actions as "pantomimic" underlines that Hall's account was based on observing the re-creation of a performance of contact. These two points—that Hall only knew about Aglooka's actions through Owwer's reconstruction of them, whether or not it was accurate, and that Owwer's reconstruction was communicated as an embodied reenactment, rather than as a narrative—are crucial to keep in mind in reading what Hall describes next.

(RE)ENACTING FAILURE

Hall then described how Owwer recreated Aglooka's performance of the ship(s) being crushed:

> He then made a motion with his hand to the Northward & spoke the word oo-me-en making them to understand there were 2 ships in that direction which had as they supposed been crushed in the ice. As Ag-loo-ka pointed to the N. drawing his hand & arm from that direction he slowly moved his body in a falling direction & all at once dropped his head sideways into his hand. At the same time making a noise with his mouth a kind of combination of whirring, buzzing, wind blowing noise. This the pantomimic representation of ships being crushed in the ice. (Hall, *Fieldnotes*)

This part of Owwer's performance is not remarkable because it conveys the fact of the ship(s) being crushed: fifteen years earlier, John Rae heard similar stories and reported that "by signs the Natives were led to believe that the Ship or Ships had been crushed by ice" (*Arctic Correspondence* 275). It is not remarkable because it reveals the fate of Franklin's men: in his earlier interview with Hall, Teekeeta provided more detail than Owwer, saying that "the full meaning of what he [Aglooka] said about the ice destroying the ship and his men dying was afterward understood" (Nourse 406). To understand why the story was remarkable, it is essential to first consider its shortcomings as an archival document.

The performance did not add to the known facts of what happened. It provided no indication of when the ship was crushed, let alone the extent of the destruction or what caused it. The lone written record recovered from the Franklin expedition, the Victory Point record, does not mention the ships being badly damaged. Most histories of the expedition concur that the ships were not abandoned in 1848 because they were uninhabitable or underwater but because the men needed to find fresh meat to stave off scurvy.[5] The orientation of the sledge that McClintock's expedition found suggested that survivors made an attempt to re-board one or both ships after the initial abandonment; most histories of the expedition concur that this was the case.[6] It seems likely, although it is by no means certain, that some men returned to and lived on at least one of the ships for a time, and that the destruction Aglooka's performance referred to occurred after the April 1848 abandonment. Attempts to date when Aglooka met the Inuit are inconclusive. Hall's informants were "unanimous in stating that the encounter took place after the ice had begun to break up" in the spring (Woodman 140), but their attempts to establish the year it took place were less certain. Hall describes his attempt:

> I now request the whole company to take hold & see if they can make out the year—how many years ago since the 4 Innuit families met Crozier and party on the w. coast of K.W.L. [. . .] The result 25 winters ago. Ow-wer & Tuk-ke-ta make out 9 to the time Dr. Rae came to Pelly Bay [. . .] I get them to try again. The result, 5 winters after seeing Aglooka, Dr. Rae came to Pelly Bay & this makes it out that the paper found by McClintock corresponds with what the Innuits of this country know. (*Fieldnotes*)

The first attempt resulted in 1844, a year before the Franklin expedition left England. The second attempt dated the meeting to 1849, a more reasonable date, although one must ask if Hall's request for a recalculation influenced the Inuit. Hall ultimately concluded, in a letter written to Henry Grinnell on June 20, 1869, that the meeting took place in 1848, shortly after the initial abandonment. Dating the meeting is further complicated when one considers that John Rae believed it occurred "In the Spring, four winters past (1850)" (*Arctic Correspondence* 274), leaving two years to account for between the 1848 abandonment and the meeting. McClintock interpolated from Inuit stories that the meeting took place in 1848 (249). The meeting, in other words, could have taken place in 1848, 1849, or 1850, meaning that the event Aglooka re-created could have occurred any time before 1850. Owwer's re-creation of Aglooka's performance complicates, rather than establishes, the chronology of events following the April 1848 abandonment.

Although Hall was convinced that Aglooka was Francis Crozier, Aglooka's identity is actually uncertain. In the 1820s, Crozier traveled to the Arctic under Parry's command. While there, he traded names with an Inuk named Aglooka and became known by that name. Hall heard other Inuit stories that seemed to refer to meeting Crozier after the ships were abandoned; these strengthened his belief that Aglooka was Crozier (Nourse 589–90). But trading names was common when Inuit met British sailors and Crozier was one of several men known as Aglooka. Both John Rae and James Clark Ross were also known by the name, which simply means "long strides" (Eber 42) and "could legitimately be given to any tall purposeful white man" (Woodman 195). David Woodman argues that there is no reason to assume that Crozier must have been the Aglooka who met Owwer and argues, based on Inuit descriptions of Aglooka's appearance, that Henry Dundas Le Vesconte, a lieutenant on the *Erebus*, is a more likely candidate for Aglooka (160).

Despite these uncertainties, one can make some speculations about the encounter. Although it is unclear who Aglooka was, he was probably the senior officer in command of the group, since he came forward to meet the Inuit and gave orders to the man with the gun. The detachment of men slowly dragging their sledges south were likely suffering from advanced scurvy, exhaustion, and exposure. One can imagine that months or years after leaving their ships, the sight of Inuit hunters must have given Aglooka and his men a rush of hope. Most British explorers believed Inuit were excellent hunters and that "where the Esquimaux can live [...]—what should have prevented Sir John Franklin and his party from subsisting too?" (King 107). Inuit presence provided both the hope of assistance and the assurance that the land was not completely barren. Aglooka told the Inuit where he planned to go and asked for food. The Inuit provided Aglooka and his men with some seal but only what they could spare: it must have become clear that this small group of Inuit could not, as Aglooka might have initially hoped, save them from starvation or scurvy.

Finally, Owwer's reenactment of Aglooka's performance provided no indication that Aglooka told the men about his ships being crushed to elicit sympathy, in the form of extra food or assistance. To summarize, the story served no purpose: telling it did not help the men with their immediate goals of finding food and reaching help. It was also unclear: although it communicated information about the event, it obscured the details. If Aglooka wanted Inuit to pass on details to British search parties in the hope of rescue, he could have communicated his message in more precise terms. This raises the question of why Aglooka used abstract gestures and sounds to communicate: why was it necessary for him to pass on the story, and why did he do it in such a strange way?

Owwer's performance is remarkable not because of its factual content but because of *how* it represents Aglooka's enactment of the ship(s) being crushed. Hall again uses the term "pantomimic" to describe the performance, referring not to generic qualities but to Owwer's—and Aglooka's—reliance on gesture, movement, and sound. Aglooka did not, according to Owwer's reenactment, use any of the performance tactics he had used earlier: he did not use props to represent the ice or the boat, as he did when he used ice chips as food; he did not use his knife to draw an image on the ice; he did not use his hands or arms to represent the boat and the ice. All these choices could have communicated what happened in more precise terms. But these performance strategies would have represented the boat and ice in objective and relatively equal terms, situating Aglooka outside of the event as an observer rather than as a participant affected by it. Aglooka's choices suggest that this was not what he wanted to do.

According to Owwer, Aglooka used minimal words to explain what had happened: he spoke only the word "oo-me-en," indicating that he was referring to a boat.[7] Again, this is a strange choice. It is not a stretch to imagine that someone who knew the words "man-nik-too-me," "c'hi-mo," and "oo-me-en" might also know Inuktitut words for ice or broken. If Aglooka was Crozier, as Hall believed, he had spent considerable time in the Arctic and his Inuktitut vocabulary, though limited, probably would have allowed him to use more than a single word to explain what happened. Furthermore, Hall's translators were "almost certain" that Aglooka was with Dr. Alexander McDonald, whom they had met in the 1830s while McDonald was serving under Captain Penny. The man Owwer and his companions described, who matched McDonald's description, could "speak with the Innuits [...] so that they could understand him better than they could Aglooka" (Hall, *Fieldnotes*). If Aglooka was Crozier, or if Aglooka was accompanied by McDonald, one must ask why one of them did not at least attempt to use words to explain what happened to his ship, particularly because the significance of Aglooka's gestures was not, according to Teekeeta, understood until later (Nourse 406).

Hall's description of Owwer's performance has a quality of absence, as though his words couldn't quite capture what Owwer did, as though his writing misses something crucial about what he saw. Erasing Owwer's presence in describing Aglooka's actions, Hall records that *Aglooka* gestured to the north and said "oo-me-en [...] making them [Owwer and his companions] to understand that there were 2 ships in that direction which had as they supposed been crushed in the ice." It is unclear how Inuit came to understand there were two ships or that the ships had been crushed: Hall erases his editorial process, either omitting a detail of Owwer's performance or retroactively explaining something that was initially unclear.

Aglooka then, according to Owwer's re-creation, performed a complex movement: pointing to the north, "drawing his hand & arm from that direction, he slowly moved his body in a falling direction & all at once dropped his head sideways into his hand." Breaking the gesture into individual moments—head and arm, torso, head and hand—reveals a range of possibilities: Did Aglooka draw his arm across his body or in toward himself? Did he fall to the ground or did he perform a gesture that suggested falling? Was he on the ground or upright when he dropped his head into his hand? Considering the sounds Aglooka made—the "combination of whirring, buzzing, wind blowing noise"—raises still more questions: was Aglooka representing what he heard as the ship was crushed? Was he making sounds to clarify what happened for his Inuit audience? Was he both recreating his experience and reproducing the sounds he heard? Still more questions arise if one considers whether Aglooka's body was meant to represent itself in the past moment or something else altogether: Was Aglooka demonstrating what he felt as the ship was crushed, falling to the ground at the moment of impact? Was he representing his experience in a symbolic way, dropping his head into his hand to signify defeat? Did his body represent the body of the boat, with his arm signifying, perhaps, the mast collapsing? And again, one returns to the question raised earlier: why represent the ships being crushed in this way at all?

Something about the performance and the event it represented was vitally important to Aglooka. His rejection of "normal" representational modes, his refusal to textualize his experience by explaining it in words, and his performance's earlier excessive qualities suggest that his performance fell outside the bounds of conventional definitions of mimesis: it was not an imitation of an event. The performance's strangeness, its abstraction, the ambiguity surrounding its referents suggest that Aglooka was not making conscious choices in order to reproduce the details of what happened but was struggling to represent his *experience* of the event. Why might this be? The ships' destruction, the event that Aglooka's performance represented, was a catastrophe. It constituted a monumental loss to the expedition. If Aglooka's performance literally represented ice crushing his ships, the event would have been horrifying, likely accompanied by a significant loss of life. Losing a ship was also, to a commanding officer, a monumental personal and professional failure: in the world of a wintering ship, where the captain was a father to his men, failing to save the ship was akin to failing to protect one's children. Moving away from thinking of the ships being crushed as a literal, singular event presents another possibility: for Aglooka, the event of the ships being crushed stood for the greater catastrophe that affected the expedition. Perhaps the ships being damaged was the catalyst for other disastrous events, perhaps it was the last in a chain of disasters. In any case, it is possible that Aglooka used the ships being crushed metonymically, to stand in as a concrete event that symbolized the failure of the expedition in general.

Aglooka's performance of the ships being crushed is not mimetic in an Aristotelian sense, but it fits precisely with Alice Rayner's description of mimesis, which arises when "the experience of loss generates a demand for a substitute" (129). Mimesis, in Aglooka's performance, emerges from the compelling need to testify to a horrific experience, to a monumental failure that he could not represent using words or imitative representation. Aglooka didn't mime the ship and ice, he didn't draw a picture, and he didn't use rudimentary Inuktitut to say something like "boat...broken...ice," not because he didn't think of these things, but because these were inadequate for expressing what he needed to convey. Aglooka's performance expresses his experience of a traumatic loss, an event that created a "wound that cries out" and demanded expression (Caruth 4).

Knowing very little about what occurred after the 1848 message was deposited means that one cannot reconstruct precisely what Aglooka felt compelled to reenact. It seems likely that, as commanding officer, the "wound" resulted from his failure to adequately protect or lead his men. One possibility, drawing on Richard Cyriax's conclusions and Hall's assumption that Aglooka was Crozier, is that Aglooka knew that his decision to abandon his ships so early in 1848 would ultimately doom most of the men. Crozier, Cyriax speculates, abandoned the ships because his men, suffering severely from scurvy, needed fresh meat; this decision would have resulted in the deaths of the weakest men: "it was probably only too evident that so many would fall by the way that it would not be difficult to procure enough food for the survivors when the provisions taken from the ships were exhausted. Confronted, as he apparently was, with a severe outbreak of scurvy, the utmost he could hope for was the survival of the strongest few." (*Sir* 151). One might speculate that Crozier's conscious choice to sacrifice many of the men under his command in the hope of saving a few was the source of his monumental feelings of failure. There are, obviously, other possibilities: Aglooka may have known that the ships' destruction would result in the loss of the one shelter available and the loss of remaining food stocks; by failing to save the ships, he guaranteed his men's deaths in other ways. The precipitating event could have been more ominous: Aglooka's performance might have used the ships' destruction to symbolize other catastrophes, for example, the cannibalism that almost certainly occurred among some survivors. Thinking of the performance figuratively, one cannot pinpoint the loss to which the gestures referred, but whatever it was, it seems to have demanded Aglooka act as a surrogate for what was lost—the ship, men's lives, national pride, civilized values. Aglooka used his body to enact this monumental loss, representing what happened by engaging in mimesis through substitution. The mysterious quality of Aglooka's performance, the inability of witnesses to capture its referent and its compelling qualities, suggest that it was indeed the expression of a traumatic event that could not enter Aglooka's spoken language or enter representation by conventional means.

Aglooka's performance, whatever it meant, remained with Owwer, compelling him to reproduce it when he met Hall. It is not surprising that a story of an encounter with *qallunaat* would survive in Inuit oral history. But Owwer apparently remembered the strange performance in perfect detail, remembering it not as a narrative but as a series of gestures. In order to tell Hall about what happened when he met Aglooka, Owwer had to enact it. If Aglooka's performance represented an unrepresentable traumatic event, a catastrophic failure to act or to protect, one which he had to pass on, one might hypothesize that witnessing the representation of this trauma somehow compelled Owwer to preserve it in his body and to pass it on as well. How can one explain how Aglooka passed on not only the story of the event but the compellation to reenact it? Stories of trauma have at their heart "a kind of double telling, the oscillation between a *crisis of death* and the correlative *crisis of life*: between the story of the unbearable nature of an event and the story of the unbearable nature of its survival" (Caruth 7). Aglooka's ships were destroyed; many of his men were dead; he was perhaps aware that some of his men had committed the ultimate transgression, consuming human flesh. He had, by the time he met Owwer, survived the ships' destruction, scurvy, and starvation. He had become a captain whose ship was destroyed and whose men were mainly dead. Although he was a survivor, he must have realized that it was unlikely he would live to tell his story at home. He was compelled to pass on the story of what it was to survive catastrophe and what it was to fail his men, and he passed it on through his gestural performance.

Why might Owwer have been compelled, as I suggest he was, to pass on what happened? As with Aglooka's performance, one cannot reconstruct what motivated Owwer to reproduce what he saw. But a discrepancy Hall notes between Owwer and Teekeeta's accounts of the meetings suggests one possible explanation for why Owwer had to reproduce Aglooka's performance. Owwer and Teekeeta's stories were remarkably consistent, except in their explanations of how the groups parted. Hall records that Teekeeta told him they:

> Saw Aglooka next morning—that is next morning after first meeting him. Aglooka came along side of Innuits tents—A CORRECTION. The Innuits took down their tents early the next morning & as they proceeded on their journey passed by Aglooka's tent. Aglooka was standing on the outside of the tent when the Innuits passed it. *Aglooka tried to make them stop*—put his hand to his mouth and spoke the word 'Net-chuk' or 'Nest-chuk' (seal). But the Innuits were in a hurry—did not know the men were starving. (*Fieldnotes*)

Hall earlier had heard a version of the story that had Aglooka visiting Inuit in their tent that morning. This inconsistency highlights two problematic questions: Why did the Inuit leave so quickly? Did they realize Aglooka and his men were starving? Teekeeta's account claims they did not; however, Hall came to believe that the Inuit left them "although supposing they were abandoning starving men" (Nourse 406). Other Inuit stories, recorded by Dorothy Eber, suggest that the Inuit left both because they could not support the white men's needs and because the *qallunaat*'s erratic behavior was disturbing (77–80). Inuit, familiar with starvation in their own culture, would have recognized the signs in the white men. They also may have recognized the signs of mental deterioration caused by scurvy and vitamin deficiency and worried for their own safety. Their decision to leave was not callous, as Hall implies: four hunters could not support thirty additional men and attempting it would have jeopardized the Inuit's chances of survival. But the fact remains that the Inuit, like Crozier in Cyriax's explanation, chose to save themselves over saving the strangers. They, like Crozier, chose survival. It is possible that some trace of that experience—of failing to save others and choosing survival—was embedded in the gestural performance, remaining even as it "jumped" bodies because it resonated with Owwer, who also chose survival at the cost of failing to save others.

SURVIVING GHOSTS

Claiming that Owwer was compelled to reproduce Aglooka's performance because the experience it contained—choosing to survive by failing to help—resonated with him is not to say that Aglooka passed on his experience of trauma to Owwer or to suggest that trauma is somehow contagious, transmitted from person to person. The story of Aglooka's and Owwer's performances continues to resonate, I suspect, because it illustrates how a remembered performance can be almost—but not quite—captured in words. While the "missed encounter," the encounter with the past that preserves but fails to fully capture or express it, is symptomatic of traumatic experiences, in this case, the performance's transmission over time and across bodies makes it difficult to reconcile with theories of individual trauma. Aglooka's performance communicated something crucial but intangible about the experience of the ships being crushed; this performance then resonated in Owwer's imagination for approximately twenty years before he shared it with Hall; Hall's fieldnotes evoke something about his experience of watching Owwer's reproduction of Aglooka's performance. Hall's account not only reflects how Aglooka's performance demanded Owwer's and Hall's attention but also compels our attention: its ambiguity forces the reader to imagine what happened. This process of looking harder, of straining to interpret, ultimately engages one in a sustained relationship with Aglooka and his lost men. Trauma theory does not, on its own, adequately explain the story's affective pull or the performance's mysterious transmission across bodies and over time.

Inuit recall their encounters with Franklin's men using language reminiscent of ghost stories. Cathy Towtongie, an executive in Iqaluit, remembers her grandmother's stories of seeing Franklin survivors: they were "a raggedy bunch and their clothing was not well made. Their skins were black and the meat above their teeth was gone; their eyes were gaunt. Were they *tuurngait*—spirits—or what?" (qtd. in Eber 9). Alice Anguttitauruq, an Inuk elder in Gjoa Haven, told Dorothy Eber that her parents "used to talk about the doomed strangers in strange clothing—'all black, no fur'— who had appeared on the shore of King William Island about seventy-five years before her birth" (xx). Anguttitauruq recalled that Inuit "saw strange creatures, strange beings wearing dark clothing, pulling a small object behind them. When the Inuit saw them, they thought they were spirits. They would never go close—they were always afraid" (qtd. in Eber xx). I suspect that it is not insignificant that Inuit described Franklin survivors as ghostly, strange beings. To Owwer, as to Towtongie's grandmother, Aglooka and his men must have looked disturbing, even inhuman, suffering as they must have been from scurvy and starvation. In Hall's account, as in Inuit stories, Aglooka is a ghostly presence, in both a literal sense— he was dead when the story was told—and metaphorically, haunting the text and the reader. Hall spent the better part of a decade searching for Franklin's men: hearing the story must have had an eerie effect, particularly because Hall's encounter with the story provided only a glimpse of an event that was irretrievable. One can imagine Hall, watching Owwer's performance with the strange sense—because he had heard similar stories before, because he had spent so long searching for traces of Franklin's men—of the uncanny, of "the strangeness or 'secret' aspect in someone or something familiar" (Rayner x).

Alice Rayner's work on theatrical ghosting allows one to theoretically position the story's lingering affective power. Rayner writes that ghosts "animate our connections to the dead, producing a visible, material, and affective relationship to the abstract terms of time and repetition [...] absence and presence [...] A ghost, particularly in the theater, ought to startle the audience into attention with a shiver. Doubt rationalizes the shiver, but it also signals an encounter" (xiii). Hall's account of Owwer's reenactment of Aglooka's performance has this quality of absence/presence: Aglooka is present in Owwer's reenactment, but the reenactment draws attention to his actually missing body. Aglooka's manifestation through Owwer's performance, which Hall's discursive erasure of Owwer underlines, produces the shiver, the sense of a close but missed encounter. Rayner argues that ghosts' mysterious power emerges because "they are fully embodied and material but are unrecognized without a certain mode of attention, a certain line of sight that can perceive the mysterious object that is distinct from, yet embodied by, the theatrical object" (xvii). This sense of oscillation is apparent in Hall's language: Aglooka moves in and out of presence, allowing Hall to forget, but only for a second, that the story is not about Aglooka's actions but about Owwer's. The performance achieves its staying power not because of its content, which remains ambiguous and ephemeral, but because of its affect, because of the shiver. Attempting to parse the performance into its constituent parts—to isolate what Hall did from what Owwer did and from what Aglooka did—is impossible. According to Rayner, this impossibility is symptomatic of a ghostly presence: a ghost is "no-thing. It is not the sort of object that can be examined, unearthed, analyzed: there is nothing to be dissected, parsed into constituent elements, revealed, or critiqued. Instead a ghost appears only from an oblique perspective and emerges only from the sideways glance at the void of death or the blanks in memory" (xxii).

Hall's account, as it survives as an archival document, erases both Owwer as performer and Hall as interpreting spectator. This is clear in his ambiguous use of the pronoun "he" and his reference only to "Aglooka" in the following passage:

> He then made a motion with his hand to the Northward & spoke the word oo-me-en making them to understand there were 2 ships in that direction which had as they supposed been crushed in the ice. As Ag-loo-ka pointed to the N. drawing his hand & arm from that direction he slowly moved his body in a falling direction & all at once dropped his head sideways into his hand. At the same time making a noise with his mouth a kind of combination of whirring, buzzing, wind blowing noise. This the pantomimic representation of ships being crushed in the ice.

In the space created by the double erasure of Hall and Owwer, the ghost appears. But is the ghost actually Aglooka? Or is it something abstract, the unknowable thing that was the catalyst of the disaster that doomed the expedition, the "thing" Aglooka's performance expressed and that, in Hall's story, Aglooka came to stand for? Was Aglooka, like Owwer, a vessel through which a ghost emerged? And if so, what was this ghost, this thing that appeared? While one might suggest that the ghost, the thing, was the event of the ships being crushed by ice floes, it also might have been something less tangible: a series of events, a failure to create an event (of saving the ships, of finding aid), a failure to act. Ultimately, this may be an impossible question: Rayner reminds us that "[i]f words are successful in naming the ghost, there is no ghost" (xxiii).

It is the ghost that appears in Owwer's performance, the ghostly repetition of Aglooka's strange actions, which continues to engage. It is the ghost that reaches out to the reader who attempts to imaginatively reenact Owwer's encounter with Aglooka, who imagines the horror of the final days of the Franklin expedition; it is the ghost that makes Hall's story meaningful and compelling today. The ghost becomes visible at the point where the secret of what happened lies—where the horrible thing that Aglooka's performance was about, where whatever caused the Franklin expedition to descend into cannibalism and death, exists. But ghosts are rarely laid to rest, and this is part of why the fate of the Franklin expedition still generates interest. Rayner writes, "ghosts hover where secrets are kept and demand that secrets come out from the crypts of time, they are everywhere [...] Some secrets can wait forever. Some compel their ghosts to appear, and the ghosts are impatient for the living to set them right, do them justice, and release them into time" (xxxv). The no-thing that happened to the Franklin expedition, the mysterious event or events that historians endlessly speculate about, is what Hall's story, ultimately, refers to. It defies archival scrutiny not only because of banal questions about who was involved, when it occurred, and what exactly happened, but because it is, more precisely, the story of a secret. And, considering recent Parks Canada searches and the number of literary and scientific works devoted to the question of what happened, it seems that ghostly stories of Franklin and his men continue to engage us years after the men's disappearance because they continue to mark the location of a secret that waits to be revealed.

5. The Last Resource: Witnessing the Cannibal Scene ❧

In October 1854, Dr. John Rae returned from the Arctic telling the chilling story that members of the Franklin expedition had resorted to cannibalism in their final days, mutilating the bodies of their dead companions and cooking their remains in kettles. The story, which Rae heard from Inuit who had been passing it along for at least four years, generated anger and sadness among the missing men's families, heated denials and awkward compensatory narratives in daily newspapers, and hysterical racist invectives in Charles Dickens's weekly periodical *Household Words*. Public responses to Rae's report included anger with the Admiralty for not investigating the King William Island area earlier, criticism of Rae for returning home rather than traveling to the area himself, and logistical questions concerning how the ships had been lost and the primary causes of death. In general, the public accepted that Franklin and his men were long dead, in large part because Rae had returned with personal artifacts that undoubtedly belonged to the missing men. The allegations of cannibalism, however, lead many to question whether Inuit were trustworthy witnesses and whether they accurately understood the remains they found.

Charles Dickens's responses to Rae's report appeared in *Household Words* on 2 and 9 December 1854. The articles, both of which were titled "The Lost Arctic Voyagers," ostensibly absolved Rae of responsibility for the allegations and actually discredited both Rae and his informants, not only arguing that Inuit were mistaken or lying, but also implying that believing these stories was akin to savagery, casting the shadow of the cannibal over Rae himself and anyone who believed him. Dickens questioned the content of Inuit reports and the way Rae had gathered his information, arguing that oral transmission did not produce reliable knowledge. Lacking hard evidence to counter Rae's arguments—Rae had, after all, brought back both stories and material relics to support his report— Dickens attempted to discredit storytelling as unreliable, suspect, and

savage and to align rhetorical power with truth, morality, and civilization. Several critics have suggested that Dickens's hyperbolic response to
Rae demonstrates his own growing obsession with cannibalism: Dickens
was both attracted to and repulsed by the cannibal scene. In discrediting
Rae's report, he not only denied the truth of what had happened but also
attempted to erase the horrifying ethical dilemma of survival cannibalism—one which he played out extensively in his own writing—from the
sphere of British knowledge.

Despite Dickens's attempts at erasure, the choice made by Franklin's
men was preserved elsewhere. Charles Francis Hall recorded Inuit stories
about encountering Franklin's men after they turned to cannibalism and
discovering mutilated and partially consumed bodies. One of the most
moving of these stories concerns an Inuk woman who took a pocket watch
from the corpse of a dead officer: the woman used a heavy rock to chip
away at the ice encasing the man's body to get at the watch. Her story not
only relates her discovery of evidence of cannibalism but also brings the
officer's trangressive choice—his body was in perfect condition, implying
that he was one of the last to die and had consumed his fellow men to
survive—into presence. The woman did not commit cannibalism, but she
broke cultural taboos by touching and damaging the man's corpse when
she took the watch. In so doing, she chose to see a body as a commodity
rather than a corpse: her choice and her act paralleled the dead officer's. In
the years that followed this encounter, the woman told and retold her story
and kept the officer's watch, preserving and commemorating her experience. The woman became a witness to the horror of the man's choice to
commit survival cannibalism through her own choice to take the watch;
her later repetition of the story suggests that she was ethically compelled to
testify to what she saw and did.

Reading the woman's testimony against Dickens's vehement denials
reveals the tensions between rhetoric and story, between written and oral
preservation of knowledge, and between imagining and witnessing that
emerged in the wake of Rae's report. Her story sharply contrasts Dickens's
responses: in his fiction, Dickens recognized the central horror of survival
cannibalism—that anyone could give into cannibalistic desires in times of
extreme deprivation—but in his responses, he refused to acknowledge it,
instead displacing the anxieties provoked by Franklin's men's actions into
racist rhetoric. While Dickens located cannibalism outside the self, the
metropole, and civility, the woman's story demonstrated that the terrible
decision Franklin's men had to make in order to survive was one of human
necessity that called out to be witnessed.

THE CONTENTS OF THE KETTLES

Rae's letter to the Hudson's Bay Company related that Inuit told him that four years earlier, in 1850, families hunting seals had met approximately forty white men near Washington Bay. These white men could not speak Inuktitut "so well as to be understood, but by signs the Natives were led to believe that the Ship or Ships had been crushed by the ice, and that they were then going to where they expected to find deer to shoot" (*Arctic Correspondence* 275). The story, to this point, echoes Owwer's Aglooka story. Rae's version continues, recounting a story of discovery:

> At a later date the same Season but previous to the disruption of the ice, the corpses of some thirty persons and some Graves were discovered on the Continent, and five dead bodies on an Island near it, about a long day's journey to the north west of the mouth of a large stream, which can be no other than Backs Great Fish River [...] Some of the bodies were in a tent or tents; others were under the boat which had been turned over to form a shelter, and some lay scattered about in different directions. Of those seen on the Island, it was supposed that one was that of an Officer, (chief) as he had a telescope strapped over his shoulders, and his double barreled gun lay underneath him.

> From the mutilated state of many of the bodies and the contents of the kettles, it is evident that our wretched Countrymen had been driven to the last dread alternative, as a means of sustaining life. A few of the unfortunate men must have survived until the arrival of the wild fowl, (say until the end of May,) as shots were heard, and fresh bones and feathers of geese were noticed near the scene of the sad event. (*Arctic Correspondence* 275–76)

After meeting Aglooka, Owwer and his companions found both the macabre campsite that bore evidence of cannibalism and the island site where the officer's body lay. The first men to die had been properly buried, while those who died later were left where they fell. The final survivors consumed the unburied men's flesh, cooking it in kettles to make it palatable.[1] Rae's July 29 letter to the Admiralty was published in the *Times* on October 23, 1854 and quickly reprinted in other dailies. The *Times* also included comments from Rae's journal: this meant that the *Times* not only included the allegation that "from the mutilated state of many of the corpses, and the contents of the kettles, it is evident that our wretched countrymen had been driven to the last resource—cannibalism—as a means of prolonging existence,"[2] but also reiterated the accusation: "from the mutilated state of many of the bodies and the contents of the kettles, it is evident that our wretched countrymen had been driven to the dread

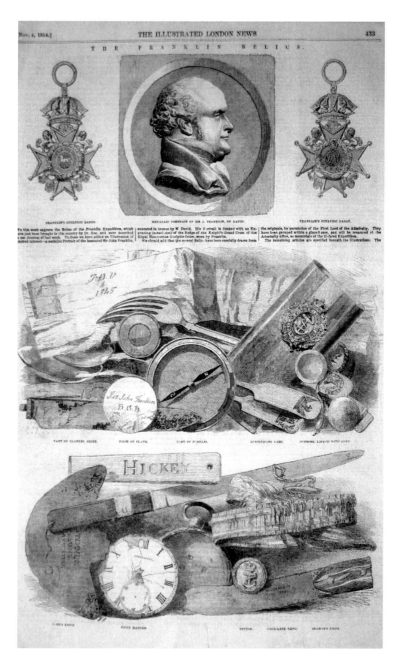

Image 5.1 Artifacts Retrieved by Rae.

alternative of cannibalism as a means of sustaining life." The article was reprinted, with this repetition, in a number of papers: this suggests that the accusation of cannibalism was initially central to the meaning of Rae's report; while shocking, it was not unbelievable or unspeakable.

The initial response to Rae's report indicates that journalists accepted Inuit testimony as substantially true, particularly because it was corroborated by the artifacts Rae had retrieved, but were hesitant about how to address charges of cannibalism. Some responses avoided the accusation altogether while others, even in the same papers, openly suggested that Inuit were mistaken in interpreting the remains as evidence of cannibalism. The *Morning Herald* avoided mentioning cannibalism explicitly but expressed sadness at "the melancholy certainty that Sir John Franklin and his gallant companions have perished, under circumstances too horrible to be thought of but for a warning" (25 October 1854). The same issue, however, included an editorial that conceded the Inuit story "seems too consistent in itself, and too conformable with probability" to be doubted, but claimed that accusations of cannibalism "may be disproved" (25 October 1854). The *Sun* also acknowledged that Rae's report contained a significant measure of truth but questioned Inuit reliability: "even civilised and educated men can distort the truth [. . .] Much more must this be the case among men of a limited range of ideas [. . .] The details of their horrible fate may be received with more or less of scepticism, but there appear no reasonable grounds of doubt that it has a substantial basis of truth" (24 October 1854). The *Times* went further, arguing Inuit were not mistaken but liars: "Like all savages, [Inuit] are liars, and certainly would not scruple at the utterance of any falsehood which might [. . .] shield them from the vengeance of the white man" (26 October 1854). Implying Inuit lied to hide their involvement, the editorial suggested that although they were known as "a harmless race, strongly inclined to pilfering and petty crime, but with little inclination or energy for deeds of blood [. . .] their constitutional timidity might have been overcome when they found the white man enfeebled and emaciated by disease and starvation" (26 October 1854). Although the personal effects Rae had retrieved made it difficult to claim the Inuit reports were completely false, the second-hand nature of the testimony, long-standing stereotypes about "savages," and the vague details of Rae's report provided fodder for those who wanted to dismiss accusations of cannibalism.

An editorial in the *Observer*, surprising because it acknowledged that cannibalism could and did occur, suggests that by the end of October, Rae's accusations weighed heavily on the British public: "The idea of the survivors being at last obliged to resort to cannibalism to keep body and soul together is almost too horrid to contemplate, and yet dreadful as it is, it is unquestionably true that a similar course has before this been had recourse to, in such fearful emergencies" (30 October 1854). Crafting rational denials, rehearsing old arguments about race and culture, and proposing counternarratives were exhausting in the face of the horror of cannibalism. This might explain why the *Sun* changed its tactic by month's end, moving from measured argument to impassioned rhetoric in claiming that Franklin's character and the taboos against cannibalism were sufficient evidence that the allegations were false: "No—they never resorted to such horrors. [...] Cannibalism!—the gallant Sir JOHN FRANKLIN a cannibal—such men as CROZIER, FITZJAMES, STANLEY, GOODSIR, cannibals! Man eating man—civilized man daring to meet his Maker in a country in which cannibalism has no place—in a condition in which the 'savages,' so called, of the Great American Continent, thank GOD, never dare to meet their Maker" (31 October 1854). With no evidence to prove or disprove the accusations, concerned parties resorted to rhetorical fervour to defend their standpoints. This tactic—denying Rae's allegations by arguing that the character of the "civilized" British sailors trumped the word of Inuit "savages"—emerged as the mainstream response to Rae's report in the months that followed.

ENTER CHARLES DICKENS...

The rhetorical strategies Dickens employed in his responses built upon press reactions, but his reputation and command over the reading public meant that his opinion carried far more purchase: he ensured that reports of cannibalism were dismissed for many years.[3] It appears that Jane Franklin prompted Dickens to join the public debate.[4] Shortly after he returned to England, Dr. Rae visited Lady Franklin and she apparently told him his "allegations should never have been committed to paper" (McGoogan, *Fatal* 210–11). After this meeting, she contacted Dickens, and "the desperately busy author dropped everything" to visit her (McGoogan, *Lady* 340). While no record of their discussion survives, it seems likely she approached Dickens because the famous author, whose views on "savages" were well-known, could successfully refute Inuit accusations. On June 11, 1853, Dickens had published "The Noble Savage" in *Household Words*; the piece, although less overtly racist than his later works,[5] was a scathing criticism of "savage" races and those who romanticized them.[6] The article began by asserting: "I have not the least belief in the Noble Savage. I consider him a prodigious nuisance. [...] His calling rum fire-water, and me a pale face, wholly fail to reconcile me to him. I don't care what he calls me. I call him a savage and I call a savage something highly desirable to be civilised off the face of the earth" (337).[7] Dickens then describes watching Zulu Bushmen sitting around their brazier and remarks: "I have sincerely desired that something might happen to the charcoal smouldering therein, which would cause the immediate suffocation of the whole of the noble strangers" (338). These fantasies of extermination, although included for their rhetorical effect, provide insight into Dickens's views on race: he rejected the idea of the "Noble Savage" because he identified "the cream of civilization with those who develop their God-given propensities to be useful;" the undeveloped savage "was rarely noble and never natural" (Marlow, "English Cannibalism" 654).[8] Dickens's well-publicized views on "savages" qualified him to make the defense Lady Franklin imagined: Dickens was both influential and completely unlikely to defend Rae's informants.

In turn Dickens, obsessed with cannibalism since childhood, was predisposed to accept Lady Franklin's request. Harry Stone suggests that "his innate temperament made him thrill with horror at each faint suggestion of eating human flesh and caused him to dwell on and retain such suggestions, while his earliest experiences and then his special childhood exposure to such lore enlarged and shaped the very things it fed upon" (*Night* 77). Although Dickens's major works thematizing cannibalism followed the *Household Words* debate, he had already begun to explore the sensational potential of cannibal narratives. This can be seen in his 1853 story "The Long Voyage," which includes two separate narratives about cannibalism. The first story introduces escaped convicts who resort to cannibalism, focusing on one man who acquires an "inappeasable relish for his dreadful food" (370).[9] The second story, about the shipwreck of the *Grosvenor*, concerns a seven-year-old boy cared for by survivors.[10] By exemplifying "the natural heroism and self-denial of ordinary human beings," the story served as "incontrovertible evidence that men are not by nature 'solitary monsters'" (Marlow, "Sir John" 98). Taken together, the two parts demonstrate that Dickens was both exploring the terrifying shiver produced by cannibal tales and reinforcing the boundary between civilization and savagery. Marlow adds that after 1854, Dickens's attitude toward cannibalism changed: "He was no longer concerned only about being the victim of cannibalism; the close identification he made between himself and Franklin suggests that the opposite dread had grown strong within him" ("English Cannibalism" 651–52). Dickens, attracted and simultaneously repulsed by the cannibal scene, deeply anxious about what divided "civilized" and "savage" peoples, could hardly help himself when the opportunity arose to respond to Rae's report: firmly identifying himself with Franklin, he nominated himself to defend Franklin's reputation and the boundaries of civilization.

Dickens begins his response by claiming that "we find no fault with Dr. Rae, and [...] thoroughly acquit him of any trace of blame" for the shortcomings of his informants ("Lost" 361), but uses this comment to introduce his critique. First condemning Rae's translator as incompetent and prone to exaggeration ("Lost" 361–62), Dickens then asks whether the gestures Rae's informants apparently used could provide precise information: "the gesture described to us as often repeated—that of the informant setting his mouth to his own arm—would quite as well describe a man having opened one of his veins, and drunk of the stream that flowed from it" ("Lost" 362). Following this, Dickens points out that Rae's information was second hand, calling it "an incoherent Esquimaux story, collected at 'various times' as it wandered from 'various sources'" ("Lost" 362–63). These three criticisms—of incompetent translation, of gestural communication, and of oral transmission—introduce Dickens's central argument against oral history.[11]

After briefly critiquing the "facts" of Rae's report—asking: "If it be inferred that the officer who lay upon his double-barrelled gun, defended his life to the last against ravenous seamen [...] how came his body to be found? That he was not eaten, or even mutilated" ("Lost" 362) and why, if there was no fuel available, "would the kettles have been defiled" for the purpose of cooking flesh ("Lost" 362)[12]—and proposing alternate explanations for what Rae heard—suggesting that either animals or scurvy could cause "dreadful disfigurement" ("Lost" 362)—Dickens, on argumentative thin ice, makes a sudden rhetorical jump. Abruptly changing strategies, he suggests that Inuit set upon Franklin's men: "Lastly, no man can, with any show of reason, undertake to affirm that this sad remnant of Franklin's gallant band were not set upon and slain by the Esquimaux themselves" ("Lost" 362). Rae, who saw this suggestion as patently absurd, used personal experience to counter Dickens's accusation ("Lost" 434), but his experience living among Inuit had no place in the economy of racial difference Dickens conceived. While Dickens acknowledged that Inuit could appear deferential and gentle, he claims they could always revert to natural "savagery": "We believe every savage to be in his heart covetous, treacherous, and cruel; and we have yet to learn what knowledge the white man—lost, houseless, shipless, apparently forgotten by his race, plainly famine-stricken, weak, frozen, helpless, and dying—has the gentleness of Esquimaux nature" ("Lost" 362).[13]

Dickens's next move is logically dodgy but affectively compelling. He suggests the "suppositious case" of lost and starving men who "lay down side by side, calmly and even cheerfully awaiting their release from this world," then asks: "if Franklin himself [...] had been [...] the Chief of this very expedition, infusing into it [...] the force of his character and discipline, patience and fortitude; would there not be a still greater and stronger moral improbability to set against the wild tales of a herd of savages?" Dickens dramatically answers his own question: "Now, this *was* Franklin's case" ("Lost" 363–64). While Dickens was correct—Franklin survived starvation during his first expedition without resorting to cannibalism—he also had to make the uncomfortable admission that even this exemplary expedition was stained by cannibalism. By carefully laying blame on Michel Teroahauté, the Métis guide, Dickens exonerates Franklin's officers and men, claiming that "so far off was the unnatural thought of cannibalism from their minds [...] that no suspicion of the truth dawned upon one of them, until the same hunter shot Mr. Hood dead" ("Lost" 365). Dickens implies that only debased men like Teroahauté who were "ignorant of the duties inculcated by Christianity" could choose cannibalism, effectively isolating the practice as something that occurred outside the bounds of civilized society ("Lost" 365). Redeeming his example by containing cannibalism as the act of ignorant "savages," Dickens effectively introduces the second part of his response, which examines specific cases of survival cannibalism.

The second part of Dickens's response, published on December 9, was intended to demonstrate that cases of cannibalism "are few and exceptional" ("Lost" 365); however, its overwhelming list of examples and his absolute denial that cannibalism could occur among British officers underline Dickens's extreme anxiety about the practice. Although Dickens's examples seem to "indicate a thriving cannibal culture" (Hill 126), they do ostensibly support his point that only uneducated, undisciplined, and godless men gave into the "last resource." For example, Dickens carefully points out that alcohol played a major role in the crew's descent into cannibalism aboard the *Peggy*:[14] "The crew were incessantly drunk from the first hour of their calamities falling upon them. They were not sober, even at the moment when they proposed the drawing of lots" to determine who among them should be killed for consumption ("Lost" 386–87). Similarly, Dickens calls the men of the *Medusa* "the scourged and branded sweepings

of the galleys of France" and blames cannibalism on the fact that "no discipline worthy of the name had been observed aboard the Medusa" ("Lost"
388). Comparing these debased men to "the flower of the trained adven-
turous spirit of the English Navy," Dickens appears to have made his point.
He was not, however, finished. Following this, he provides examples of
British sailors who, shipwrecked or lost at sea, refused to give into cannibalistic urges. Then, after providing four further examples of cannibalism,
Dickens explicitly states: "It appears to us that the influence of great priva-
tion upon the lower and least disciplined class of character, is much more
bewildering and maddening on sea than on shore [...] even men who
might be in danger of the last resource at sea, would be very likely to pine
away by degrees, and never come to it, ashore" ("Lost" 391).[15]

Critics have noted that Dickens's exhaustive list of examples "reveals a
fascination that exceeded all necessity" (Potter 145), "throw[ing] more light
on his own excitable and anxious state of mind than upon the ostensible
subject of his concern" (Ackroyd 713), and "bring[ing] to light Dickens's
investment in the affective mechanics of cannibal tales" (Hill 126). I also
see in the list of examples Dickens's absolute refusal—surprising for a nov-
elist who spent his career detailing the inner workings of his characters'
psyches—to address the psychological reality of the decision to commit
cannibalism, achieved by situating cannibalism as a phenomenon that only
occurred among "savages." "Savages," as Dickens's examples show, were not
necessarily indigenous: lower-class Britons, French sailors, and Americans
could all "become savage" by forgetting cultural taboos. Dickens's conclusion makes the alignment of "savagery" with cannibalism clear, contrasting
Rae's informants with Franklin's men and locating cannibalism entirely
outside the metropole. Reiterating his racist diatribe against "savages" in
list format, Dickens demonstrates that he had moved from the territory of
reasoned argument into the realm of hysterical sensationalism:

> The word of a savage is not to be taken for it [the occurrence of cannibalism];
> firstly, because he is a liar; secondly, because he is a boaster; thirdly, because he
> often talks figuratively; fourthly, because he is given to a superstitious notion
> that when he tells you he has his enemy in his stomach, you will logically give
> him credit for having his enemy's valour in his heart. Even the sight of cooked
> and dissevered human bodies among this or that tattoo'd tribe, is not proof.
> Such appropriate offerings to their barbarous, wide-mouthed, goggle-eyed
> gods, savages have been often seen and known to make. ("Lost" 392)

Dickens is coasting on his own rhetoric, but his derision of Rae's witnesses
emphasizes the difference between "savages" and the cream of the Royal

Navy, reducing Inuit oral history to "chatter" and aligning Inuit material practices with barbarism: "We submit that the memory of the lost Arctic voyagers is placed [...] high above the taint of this so easily-allowed connection; and that the noble conduct and example of such men, and of their own great leader himself, under similar endurances [...] outweighs by the weight of the whole universe the chatter of a gross handful of uncivilized people, with a domesticity of blood and blubber" ("Lost" 392).

After carefully creating an "us"—readers and Franklin's men—to contrast "them"—"savages" who worshipped "barbarous, wide-mouthed, goggle-eyed gods"—Dickens argued that the British public had a patriotic duty to remember Franklin and his men as heroes, claiming that the lack of evidence and the fact that Franklin could not return were reason enough to discard Inuit oral history. His final passage showcases his rhetorical command:

> Utilitarianism will protest 'they are dead; why care about this?' Our reply shall be, 'Because they ARE dead, therefore we care about this. Because they served their country well, and deserved well of her [...] Because no Franklin can come back, to write the honest story of their woes and resignation [...] Because they lie scattered on those wastes of snow, and are as defenceless against the remembrance of coming generations, as against the elements into which they are resolving and the winter winds that alone can waft them home [.'] [...] Therefore, teach no one to shudder without reason, at the history of their end. Therefore, confide with their own firmness, in their fortitude, their lofty sense of duty, their courage, and their religion. ("Lost" 392–93)

With no written evidence of what happened, Dickens gave readers a choice: to believe second-hand Inuit stories, sympathizing with the blood-thirsty, blubber-eating Inuit and the desire to commit cannibalism, or to affirm ideals of British heroism, confirming Franklin's reputation and comfortably dismissing Rae's accusations.

John Rae spoke truth to power in his December 23 and 30 responses, pointing out that Dickens relied upon rhetoric over experience or evidence, but Rae's criticisms did little to change public opinion. Rae conceded that Dickens, a "writer of very great ability and practice," had taken the "popular view of the question," while Rae himself had "nothing but a small amount of practical knowledge" and "a few facts to support my views and opinions" that he threw "together in a very imperfect and unconnected form" ("Lost" 458–59). He recognized that the debate was not about whether cannibalism had occurred, but about the social power that polished rhetoric exerted over oral history and about the choice of how to remember Franklin and his men. Russell Potter summarizes the choices available to *Household Words* readers: "side with the embattled Dr. Rae, who trusted the words of savages, or with Mr. Dickens, who gave articulate voice to the denials that rose like mantras on the lips of British men and women" (108). Middle-class Christian Britons identified with the missing men and didn't want to believe Rae: Dickens gave them permission to dismiss his accusations. Dickens's denial of cannibalism even came to represent the truth for officers with Arctic experience. For example, Lieutenant Bedford Pim, advocating an expedition to disprove Rae's allegations, ascribed more authority to Dickens's fiction than to Rae's Inuit witnesses:

> The writer of these pages has had no common experience in the Polar regions [...] and [...] he will not cease to urge another Expedition, if ONLY to wipe out the foul charge which it has been attempted to fix on the honoured names of his brother officers. Many, very many people in this country have the same feeling, and on the highest authority cannibalism is pronounced 'a gigantic improbability.' Let those who believe in such an act read 'The Wreck of the Golden Mary,' the most truthful and graphic description of shipwreck and suffering the language has ever produced, and all doubts on the subject must vanish. (15–16)

Dickens and Wilkie Collins's 1856 story *The Wreck of the Golden Mary*, in which shipwrecked men and women refuse to commit cannibalism, came to "truthfully" represent how Christian Britons—like Franklin and his men—responded to desperate circumstances, overwriting Rae's report.[16]

One effect of the debate was that the British public was left in a tricky epistemological position. While many Britons were comforted to believe cannibalism had not occurred, they did not know what had happened: Rae's stories were dismissed and the relics he retrieved—although accepted as evidence that the men who had owned them were dead—were mute. Although Dickens called upon his readers to commemorate Franklin and his men as heroes, it was unclear what, precisely, readers were to remember: no one knew what had happened to their ships, why the men were found wandering the tundra, or what ultimately killed them. The question of what happened appeared closed following the *Household Words* debate; however, it ballooned into a epistemological crisis after the Crimean War, when the "British public awoke anew to the old, festering anxieties that Rae's evidence had only heightened" (Potter 138). By 1856, Dickens was aware of the need for further closure. I argue in chapter 6 that *The Frozen Deep*, the drama he cowrote with Wilkie Collins, attempted to facilitate precisely the emotional catharsis that was missing after the *Household Words* debate ended.

CRACKING THE ICE

Rae's report aroused the anxiety of identification: if the best men in the British Navy could grow so debased as to give into cannibalistic urges, anyone—including Dickens himself—could. Dickens attempted, first in *Household Words* and then in *The Frozen Deep*, to erase the reality of cannibalism preserved in Inuit stories and to facilitate public forgetting on a national scale. His simultaneous denial of cannibalism and valorization of Franklin exemplifies the "complicity of memory and forgetting" that Joseph Roach identifies as emerging from the process of surrogation within a culture in crisis (6). The selective memory required for a community to address and overcome "actual or perceived vacancies" not only involves public commemoration but also "requires public enactments of forgetting" (Roach 2, 3). Roach carefully notes, however, that this process is messy and is rarely completed: "circum-Atlantic performance is a monumental study in the pleasures and torments of incomplete forgetting" (7). Although the majority of the British public, like Dickens, denied the reality of cannibalism and privileged rhetoric over oral transmission, the horror of the choices made by Franklin's men were only incompletely forgotten. The terrifying choices the final survivors had made were preserved—in strange, often displaced ways—in Inuit oral history.

Inuit, like the British, had taboos against cannibalism; however, they were somewhat more pragmatic about the practice than Dickens. Inuit stories collected from across the Arctic by late-nineteenth- and early-twentieth-century ethnographers suggest that Inuit viewed cannibalism as a generally forbidden practice that was, at times, necessary to ensure survival. "A Story of the Great Famine," an eastern Greenland story recorded by Knud Rasmussen, illustrates both the taboo concerning cannibalism and the stoicism that allowed individuals to choose survival:

> When they had nothing left to eat, and yet were loath to die, they began to eat dead bodies. When a man or woman died, the corpse was cut up and devoured; and the survivors ate those living in the same house with them; parents ate the bodies of their children, and children their parents.
>
> But it came to pass that many were seized with madness when they had eaten those they loved. Yet the few clung so fast to life when it seemed as though

death was to be the lot of all, that they preferred eating their dear ones to being eaten themselves. [...]

And, as the winter advanced, the famine became more acute. At last they were no longer content with eating those who died naturally; the stronger murdered those who were too weak to defend themselves. [...]

It is many years now since it happened that two winters followed one upon another without summer; but all we who have come after are descended from cannibals, you see. (351–52)

The story is remarkable not only for how it details the development of cannibalism within a small community but also for its suggestion that contemporary Inuit carried the burden of their ancestors' acts in their own survival: cannibalism was taboo but existed within, not apart from, the community. Other stories demonstrate a similar balance between acknowledging cannibalism as a rare reality of Inuit life and framing it as outside of appropriate sociability. Both Rasmussen and Franz Boas record the story of Igimarasugdjuqdjuaq, a "very huge and bad man, who had committed many murders and eaten the victims after he had cut them up with his knife" (Boas 225). In the version Boas heard, Igimarasugdjuqdjuaq's crimes are avenged by the community, whose members kill him with his own spear to "revenge the many outrages which he had wrought upon them" (226). The variation Rasmussen heard, from a man named Qilerneq, had the cannibal murdered by his own wife (185–86). The Igimarasugdjuqdjuaq stories differ from Rasmussen's story of famine because they acknowledge that people committed cannibalism not only as an act of survival but also as an act of antisociability and suggest that when people committed cannibalism out of sheer desire, they were subject to punishment from the community. In contrast, when people resorted to survival cannibalism, as in the story of famine, they bore a burden of guilt and shame but were not punished. Taken together, the stories indicate the nuanced views Inuit held on the ethics of cannibalism.

Inuit oral history also includes a number of accounts of encounters with strange white men who subsisted on human flesh; Dorothy Eber includes several such stories in *Encounters on the Passage*. One of her informants, Tommy Anguttitauruq, heard that even before Inuit knew *qallunaat* were consuming the remains of their dead companions, "some of them [...] didn't seem to be right. Some of the Inuit would try to help some of these white people who seemed not quite right, but they wouldn't want to receive help. They would grab them and burst out screaming" (qtd. in Eber 75). Mark Tootiak, another of Eber's informants, recalled hearing his stepfather tell how "Inuit heard that people had seen more white people, a lot more white people, dying. They were seen carrying human meat, small pieces, because they were so hungry" (qtd. in Eber 80). Tootiak's story is corroborated, according to Eber, by Francis McClintock: "Inuit who met [Francis] Leopold McClintock on the sledging journey during which Crozier's record was discovered told him that the white men had been seen carrying skulls and also bones from legs and arms that appeared to be sawn off" (Eber 80).[17]

Charles Francis Hall, like John Rae, heard Inuit stories of finding the macabre campsite. In 1869, Innookpoozheejook—one of the men Rae had interviewed in 1854—told Hall about finding a tent site near Terror Bay: "Three men, one of whom was *Tee-kee-ta*, first saw the tent. It had in it blankets and bedding, a great many skeleton bones and skulls, the flesh all off; nothing except sinews attached to them; the appearance as though foxes and wolves had gnawed the flesh; some bones had been sawed with a saw; some skulls had holes in them" (Nourse 405). An interview with Eveeshuk, an Inuk woman, corroborated some of the details of Innookpoozheejook's story; she told Hall that Inuit had seen: "One man's body [...] flesh all on, not mutilated, except the hands sawed off at the wrists; the rest, a great many had their flesh cut off as if some one or other had cut it off to eat" (Nourse 608). Further questions Hall put to Eveeshuk suggested the bodies were near Point Richardson, a significant distance from Terror Bay. This discrepancy raises the possibility that men practiced cannibalism both at Terror Bay and as they traveled south, suggesting the practice may have been widespread among Franklin survivors. The questions raised by variations in Inuit stories illustrate the difficulties that emerge from considering oral history as "beads on a rosary": it is very difficult—as David Woodman's *Unravelling the Franklin Mystery* illustrates—to resolve all the discrepancies between Inuit stories. At the same time, the similarities between stories—their suggestions that evidence of cannibalism was unmistakable, the way they attend to the practical questions of *how* Franklin's men committed cannibalism—not only indicate that the stories refer to real events but also point to their staying power. The reiteration of and within Inuit stories and the survival of these stories in present-day Inuit cultural memory reveal the lingering affective power of the events the Inuit witnessed. This persistence suggests that these stories, like Owwer's story of Aglooka, preserve something crucial about the experiences of those who committed and witnessed cannibalism.[18]

Hall heard one of the most evocative stories about visiting the tent site from an old woman named Ookbarloo in 1864; Ookbarloo had heard the story from Innookpoozheejook's mother-in-law, whom Hall does not name. Tookoolito brought Ookbarloo to meet Hall after Ookbarloo told Tookoolito that she saw a woman wearing a watch, resembling Hall's own watch, that "once belonged to one of the many Kob-lu-nas that had died near Neitchille" (Nourse 595).[19] J.P. Nourse rarely reproduced Hall's accounts of Inuit stories in full, tending instead to integrate quotations from Hall's notes into his own narrative. It is a signal of the story's significance that Nourse reprinted it in its entirety.

Hall begins by explaining how he heard the story: "Through Too-koo-li-too [Ookbarloo] said: 'When she was at Ok-kee-bee-jee (Pelly Bay), which was in the winter of 1853–4, she saw a woman who had a watch with chain and key, which she always kept carefully by her. This mother was mother-in-law of In-nook-poosh-ee-jook, the man who told her (Ook-bar-loo) what she related to me the other day. This mother of In-nook-poosh-ee-jook told her all about where and how she got the watch" (595). By explaining how the story traveled—from Innookpoozheejook's mother-in-law, to Ookbarloo, to Tookoolito, to Hall—Hall provided the genealogy of the story's transmission. Hall's account of the story, which I reprint here in full, continues:

> She and her husband went to a big tent not very far from Neitchille, and among the frozen mass of human bones and bodies that were lying around in it she saw one Kob-lu-na body that had a bright white (probably silver) chain around the neck. She knew at once what the chain was for, as some of the other Neitchille Innuits had just come into possession of several watches and chains, which she saw.
>
> The body of this man was lying on one side, and was half imbedded in solid ice from head to feet. The way the chain was about the neck and running down one side of the body indicated that the watch was beneath it; and therefore, to get at the watch, she found a difficult and disagreeable task before her. Neither she nor her husband had any instrument with them that they would use for any such purpose as was desired; therefore, while the husband was seeking around, in and about the tent, collecting such things as he fancied would best suit him, she procured a heavy sharp stone, and with this chipped away the ice from all round the body till it was released. Continued old mother *Ook-bar-loo*, in a truly sorrowful tone of voice: This woman told her that she could never forget the dreadful, fearful feelings she had all the time while engaged doing this; for, besides the tent being filled with frozen corpses—some entire and others mutilated by some of the starving companions, who had cut off much of the flesh with their knives and hatchets and eaten it—this man who had the watch she sought seemed to have been the last that died, and his face was just as though he was only asleep. All the while she was at work breaking the ice near the head, especially the ice about the face, she felt very, very bad, and for this

reason had to stop several times. She was very careful not to touch any part of the body while pounding with the sharp stone. At last, after having pounded away the ice from around and under the body, her husband helped her to lift it out of its icy bed. Still she was troubled to get the watch from the frozen garments with which the body was completely dressed. Finally, the watch and key and chain were obtained entire; and the woman now keeps them very choice, in commemoration of the terrible feelings she had when getting them from the dead Kob-lu-na, whom she dug out of the ice with nothing but a heavy, sharp stone. (Nourse 595–96)

The woman and her husband went to the tent site thinking they would find valuable goods and discovered a campsite littered with human remains. They entered the tent, which they must have anticipated would be a macabre space, and were confronted not only by a number of frozen corpses but by unmistakable evidence of cannibalism: some corpses were "entire and others mutilated by some of the starving companions, who had cut off much of the flesh with their knives and hatchets and eaten it." It is unclear, in Hall's account, whether Ookbarloo told Tookoolito that the bodies had been deliberately mutilated by starving men or whether Hall (or Tookoolito) drew this conclusion. Similarly, one must ask who—the unnamed woman, Ookbarloo, Tookoolito, or Hall—concluded that the man with the watch, because his body was unmutilated, was "the last that died." Lacking evidence to the contrary, I will take Hall's text at face value and assume that the woman herself believed the man was the last to survive and was, therefore, responsible for some of the deliberately mutilated corpses.

The woman's desire for the watch is hardly surprising. She had seen other Inuit with similar items and must have suspected that the watch and chain were valuable. In a culture with limited access to wood and metal, European goods were sought after and were either traded or creatively repurposed. Vilhjalmur Stefansson noted that HMS *Investigator*, a British search ship abandoned in 1853, was "a veritable treasure house" to Inuit, who "made long trips there to get material for knives, arrow points, and the like" (240–41). Food and clothing were of little value to Inuit, but "two classes of article [. . .] were to them beyond price—the iron and other metal work, and the soft wood" (360). Inuit used these items for a wide range of purposes; for example, metal plate and chair legs salvaged from the Franklin expedition were used to make knife blades and spear handles.[20] Although Inuit did not use watches to tell time, the officer's watch could have been repurposed for another use; I suspect, however, that its primary value to the woman was either as a status symbol or a tradable good. Like other decorative items Inuit salvaged from Franklin's ships, the watch was comparatively rare and thus could be traded with other Inuit or *qallunaat* or worn by the woman to signify her social status.

While one cannot reconstruct exactly why the woman took the watch, it seems certain that she decided to take it because she believed it would be valuable; once she got the watch, however, its value to her changed. Inuit retrieved scores of objects from the tent site and other caches of Franklin relics. Throughout the 1850s, they traded these items with Inuit and *qallunaat* in exchange for other useful or desirable supplies. For instance, when John Rae met Inuit at Repulse Bay, he bought "a small silver plate with 'Sir John Franklin K.C.B.' engraved thereon, a star of the Hanoverian order of Knighthood, and a number of Silver spoons and forks, on which are marked the initials of several of the officers of *both* ships" (*Arctic Correspondence* 288). While the woman might not have predicted *qallunaat* interest in the watch when she took it, by the time she told her story she certainly would have been aware of the watch's value. Yet she held on to the watch for years. It is, of course, possible that she kept the watch in order to exchange it at a later time or simply because she appreciated it as a luxury item. A comment at the end of the story, however, indicates this was not the case: Hall specifies that the woman kept the watch "in commemoration of the terrible feelings she had when getting them from the dead Kob-lu-na, whom she dug out of the ice with nothing but a heavy, sharp stone." The watch was transformed, by the act of retrieval, from an item with economic or social value to one with commemorative, affective value.

Where did the woman's "terrible feelings" come from? Taking the watch was a difficult and gruesome act. The woman used a heavy stone to chip away the ice encasing the man's body. The story's language suggests the violence of her actions: she had to pound at the ice to break it and she almost certainly damaged the man's frozen flesh by hitting it with the stone. Although the woman was overwhelmed by the horror of breaking the ice around the man's face, pausing several times because of her "very, very bad" feelings, her desire to take the watch was stronger than her repulsion. Once she broke the ice away, she was faced with another problem: the man's clothes were frozen and held the watch fast, leaving the woman "troubled to get the watch from the frozen garments with which the body was completely dressed." Hall's account of the woman's story jumps ahead here, skipping an explanation of how the woman got the watch free from the man's clothing, and stating only: "Finally, the watch and key and chain were obtained entire." Considering the story's level of detail, this silence is surprising and suggests that there was something unpleasant or even unspeakable about how the woman removed the watch from the frozen clothing. The woman, Hall specifies, was careful not to touch the body when she was breaking the ice with the rock, but removing the watch from the clothing would have been almost impossible for her to achieve without using her hands to touch the man: the act of touching the corpse was, I suspect, one source of the woman's terrible feelings.

Many Inuit cultures believed that a dead body was fundamentally unclean and that it contaminated those who came in contact with it. This perspective structured many customs surrounding death and dying. Franz Boas notes that among Baffin Island Inuit, only immediate relatives were allowed to touch the body of the deceased and that they buried or entombed the body as quickly as possible. After burying a body, relatives of the deceased locked themselves in their hut or igloo for three days to mourn, then left the home forever (205–06). In Greenland Inuit culture, not only the body but also the belongings of the deceased were considered contaminated, according to Hans Rink: "If any one happened to die in a house, everything belonging to the deceased was brought outside to avoid infecting the living. All the housemates likewise had to bring out their belongings, and take them in at night after they had been well aired. The persons who had assisted in carrying the corpse to the grave, for a time were considered to be infected, and had to abstain from taking part in certain occupations" (55). Hall became aware of similar customs among Inuit he encountered across the Arctic and learned that the possessions of a dead person were considered untouchable if they were present when the person died. Hall's account of his first expedition includes a story of seeing "the skeleton of an Innuit, or Esquimaux woman, just as she had died some three years before! She had been sick, and was left to take care of herself. The remains of her tent—her skin bedding, her stone lamp, and other domestic articles, were still by her side. This inattention to the sick and dead is a custom of the Esquimaux" (*Life* 84). Hall realized that what he initially saw as inattention was actually the reflection of a deeply felt repugnance to "touch anything belonging to an igloo covering the dead" (*Life* 448). Although it is impossible to reconstruct the woman's beliefs, it is likely that she, like many Inuit, believed that touching a dead body was a fundamentally unclean act: touching the man's body to remove his watch from his clothing would have been a taboo act.

Furthermore, Inuit believed that the soul survived after the body died and developed practices to ensure that the soul of the deceased did not threaten the living. Bennett and Rowley note that Inuit believed "the soul of the deceased was aware of visitors" (223). This awareness permeated many posthumous customs. Hans Rink remarks that in Greenland Inuit cultures, a "dead man is considered as the inua [ruler] of his grave, and of the personal properties he left" (44). While the deceased could act as a guardian to the living, he could also avenge himself on those who had injured him in life; for this reason, "Danger is more or less connected with everything appertaining to, or having been in any contact with, dead bodies, or used at funerals, the invisible rulers in some cases being apt to take offence, or *have smoke or fog of it*—viz., causing bad weather and bad hunting on this account" (45). To appease and help the deceased, Inuit left personal items with a body when it was buried or entombed: "The man's hunting implements and other utensils are placed by the side of his grave; the pots, the lamps, knives, &c., by the side of that of the woman; toys, by that of a child" (Boas 205). Family members also visited the burial site at predetermined intervals and sometimes left food as a token to placate the deceased (Boas 206). Though it is unclear whether these beliefs applied to the souls of dead *qallunaat* or only Inuit, the woman might well have believed that the dead officer's belongings remained his property and that his soul had the power to avenge itself on those who injured him, as she did by taking his possessions. It seems likely that the woman's terrible feelings were partially engendered by cultural taboos concerning the treatment of dead bodies and beliefs about the survival of the soul after death.

I suspect, however, that the woman's feelings were heightened by another factor: the man's supposed cannibalism. The woman believed that the officer, because his body was in good condition, was the last to die and that he had survived because he consumed human flesh: he was responsible for at least some of the mutilation she saw around her. Inuit stories indicate not only that they were familiar with the horror of cannibalism but also that the act was regarded with repugnance. Some Inuit believed that those with antisocial and selfish tendencies were most susceptible to cannibalistic desires: "Those who did not share were held in fear and disdain. People regarded them as the most likely to resort to cannibalism" (Bennett and Rowley 89). In a culture that held food sharing within and between families as sacrosanct, the term *iqattajattuq* described individuals who kept food to themselves in times of famine. Rachel Uvarasuk Amitturmiut explains that "when the people begin to die of starvation this individual will be drawn by his desire for food and will therefore look at the corpse with the idea of eating the flesh [...] These types of individuals were feared when they started to keep food to themselves without the slightest intent of sharing" (qtd. in Bennett and Rowley 89). While Inuit recognized that cannibalism could be an unfortunate necessity, they also believed that it was an antisocial behavior that could often be prevented by maintaining and strengthening food sharing relationships. In the woman's worldview, the man in the tent was, because he was the last to die, *iqattajattuq*, one who had survived at the expense of his community.

It is difficult to imagine precisely how the man in the tent obtained the human flesh he consumed, but speculation is possible. Bodies, even in the shelter of the tent, froze quickly. It is unlikely that the officer possessed the strength or desire to fully dismember the body. Although Inuit reported seeing men carrying body parts as a portable food supply and Innookpoozheejook reported finding bodies that appeared to have been dismembered with saws, the tent site was a semipermanent encampment and the men there would have had easy access to their "food" supply. Innookpoozheejook and Eveeshuk both found body parts that appeared to have been "gnawed" or "had their flesh cut off." Since the officer was found in the tent with the bodies—he did not travel with a food supply—it seems more plausible that he and his remaining companions removed the flesh from the bodies in small pieces, as required, rather than all at once. In order to remove small amounts of flesh from a frozen corpse, the officer probably used some kind of tool—a hatchet, a knife—to scrape and hack away at the body. These actions would have mutilated the surface of the body, leaving the corpse disfigured.

The woman used a sharp stone to scrape the ice away from the man's body. Considering that the ice was frozen to the man, it is likely that the woman's actions damaged the man's flesh, leaving him mutilated and resembling the other corpses in the tent. The woman, by scraping away at the ice and disfiguring the man's body, physically replicated what the man had done to his companions. The woman believed the officer was responsible for some of the mutilation she saw around her and imagined him cutting flesh off the bodies of his tent mates. The "dreadful, fearful feelings" she experienced while breaking the ice around his body resulted, I suspect, from the way her actions mirrored those she imagined the man performing. The relationship between the woman's and the man's actions went further: not only did the woman replicate the man's actions, she also replicated his choice to break a taboo. The British officer disobeyed long-standing cultural injunctions against cannibalism, mutilating and consuming parts of a human body rather than passively accepting death. The woman, likewise, defied cultural prohibitions against touching dead bodies and interfering with the possessions of the dead in taking the man's body. The man chose to consume human flesh to survive; the woman chose to do violence to a dead body to obtain a watch. Both saw human bodies not as corpses to be treated with respect but as potentially valuable commodities: each committed a deliberate act of misrecognition, mistaking a human body for a thing.

There is no record of how the man felt after he consumed his companions' flesh, but we do know something about what the experience of taking the watch did to the woman. The story of taking the watch is not a story of encounter or discovery, but a story of a horrible choice and its effects on the woman. It is a story about choosing to treat a human body as a commodity in order to survive. Her act of taking the watch was doubly transformative: she temporarily transformed the man's body into a commodity to obtain the watch; the watch she obtained through this misrecognition was also transformed, from a commodity into a relic that commemorated her terrible act. Taking the watch changed the woman, compelling her to keep the watch and to retell the story of the taboos she broke in order to get it. The woman bore witness to her own terrifying choice and, through her repeated act of bearing witness, performed each time she retold the story, she also allowed—in a displaced, indirect manner—the choice the man made to commit cannibalism to survive as a performative remain. The woman's story not only preserves the chaos of the scene in the tent, the "frozen mass of human bones and bodies" that remained as the final days of the expedition came, but also allows the ghostly remains of the men's choices to become cannibals to emerge in the woman's actions. The repetition of the ethical dilemma resurfaces and becomes visible in the evocative gesture—the hacking at the corpse—that the woman replicated in her actions. In this way, Inuit oral history held open the horrifying space in memory, the terrible moment of choice, that Dickens, through his heated rhetoric, attempted to erase.

6. The Designated Mourner: Charles Dickens Stands in for Franklin ✎

Two thousand people sit "rigid and frozen together" in the Manchester New Free Trade Hall (Dickens, "Letter to Mrs. Richard Watson" 488). All eyes are focused on the stage where the most famous author in England—in the role of Richard Wardour in *The Frozen Deep*—is dying. With his head in the lap of Clara, his true love, and his hand on the head of his former nemesis, Frank, he speaks his final pathetic lines: "You will remember me kindly for Frank's sake? Poor Frank! Why does he hide his face? Is he crying? Nearer, Clara—I want to look my last at *you*. My sister, Clara! Kiss me, sister, kiss me before I die!" (Collins and Dickens 160). The pathetic scene draws tears "from grey heads and young hearts" alike, moving not only the audience but also the actors on stage (*Manchester Times* 22 August 1857). Maria Ternan, playing Clara, weeps, her tears falling onto Dickens's beard and clothes, pouring "all over [him] like Rain." Dickens whispers words of comfort to her: "My dear child, it will be over in two minutes. Pray compose yourself," but Ternan is inconsolable: "it's no comfort to me that it be soon over [...] Oh it is so sad, it is so dreadfully sad. Oh don't die! Give me time, give me a little time!" Other actors—including Mark Lemon, a founding editor of *Punch*, who frequently appeared in Dickens's amateur theatricals—begin to weep, and as the curtain falls, the audience, cast, and even the carpenters at the sides of the stage are joined in communal tears (Dickens, "Letter to Mrs. Richard Watson" 488).

The August 1857 performances of *The Frozen Deep* mark the chronological and emotional culmination of the fragmented run of the play, which began in January 1857 at Dickens's Tavistock House and included performances at the Gallery of Illustration in July. Dickens's December 7, 1857, letter to Mrs. Richard Watson indicates his belief that the final moments of the play electrified the audience, prompting an outpouring of grief from actors and audience alike. Robert Louis Brannan notes that Dickens remembered "the tears were apparently more numerous at Manchester than they had been earlier; Dickens had mentioned several times that his audiences had been 'strongly affected,' but had not remarked on any event comparable to that at Manchester" (73). If Dickens's memory is to be trusted, one must ask why this heightened response occurred. Were the actors and audience members crying for Richard Wardour's death alone? Were they recalling the recent death of playwright Douglas Jerrold, for whose family the performances were a benefit? Or was Wardour's death a theatrical substitute for a third death—John Franklin's—that had not been fully mourned by the public? Russell Potter claims that the "public outpouring of emotion at this event exceeded any other of its kind, becoming almost a double memorial" and emphasizes his argument with the rhetorical question: "Could it have been Dickens's performance only [...] that had such a striking effect on the crowd? Or must Franklin's own loss, so lately in the public eye, have been the great, displaced sorrow that, like some ice-choked river overflowing its banks, found its necessary and inevitable outlet in these otherwise modest performances?" (147). In this chapter I probe Potter's contention, examining how *The Frozen Deep* allowed displaced sorrow at the loss of the Franklin expedition to be publicly expressed.

As his passionate responses to Dr. Rae's report indicate, Dickens was deeply invested in the question of what happened to the Franklin expedition. Although his *Household Words* articles convinced many readers not to trust Rae's Inuit informants, they also highlighted the extent to which what actually happened remained unknown. Sarah Moss eloquently links Rae's reliance on Inuit testimony and his allegations of cannibalism with the epistemological anxiety surrounding the expedition:

> The idea of cannibalism and the idea of Inuit testimony [...] collapse into each other. It is unspeakable that the British Navy should have resorted to eating each other and unbearable that savages *who will not write things down* should be the ones to tell the *Times* about it. All savages lie [...] and no gentleman eats a colleague; these things are simply not admissible and will not be admitted. There is an imperial need for everything that happens to be collated and to make sense in the metropolis, and the idea that Franklin's story might exist only in Inuktitut, only in places that the British have not yet mapped, is as intolerable as the idea that a hundred and thirty five of the Navy's finest men might have been so changed by their experience of a foreign land that they ate each other. (143)

Moss's comment explains Dickens's vehement denial of cannibalism and draws our attention to two interrelated epistemological problems. First, Inuit provided Rae not only with stories but with personal articles that undoubtedly belonged to members of the Franklin expedition: these items proved that Inuit had either met Franklin survivors or had discovered their remains. In contrast, British search parties failed to uncover any significant remains of the expedition apart from those at Beechey Island. Inuit possession of Franklin relics was physical evidence that they had seen more—and thus *knew* more—than the British. Second, whether Rae's report was true or not, what happened to the expedition remained largely unknown: even if Inuit discovered the thirty or forty corpses Rae claimed they had, almost 100 men, two large ships, and tons of cargo remained unaccounted for. In 1857, no written records from the expedition had been retrieved and the causes of the expedition's failure remained unknown.

This two-pronged epistemological crisis—that Inuit witnessed more than the British search parties and that the British could not reconstruct what happened—had psychological implications. Because the British public did not know what happened to the men, the loss of the expedition could not fully enter public consciousness: the public could not mourn its loss because it was stuck in a melancholic engagement with the missing men. Freud, contrasting mourning and melancholia, argues that both conditions arise from the loss of a loved object, but that in cases of melancholia the lost object remains outside consciousness: "one cannot see clearly what it is that has been lost, and it is all the more reasonable to suppose that the patient cannot consciously perceive what he has lost either. This, indeed, might be so even if the patient is aware of the loss which has given rise to his melancholia, but only in the sense that he knows *whom* he has lost but not *what* he has lost in him" (245). Those affected by the expedition's disappearance knew they had lost their husbands, sons, and brothers, but—because they did not know precisely what had happened—did not understand what they had lost in losing the men: mourning the loss of a husband who died heroically is very different than mourning one who sustained himself by consuming the flesh of his dead shipmates. It was, furthermore, impossible to imagine exactly what happened because so many events *could* have happened: Dickens's litany of examples of cannibalism and the avoidance of cannibalism demonstrates the range of possible outcomes. Melancholia is also "complicated by the conflict due to ambivalence [...] countless separate struggles are carried on over the object, in which hate and love contend with each other" (Freud 256). Whether cannibalism occurred or not, Franklin's men failed in their object—finding the

Northwest Passage and returning home—and this failure hung over their reputations, even as they were heroized for sacrificing themselves for the sake of the Arctic mission. This failure allows one to argue that the missing men were objects of ambivalence even before Rae's report appeared, and that Rae's allegations that Franklin's men had descended to the level of "savages" only heightened these mixed feelings. Considering how the specific circumstances surrounding the expedition's disappearance prohibited "normal" mourning and facilitated melancholic engagement allows one to locate Russell Potter's provocative claim that *The Frozen Deep* served as the "last great public catharsis of [the Franklin] tragedy" (139) within the discursive framework of Freudian psychoanalysis. The epistemological and psychological anxiety that lingered in the wake of the *Household Words* debate centered, I contend, around the question of how the public could mourn an unknown loss. *The Frozen Deep*, which Dickens wrote with Wilkie Collins, intervened in this cultural crisis by producing a "knowable" loss for the public to witness and mourn.

Because *The Frozen Deep* has received more critical attention than any other performance considered in this book, it is essential to briefly locate my argument in relation to other assessments of the cultural work the play attempted to perform. Jen Hill makes the compelling argument that in the play, "cannibalism remains the powerful, if not fully articulated organizing force around which Dickens constructs a stable, white national identity" (116) and, connecting melodramatic affect to the sensation novel, claims that the play played a fundamentally conservative role: "In the schematic nature of melodrama, there can be only one conclusion: the reassertion of social norms [...] in the melodrama, transgression is recuperated by its conservative mechanics to unify audiences into the reaffirmation of shared values" (134). In other words, Hill argues that *The Frozen Deep* responded to the question of whether cannibalism occurred by containing it through the reaffirmation of national values. In arguing that *The Frozen Deep* functioned as an epistemological intervention, I diverge from Hill by contending that cannibalism did not constitute the most profound anxiety remaining from the *Household Words* debate. This is not to say that cannibalism was no longer a source of anxiety[1] or that the play ignores the issue: cannibalism certainly emerges as a theme in the play. But to understand how the play performed the cultural work of mourning, it is essential to consider what was imagined as lost. Without going so far as to claim that the loss of the Franklin expedition constituted a national trauma, one can say that the language of trauma helps illuminate the contours of loss. As Alice Rayner notes: "Trauma is characterized by the impossibility of an event, in its singularity, to enter any representation" (26). Paying attention to what falls outside the play's representational economy, to what is absent from the play, allows one to acknowledge the extratheatrical absence—the actual loss—to which the play responded.

The play's engagement with cannibalism suggests that Dickens had managed to discursively contain the practice, indicating that it was no longer the sole or primary source of angst. The script makes numerous references to cannibalism, even employing it as a comic device. For example, in the second act, John Want, a cook whose name suggests appetite, feeds the men ambiguously named "bone soup."[2] Cannibalism is evoked more ominously at the end of the act when Wardour tells Aldersley to come with him "over the road that no human footsteps have ever trodden, and where no human trace is ever left!" (140–41). The lines suggest that no trace of Aldersley will remain because Wardour, consumed by desire for Aldersley's fiancée, will instead consume Aldersley's remains. Collins and Dickens even increase the chances that cannibalism will occur by making Wardour and Aldersley romantic rivals and by stranding them at sea during their time alone. Recalling Dickens's *Household Words* articles, this implies that if Wardour refused cannibalistic urges in circumstances far worse than Franklin's men faced, it was impossible to imagine that *any* British officer could give into the desire.

In contrast, the play fails to represent or even mention Inuit. This suggests that anxiety was centered on the specter of Inuit witnesses and that the play engaged not with the trauma of cannibalism but with the trauma of the British failure to witness what happened.[3] Collins's and Dickens's decision to erase Inuit from the Arctic landscape was nothing new: many contemporary representations of the Arctic depicted it as empty of human inhabitants.[4] Their decision is, however, surprising when one considers Dickens's obsession with accurately depicting Arctic life. He insisted, for instance, on replacing a table with a cask and wooden bunks with hammocks because explorers would not have carried tables when they abandoned their ships, and only officers slept on wooden bunks (Brannan 75).[5] Dickens knew, from his extensive reading on exploration, that virtually every Arctic expedition encountered Inuit at some point. But there was no way for Inuit to appear on stage—as bumbling comic relief, as guides, even as villains—without affirming their presence in the Arctic and without, by extension, underlining the actual absence of British witnesses. The experience of loss expressed in the play emerged from the traumatic—unspeakable—failures of the British to locate the men in time or to bear witness to what happened to them.

The Frozen Deep was Dickens's attempt to intervene in the epistemological and psychological crisis that lingered after the publication of his
Household Words articles. The Collins and Dickens script rewrote the tragic
narrative of Rae's report as an emotionally satisfying and conclusive melodrama. In contrast to the real event of the ships' disappearances, which
was dramaturgically messy and inconclusive, the play produced a fantasy
of rescue and reconciliation, providing anxious audience members with
comforting closure, leaving no loose ends to be tied up. *The Frozen Deep*
also attempted to resolve the psychological hangover left by the *Household
Words* debate by presenting a theatrical death that audience members
could witness and actually mourn. While I cannot take credit for arguing that the play provided audience members with a "real" experience—
Potter implies, through his comment that the play allowed catharsis to
take place, that *The Frozen Deep* produced a visceral, affective experience
for audience members, and Hill suggests that the play allowed audience
and actors, through sensational aesthetics, "to experience 'truth' in the
melodramatic *present*" (138)—I contend that this experience of "reality"
can only be understood by contextualizing it in relation to contemporary
acting practices and to theories of surrogation. Dickens's proto-verisimilar
acting allowed audience members (and Dickens himself) to "forget" they
were watching a play and "really" see a pathetic heroic death, experiencing
in the theater what was impossible in life. Dickens's onstage death produced this uncanny form of catharsis because of the strange operations of
surrogation: as a surrogate for Franklin, Dickens created an effigy—Wardour—who could be sacrificed, night after night, in Franklin's place. The
effigy allowed audience members to mourn the loss of Franklin by witnessing and mourning the death of a real but surrogatory victim. This chapter
concludes by briefly considering the command performance of the play,
held in July. Dickens orchestrated the command performance in order to
create a "legitimate" set of spectators—the Queen and her entourage—to
replace the "illegitimate" Inuit witnesses upon whom Rae's report relied.
The imperial audience's appreciation of the play sanctioned Dickens's version of events as the truth and effectively obliterated Inuit histories of what
happened, laying the epistemological problem of Inuit witnesses to rest.

MELODRAMATIC (UN)CERTAINTY

Although Dickens and Collins collaborated on the script of *The Frozen
Deep*, Dickens consistently overrode Collins's intentions and the surviving

script reflects Dickens's vision of the play as a displaced memorial to Franklin's heroism. The idea for the play arose while Collins was visiting Dickens in Paris in early 1856. On April 6, Dickens wrote to W.H. Wills, telling him, "Collins and I have a mighty original notion (mine in the beginning) for another play at Tavistock House" (Dexter, ed., *Letters*755–56). The letter included details of the setting and characters, indicating that Collins and Dickens had already discussed some specifics of the play. Busy with *Little Dorrit*, Dickens asked Collins to write the first draft. By September, Dickens sensed their ideas were diverging: Collins, for example, wanted to represent class conflicts among the shipwrecked men, resulting in a less-heroic depiction of the voyagers than Dickens desired. Dickens wrote to Collins with a number of "suggestions" (Nayder 63–64) and, when he received Collins's script in October, he made substantial changes that increased the emphasis on Wardour and developed "suspended interest" to ensure the conclusion had the emotional impact he imagined (Brannan 33–34).[6] Brannan argues that Dickens conceived *The Frozen Deep* "as a peculiar kind of stage performance with the script to be merely an essential means for implementing this performance. The performance, not the script, excited Dickens and his audiences. [...] Dickens was able to achieve this kind of performance because his conception of the play was partly independent of Collins' script" (4–5). While Brannan's assessment that the script was secondary to the overall production is apt, it is critical to consider how the script diverged from the known facts to understand how the play responded to the uncertainty concerning what happened to the Franklin expedition.

Dramatizing "the revisionist history of the Franklin expedition that [Dickens] had related in *Household Words*" (Nayder 63) placed Dickens and Collins in the awkward position of balancing their desire to accurately represent the realities of Arctic exploration against the need to overwrite questions surrounding what happened to Franklin and his men. Instead of imagining an expedition that ended in catastrophe and disappearance, they imagined one that almost met this fate, but was saved. In *The Frozen Deep*, the *Sea Mew* and the *Wanderer* leave for the Arctic and become trapped in pack ice. Three years pass and the health and morale of the expedition deteriorate, leading Captain Ebsworth to send a detachment to seek help. The party succeeds and the men and officers are evacuated to Newfoundland, where their families greet them. All but one of the men return to England; Dickens's Richard Wardour is the expedition's lone casualty. In his revisions to Collins's draft, Dickens delved more deeply into the psychological implications of the situation, characterizing

Wardour as more complex than conventional melodramatic villains. Despite this, Dickens and Collins downplay the actual conflict inherent in Arctic exploration—man versus nature—to develop a narrative centering on the rivalry between Wardour and Aldersley and on Wardour's ability to overcome his baser feelings and sacrifice himself for Aldersley.

The prologue, which Dickens wrote and performed at the Gallery of Illustration and at Manchester,[7] refers to the Franklin expedition but clarifies that the play rewrites its story as fiction. Dickens, his voice underscored by soft music, emerges from "mists and darkness" to ask the audience to "Pause on the footsteps of heroic men,/Making a garden of the desert wide/Where PARRY conquer'd and FRANKLIN died" (Collins and Dickens 97). Acknowledging that Franklin is dead, Dickens tells the audience: "That in the fiction of a friendly play,/The Arctic sailors, too, put gloom away,/Forgot their long night, saw no starry dome,/Hail'd the warm sun, and were again at Home" (98). These lines imaginatively link audience members to the missing men. First, by reminding audience members of the practice of staging theatrical performances aboard Arctic ships, Dickens hints that Franklin's men used the "fiction of a friendly play" to dispel gloom, linking audience and performers with the missing through theatrical practice. Second, the lines suggest that the "friendly play" will bring the sailors home, allowing their ghosts to be laid to rest and assuaging the melancholia lingering from the expedition's disappearance.

The play opens in a *"pleasant room in a country-house"* in Devonshire (101), introducing the women left behind by the officers: Rose Ebsworth, Captain Ebsworth's daughter; Mrs. Steventon, Lieutenant Steventon's wife; Lucy Crayford, Lieutenant Crayford's sister; and Clara Burnham, Frank Aldersley's fiancée. By 1857, the women left behind—specifically Jane Franklin—had become the public face of the missing men. The decision to begin *The Frozen Deep* by showing the women left behind replicated how Franklin's men remained "visible" in England through waiting women. Russell Potter notes the parallel between the four women in the play and the "tragic trinity of womanhood" composed of Lady Franklin, Franklin's daughter Eleanor Gell, and his niece Sophia Cracroft: Collins and Dickens "simply added a fourth figure to an already well-known public grouping" (Potter 143). The women in the play were, however, imperfect replicas: Rose Ebsworth's situation resembled Eleanor Gell's, but Mrs. Steventon, Potter's candidate for "Jane," is married to a lieutenant, not the commander, and Clara Burnham, unlike Sophia Cracroft, is engaged to one officer (Aldersley) and has spurned another (Wardour).[8] This is the first of many moments when Collins and Dickens reference the Franklin expedition but subtly distance their play from reality.

The first act introduces the play's central conflict by revealing Clara Burnham's dark secret and foreshadowing the threat Wardour poses to Aldersley. The "naturally excitable and nervous" Clara is "wasting, still growing paler" (Collins and Dickens 104, 106): her fiancé's long absence has made her melancholic. In a scene underscored by a piano playing "Those Evening Bells," Clara reveals that years before, when her childhood friend Wardour was about to sail for Africa, he had proposed to her. When she did not reply, he assumed her consent, but while he was away, she fell in love with Frank Aldersley. Upon his return, Wardour learned that she was in love with another man and vowed that his unknown rival would come to "rue the day when you and he first met" (113). The audience then discovers the source of Clara's anguish: Aldersley and Wardour set sail for the Arctic together, and Clara fears that "one chance syllable between them might discover everything!" (115). The tension is heightened when Clara's childhood nurse Esther enters. Esther claims to have the power of "second sight"—a primitive psychic power—and tells Clara she has had a vision: "Doos the Sight show me Frank? Aye! and anither beside Frank. I see the lamb i' the grasp o' the lion. I see your bonnie bird alone wi' the hawk. I see you and all around you crying bluid. The stain is on you!" (116). The truth of Nurse Esther's vision, which anticipates Wardour attacking Aldersley, is undermined by a stage direction that has her in the room when Clara tells Lucy about Wardour's vow of revenge. Her reliability is further challenged by her Highland ethnicity, highlighted in her thick dialect. For audience members familiar with the *Household Words* debate, her Scottishness would have cited Rae's and linked them as unreliable, non-English witnesses.[9] The question of how to characterize Nurse Esther was one of the major disagreements between Collins and Dickens: Collins's draft implied Esther actually had second sight; Dickens, worried that supernatural elements would overshadow the play's central suspense, rewrote the part, highlighting Esther's "Highland primitivism" (Nayder 91) and changing Collins's stage direction so that her "second sight" could be attributed to eavesdropping (Brannan 39). By rearranging dialogue and speakers, Dickens shaped how tension developed in the first act, "minimizing the threat to Clara Burnham and subtly heightening the threat to the entire expedition" (Brannan 38); although the first act still introduced the melodramatic love triangle, Dickens's revisions provided space for tension to increase concerning Wardour's motives, anticipating his emergence as something far more ominous than a jilted lover (Brannan 38). In these revisions, one can see Dickens already exerting control over the production and shaping it to allow for the performance he imagined himself giving.

The play leaves the comforts of home and the concerns of the domestic behind in the second act, which opens in a ramshackle hut. Lieutenant Crayford gathers the crews and officers of both ships and tells them that Captain Ebsworth has decided that the able-bodied must make "another, and probably a last, effort to extricate" the group, traveling to the closest fur settlement "from which help and provisions may be dispatched to those who remain" (127–28). This is the closest Collins and Dickens come to imagining what happened to Franklin and his men, basing their representation on the experiences of other explorers, like John Ross, who found themselves similarly stranded. Then, turning away from Arctic realities, the play's solution to the problem of who should stay behind and who should seek help evokes Dickens's *Household Words* examples of survival cannibalism in which men were forced to choose whom to consume. The crew draws lots, placing their names in a pot (underlining the idea of consumption) and the officers roll dice. When the morose Wardour refuses to participate, Aldersley rolls for him. Dice rolled, it appears that Wardour will stay and Aldersley will go: one can imagine the relief

Image 6.1 Act Three of *The Frozen Deep*. From Illustrated London News. © Illustrated London News Ltd/Mary Evans

of audience members at this happy twist of fate and the dread, learned by watching melodrama, that this relief would be quickly reversed. As the detachment prepares to depart, Wardour cuts up Aldersley's bunk for firewood and discovers that Aldersley has carved Clara's initials into the wood. Wardour questions him and discovers that he is Clara's fiancé and, therefore, his own arch-rival. At that very moment, Captain Helding announces that the second lieutenant has injured himself. Without revealing his discovery, Wardour volunteers to fill the empty place alongside Aldersley. The act ends with Crayford advising Aldersley: "While you can stand, keep with the Main Body," and Wardour ominously replying "While he can stand, he keeps with *Me*" (141). In Collins's draft, Wardour was a relatively "conventional villain," but in Dickens's revised second act, he "emerged as more dangerous, but as less villainous" (Brannan 41–42). Dickens's revisions characterized Wardour as a "strong man capable of murder [. . .] but also as a man with potential nobility of sentiment and character" (Brannan 40). This departure from generic character clichés provided the space Dickens required to depart from gestural and vocal clichés in devising his performance.

When the third act opens on a *"cavern on the Coast of Newfoundland,"* it is clear that the detachment that departed in act two was successful. Privileging dramaturgical convenience over exploration reality, Collins and Dickens have the women meet the men in Newfoundland.[10] The fragile Clara has been told that the explorers divided into two parties and that Aldersley's group is still missing, but when Lucy and Lieutenant Crayford are left alone, the audience learns that the only men unaccounted for are Wardour and Aldersley. The audience's dread that Wardour did harm to Aldersley, introduced by Nurse Esther's vision in act one and heightened by Wardour's threat in act two, is confirmed when Wardour enters the cavern alone. Unrecognizable, clothed in rags, *"his hair is tangled and grey; his looks and gestures are those of a man whose reason is shaken, and whose bodily powers are sinking from fatigue"* (Collins and Dickens 155). Clearly starving, he says: "Throw me some bones from the table. Give me my share along with the dogs" (155), and then tells Steventon and Ebsworth about having been shipwrecked in a drifting boat. His disheveled appearance, his request to eat bones, and his reference to being adrift at sea all appear to confirm the suspicion that he has resorted to cannibalism. Crayford, finally recognizing Wardour, voices the audience's assumption and accuses him of killing Aldersley: "Why are you here alone? Where is Frank, you villain! Where is Frank?" (157). Clara reenters and Wardour *"breaks his way out of the cavern"* (157). This scene was one Dickens extensively revised: in

Collins's draft, Wardour is "presented as a maniac" and reduced to the role of a stock villain; Dickens avoids "the dehumanizing suggestions of 'maniac'" and instead "killed the suggestions of brutish horror and evoked limited pity for, as well as fear of, Wardour [. . .] he retained enough control and dignity to appear moments later as a self-sacrificing hero" (Brannan 44–45). Wardour's wild gestures and his abrupt exit ultimately signify his inner torture and demoralization, demonstrating that he was more psychologically complex than a conventional melodramatic villain. He reenters a moment later, bearing Aldersley in his arms, telling Clara: "Saved, saved for you![. . .]He's footsore and weary, Clara. But I have saved him—I have saved him for *you*! I may rest now—I may sleep at last—the task is done, the struggle is over" (158). The characters' and audience members' expectations suddenly reversed, Wardour is revealed as not a murderer or cannibal but as a hero who, though tempted by the "fiend within," gave "all his strength to [Aldersley's] weakness" (Collins and Dickens 158–59).

Collins and Dickens have another reversal up their sleeves: happiness at Clara and Aldersley's reunion is marred by the realization that Wardour is dying. Before he dies, however, the audience and characters learn exactly what happened while Wardour and Aldersley were alone on the tundra. Wardour describes how he overcame his desire for revenge, relating how he listened to a "tempter" whisper, "If you can't kill him, leave him when he sleeps"; Wardour "set [Aldersley] his place to sleep in apart; but he crept between the Devil and me, and nestled his head on *my* breast, and slept *here*." When the tempter's voice told Wardour to leave him, "Love him— the lad's voice answered, moaning and murmuring *here*, in his sleep" (159). With this, "the night-wind [came] up in the silence from the great Deep. It bore past me the groaning of the ice-bergs at sea, floating, floating past!— and the wicked voice floated away with it" (159). Wardour opened his heart to nurture the ailing Aldersley and overcame the fiend who told him to kill. Wardour's speech illustrates how even the most pronounced hatred could be overcome and demonstrates that even the most debased officer could choose redemption. After hearing Wardour relive how he gave up his desire for revenge, the audience witnesses his death. Wardour's final speech is in a sense conventional, resembling the deathbed speeches that became cliché in melodrama, but his apparent naiveté about the impact of his death is highly moving and his question, "Poor Frank! Why does he hide his face? Is he crying?" demonstrates Collins and Dickens's mastery of the affective power of understatement. Wardour patiently accepts his impending death, Clara and Aldersley's relationship, and the containment of his love for Clara as brotherly affection; this is seen in his final line,

"Nearer, Clara—I want to look my last at *you*. My sister, Clara!—Kiss me, sister, kiss me before I die!" (160). The Christian acceptance of death evokes the image of Franklin and his men "lay[ing] down side by side, calmly and even cheerfully awaiting their relief from the world" (363) that Dickens had promoted in *Household Words*.

The script's ending is both affecting and dramaturgically conclusive. Wardour, unlike Franklin, can say goodbye to Crayford, Aldersley, and Clara; he and the other characters experience emotional closure through the goodbye scene. A final stage direction, likely added to the fair copy for the Manchester performances (Brannan 160), adds that after Wardour dies, a "*gun is fired from ship and boat is drawn to shore*" (160). This stage direction makes it even easier for the audience to guess what will happen after the play ends—the group will return to England on the ship that just fired its gun, Clara and Aldersley will likely marry, and Wardour will fade into memory, having been appropriately mourned. The script provides the narrative closure that was lacking for Franklin's men and their families by giving the audience full knowledge of what happened and the satisfaction of witnessing a tearful goodbye.

REJECTING HISTRIONICS

To understand the emotional closure the play provided, one must consider not only the script but also accounts of the performance, with particular attention to Dickens's acting in the final scenes of the play. First, however, it is essential to briefly situate *The Frozen Deep* in relation to melodrama's affective dramaturgy. In revising Collins's conception of Wardour, Dickens transformed the character from a stock melodramatic villain into an emotionally tortured man capable of heroic self-sacrifice. This revision is indicative of the play's complex employment of melodrama. The play's "narratives of dispersal and reunion, its emphatically visual renderings of bodily torture and criminal conduct, its atmospheric menace and providential plotting, its expressions of highly charged emotion" align it with the melodramatic mode described by Elaine Hadley (3). *The Frozen Deep* also provided the audience with the "realistic" emotional experience Jeffrey Cox contends melodrama generated, making viewers "feel as if [they were] experiencing along with the characters the tensions, fears and joys evoked by the situation on stage. It is not a pictorial but an experiential realism" (170). Dickens's refusal to characterize Wardour as a stock villain suggests, however, that he was not simply adapting the Franklin narrative to fit the conventions of stage melodrama but was manipulating theatrical conventions to achieve the effects he desired. The reviews of his performance also indicate that critics recognized in Dickens's acting a surprising novelty: he rejected established melodramatic acting conventions, instead developing gestures and vocalizations that specifically represented Wardour's emotional state. This rejection of cliché was necessary for the play to perform the cultural work the melodramatic mode facilitated and create the "experiential realism" Cox describes.

Considering the sizeable body of work examining *The Frozen Deep*, it is surprising that relatively little attention has been paid to the mechanics of Dickens's acting or to how his acting choices contributed to the affective impact of the production. Hill, observing the importance of embodiment and performance in explicating the play's effect on audiences, remarks on how the play "substitute[d] its own embodied experience for the 'experience' of polar exploration and bodily suffering that Rae had privileged" (135). Recognizing that *The Frozen Deep* "reveals Dickens's theatricality as being important in and of itself, in its demonstration of Dickens's deeply held belief in the role of publicly performed affect in moral and social transformation" (131), Hill goes further than many critics in emphasizing that Dickens's cultural intervention happened *in a theater*. Her comments open the door for further investigation of how Dickens produced a "present experience"—the experiential realism Cox describes—for audience members.

Victorian acting was an ever-evolving aesthetic, responsive to changing public tastes and material conditions (Mayer, "Melodrama" 151). While it is as difficult to typify Victorian acting as to typify the acting of any period, one can note that a transition from histrionic to verisimilar acting codes occurred in the second half of the nineteenth century. Roberta Pearson contrasts the two modes, arguing that the histrionic code was based on the recognition of the actor as performer, while the verisimilar attempted to erase the actor so audience members only saw a "character." She notes that the histrionic code relied upon a highly conventionalized gestural language, while the verisimilar approach employed gestures to signify a particular character's emotional response to a specific situation. Histrionic actors "proudly displayed their skills, always striving to create a particular effect"; the code dictated that actors stood at center stage, "facing front, as close to the footlights as possible [and] at their climactic speeches, they would 'make points,' striding across the stage in deliberate fashion to call for applause" (Pearson 21). The histrionic code "imposed a certain uniformity on dramatic characters: with each emotion and state of mind represented by a certain prescribed pose or gesture, characters expressed themselves in precisely the same fashion. A young woman and an old man both portrayed grief by raising the back of the hand to the forehead" (Pearson 34). Gestures were single-unit signs that, through the precise arrangement of the body, represented an emotion or state of mind (Pearson 24). In contrast, actors following the verisimilar code displayed less awareness of the audience, delivering lines not from center stage, but from where circumstances and characterization dictated their character "should" be. Verisimilar acting used props, mannerisms, and "realistic" touches to give the impression of distinct characters. Actors did not select gestures from a stock repertoire but broadened their gestural vocabulary, attempting to create movements and expressions that represented a specific character's personality and given circumstances (Pearson 37). Verisimilar acting was and is no more "realistic" or less conventional than histrionic acting, but it attempted to provide the impression of reality by focusing on the particularities of character and situation, rejecting one set of conventions for another.[11]

Dickens, an enthusiastic theatergoer and a skilled amateur actor,[12] "had the genuine instincts of an actor" and loved "feigning to be somebody else," but he was also criticized for being "too 'hard' in performance, by which was meant too careful, too contrived, too rigid" and "better at the detail than the broad effect." Ackroyd attributes the criticisms he notes to the fact that Dickens "was thoroughly self-trained in the art;" he had "studied its effects too carefully and was too assiduous in applying them" (473–74). In reviews of Dickens's performance, one gets the sense that this "amateurishness" actually engaged the audience: Dickens's ignorance or rejection of the histrionic acting conventions popular among professional actors contributed to the novelty reviewers noticed. A close reading of reviews suggests that Dickens's lack of training and amateurishness allowed him to anticipate, perhaps inadvertently, the movement from histrionic to verisimilar conventions that peaked by the late nineteenth century. Because the verisimilar code was only emerging in the 1850s, Dickens's acting choices seemed unconventional and "new." Dickens's embrace of proto-verisimilar conventions produced the impression of a heightened emotional "reality," allowing audience members, actors, and Dickens himself to "forget" he was acting.

While reviews must always be taken with a grain of salt because they represent, in essence, a single audience member's perspective, in this case additional care is required because reviewers were undoubtedly influenced by Dickens's enormous public persona. That said, reviews of the performances at Tavistock House and the Gallery of Illustration provide details that allow one to imagine how Dickens used character- and situation-specific gestures and vocalizations to give audience members the impression they were watching not an actor performing a role but a character experiencing a situation. The feeling of watching a fellow human who was suffering, not an actor performing suffering, moved the audience members. The *Morning Herald* noted that in the final scene at Tavistock House,

> The pitiableness of his aspect, as he stood in his miserable rags at the back of the stage, his look of gaunt and intolerable suffering, and the wild hoarseness of his exclamation when he sees Clara and thrusts down all opposition that would prevent him from bringing her lover to her feet, were incidents of the most harrowing pathos, and nothing that we were ever present at upon the public stage exceeded them, as well as the closing moments of the repentant sinner, in deep and earnest truth. To this the tears of the audience bore attestation. It is not too much to say that there was scarcely a dry eye in the whole of the theatre, and that among many persons, too, not, we should imagine, much given to the melting mood. (8 January 1857)

The *Daily News* concurred in its assessment, noting that "the deep pathos of the closing scene thrilled through every heart and the audience by the plaudits, and still more by their tears, bore testimony to the power of the actor" (7 January 1857). This review also provides a sense of the tenor of Dickens's performance, his quick shifts in mood, and his range as an actor, indicating that these qualities combined to give the appearance of "reality": "his performance was a display of tragic power which has seldom been surpassed. The gloomy moodiness, interrupted by gusts of irritation, or bursting into sudden fits of passion; the manner in which he confided to his friend the story of his wrongs, revealing his deadly hate and cherished revenge; his desperate joy when he departed, with his destined victim by his side, all had an appalling reality" (7 January 1857). These early reviews suggest that Dickens, through his "miserable" costume and facial expressions representing "gaunt and intolerable suffering," gave the impression of Wardour's suffering.

July reviews provide more detail about exactly how Dickens represented Wardour. John Oxenford's review emphasizes his richly detailed yet understated performance: "we feel that if Mr. Dickens had had to describe in narrative form the situations of the *Frozen Deep*, instead of acting them, he would have covered whole pages in recording those manifestations of emotion, which, not having his pen in hand, he now makes by the minutest variations of voice and gesture. Where an ordinary artist would look for 'points' of effect he looks for 'points' of truth" (*Times* 13 July 1857). Oxenford alludes to the difference between histrionic and verisimilar acting: Dickens's concern was not with obeying convention to provoke predetermined reactions in audience members, but with depicting the "truth" of Wardour's situation. Oxenford explains how Dickens used fine details to provide the impression of character: "A specimen of humanity in which every twitch of every muscle can be accounted for is to be presented with all the elaboration of actual nature, no matter whether it be admired or not." Oxenford uses one example to explain Dickens's success, describing how he told the story of his disappointment in love in act two:

> [T]here is ample opportunity for much noisy grief and many a stride to the footlights, but Mr. Dickens dares to keep down his voice through the whole of the narrative. The effect may be monotonous—but what of that? He who talks not for the sake of display, but simply that he may relieve his mind from an oppressive and almost humiliating burden, will necessarily be monotonous [...] such a man as Mr. Dickens presents—a man strong in the command of his voice but weak in suppressing the language of his eyes and facial muscles, a man whose constant attempts to hide the internal storm by slight simulations of good fellowship, only renders more conspicuous the vastness of that which he could conceal—a man who has a habit of losing his temper in a manner that mere external circumstances do not warrant—such a man is a just object of terror. (13 July 1857).

Oxenford interprets Dickens's monotonous tone of voice—which could be attributed to amateurism—as a sign of his commitment to "truthfully" depict the inner emotions of the character. Dickens trusted the power of the script—words he wrote or revised himself—and through the dissonance between his words, his controlled voice, and his tense body gave the impression of a man whose emotions were on the edge: the "lying" voice and the "honest" body revealed Wardour's inner conflict. Oxenford's description of the details of the performance—particularly Dickens's use of the "language of his eyes and facial muscles"—suggest that his performance was not initially intended to travel to the back of an enormous hall but bore signs, even at the Gallery, of its origins in a small, private theater. These details evoke the idea of the cinematic close-up, which allowed actors to express character through minute gestures and expressions, suggesting that Dickens also anticipated film's popularization of verisimilar acting.

The *Daily News*'s review of the July Gallery performances also details how Dickens gave the audience the impression of inner turmoil, psychological complexity, and "reality," insinuating that Dickens was virtually inventing a new style of acting. Though this is obviously a flattering exaggeration, the review indicates that audience members saw something new and that this novelty, because it was not coded by histrionic conventions and reflected how Dickens imagined Wardour would express himself, gave audience members a heightened impression of reality:

> The entire interest of the piece is concentrated upon Richard Wardour, the representation of which character by Mr. Dickens is the greatest triumph of dramatic art which, in the course of a tolerably large theatrical experience, we have ever witnessed. On the English stage there is no one who can approach him in his delineation of intense power and feeling, nor was Frédéric Lemaitre,[13] in his best days, a greater artist. The power of observation, the knowledge of the workings of the human heart—all those qualities which have rendered Mr. Dickens the most popular author of modern days, are equally available to him as a dramatic artist. His voice, although always admirably modulated, is almost the least exponent of the passion represented; each muscle of the face, each motion of the hands, lends its aid to tell the story; his pathos is as touching as his rage is terrifying; the tender pressure of his lips on the board bearing the carved name of his love, after a stolen glance around to see that he was unobserved, was as perfect as the quick frantic loading of the gun and the unsuppressible howl of exultation when he finds his rival in his power. From first to last his performance was of the most finished nature, and that it was appreciated by the audience was evident from the constantly-recurring hum of approbation and frequent bursts of applause. (13 July 1857)

This review fails to provide detail about the final scene, but it does suggest the nuanced quality of Dickens's entire performance: he appeared in control of every facial muscle, every hand gesture, and he used these—as much as his words—to tell the story. The description of how he conveyed his anguish at discovering Aldersley was his rival is enlightening: rather than use a conventionalized gesture—a walk to the footlights, a hand to the forehead—to communicate his pain, he kissed the board, showing his enduring love for Clara, and then, making sure he was unobserved, loaded his gun and howled to show—not tell—that he was going to revenge himself. The signifiers Dickens developed were no less contrived or theatrical than those his contemporaries used, but their specificity to the material conditions of the play and their unfamiliarity to the audience gave a heightened impression of realism. Roberta Pearson argues that verisimilarly coded acting "has no standard repertoire of gestures, no limited lexicon. The style defined itself by the very abandonment of the conventional gestures of the histrionic code. Actors no longer portrayed emotions and states of mind by selecting from a pre-established repertoire but by deciding what was appropriate for a particular character in particular circumstances" (37). This was precisely what Dickens did in representing Wardour's anguish.

Wardour's death scene generated fewer comments in reviews, but one gets a sense of how audience members responded to it from the *Manchester Times*, which repeated earlier praise for the novelty and "reality" of the performance:

> The portrait he painted was not, indeed, like that we are accustomed to receive from the actor. The passionate utterances did not carry with them the excitement we are accustomed to experience from stage representation. We meet the haggard seaman, and heard the husky rattle, expressive of his agony, as we should meet a human sufferer in our daily intercourse. It was the absence of all stage trick, all the breadth of the action, which made the scene so true, so full of reality. The first scene in which he is engaged—the second act of the drama—contains many striking points; striking because of the quiet, unstrained manner in which they were delivered. This secured at once the attention and sympathy of the audience. It was too real for applause. There was scarcely a hand until the close of the act, when the cheers burst forth. In the last scene—that of the death of 'Wardour,' in the presence of 'Clara'—Clara forgiven, though still beloved, there was the highest artistic power displayed. Here it was that failure might have ensued, but for the most delicate treatment. It was all that could be desired. (22 August 1857)

Recognizing that the melodramatic actor had to "make inconsistencies appear truths, and yet if he tones down the colouring beneath a certain level he may probably commit as much mischief as in tearing 'the passion to tatters'" (22 August 1857), the *Manchester Times* has the highest praise for Dickens's ability to balance these demands. His performance used conventions familiar from real life, rather than those familiar from the theater, so that audience members met Wardour as they would "a human sufferer in our daily intercourse." Dickens was not not-acting, but he hid the signs of his craft, unlike histrionic actors who drew attention to their skills; this apparent lack of awareness—again a potential sign of amateurism—gave audience members the impression they were watching real life.

Accounts of the audience response in Manchester suggest that audience members were utterly absorbed in the performance. Dickens reminisced in a letter to Mrs. Watson: "It was a good thing to have a couple of thousand people all rigid and frozen together, in the palm of one's hand—as at

Manchester—and to see the hardened Carpenters at the sides crying and trembling at it night after night" (488). This corroborates the *Manchester Times*'s report that the performance, which was "too real for applause," "drew tears from grey heads and young hearts, from the sensitive and inexperienced in such matters to the old *habitué* of theatres, who has lived long enough to be familiar with all the finest acting of the present century" (22 August 1857). The review suggests that audience members, sensing the play was too "real" for applause, responded with actual sadness to the theatrical event, hinting that they temporarily "forgot" they were watching a contrived performance. This implication begs one to read skeptically: would audience members have actually forgotten they were watching Dickens? Does one ever "forget" that one is in a theater when one allows oneself to feel "real" emotions in response to a theatrical event?

This question of how one "forgets" about the play in feeling "real" emotions is central to the anecdote with which this chapter began. The story of Maria Ternan losing control, leading Mark Lemon and other actors to become overwhelmed by emotion, is about the experience of becoming absorbed in the pathos of performance; it is about the strange phenomenon of recognizing that one is watching (or participating) in fiction but is experiencing real emotions. Dickens accounted for Ternan's performance in a letter to Angela Burdett-Coutts on September 5, 1857, and in his December 7, 1857, letter to Mrs. Richard Watson. In both, he stressed that Ternan was so overcome by grief that she, no longer in character, helplessly cried during Wardour's death scene. In his letter to Burdett-Coutts, Dickens notes that when he tried to comfort her—on stage, while supposedly dead or dying, another seeming sign of amateurism—"She could only sob out, 'O! It's so sad, O it's so sad!' and set Mr. Lemon (the softest hearted of men) crying too. By the time the Curtain fell, we were all crying together, and then her mother and sister used to come and put her in a chair and comfort her [...] I told her on the last night that I was sure she had one of the most genuine and feeling hearts in the world; and I don't think I ever saw any thing more prettily simple and unaffected" (433). Dickens emphasizes the naiveté of Ternan's response, remarking she was such a genuine person that the emotion of the theatrical representation overtook her. In his letter to Mrs. Watson, he added "if you had seen the poor little thing, when the Curtain fell, put in a chair behind it—with her mother and sister taking care of her—and your humble servant drying her eyes and administering Sherry [...] and the people in front all blowing their noses, and our own people behind standing about in corners and getting themselves right again, you would have remembered it for a long,

long time" (488). Dickens's letters indicate that Wardour's death engulfed audience members, actors and stagehands in a communal experience of grief. While the audience's response is unsurprising, the stagehands' and actors' are: one would imagine that those familiar with the scene, having rehearsed it many times, could maintain a professional distance from it.[14]

Furthermore, while Dickens's letters highlight that Ternan and Lemon were overwhelmed by emotion, he also "forgot himself" in the performance. Several accounts note Dickens's total absorption in his own performance, particularly when he ran offstage to bring Aldersley on in act three. Dickens wrote to Mary Boyle after the Tavistock House run, commenting that he "terrified Aldersley to that degree by lunging at him to carry him into the Cave, and the said Aldersley always shook like a mound of jelly and muttered: 'By G— this is an awful thing!'" (277). Dickens suggests that it was Collins who had the problem, because he was terrified by Dickens's energy; however, Charley Dickens remembers that his father often lost control when rehearsing the scene:

> In his demented condition in the last act he had to rush off the stage, and I and three or four others had to try and stop him. He gave us fair notice, early in the rehearsals, that he meant fighting in earnest in that particular scene, and we very soon found out that the warning was not an idle one. He went at it after a while with such a will that we really did have to fight, like prize-fighters, and as for me, being the leader of the attacking party and bearing the first brunt of the fray, I was tossed in all directions and had been black and blue two or three times before the first night of the performance arrived. (Qtd. in Ackroyd 773)

Even offstage, Dickens remained in character to the point that he endangered his fellow actors. Comments about his complete absorption in his role suggest that his acting anticipated "System-" and "Method-" based approaches that advocated this structure of belief, and highlight the extent to which Dickens rejected histrionic self-consciousness in his performance. The indefatigable Dickens found his role emotionally exhausting, writing to Mary Boyle that "for about ten minutes after his death [...] Richard Wardour was in a floored condition. And one night, to the great terror of Devonshire, the Arctic Regions, and Newfoundland, [...] he very nearly did what he never did—went and fainted off, dead—again" (276–77). By the time the play moved to Manchester, the weight of the role had taken its toll on Dickens, leading him to ask his close friend, actor Frank Stone, to take his part in the farce that followed because "the agitation and exertion of Richard Wardour" was "so great" that he said he could not "rally my spirits in the short space of time I get. The strain is so great, to make a show of doing it, that I want to be helped out of Uncle John, if I can" (9 August 1857, 405). Dickens, absorbed in his performance, was overwhelmed and exhausted by the act of representing Wardour's "real" anguish.

LEGITIMATE EFFIGIES

Bert O. States's description of the self-expressive mode illuminates the operations of Dickens's "realistic" performance. Locating Dickens's, the audience's, and the actors' "forgetfulness" in the context of the fissure States suggests occurs in the self-expressive mode and in relation to Joseph Roach's figure of the effigy allows one to recognize precisely how Dickens's "realistic" performance allowed the play to serve as a "font of public mourning" for Franklin. States argues that in the self-expressive mode, "It is not that the actor steps out of character [...] but that he finds the fissure in the text that allows him to make his unique contribution: he self-creates the real ground of his character's ideality" (164). For Dickens, audience members, and actors this was precisely what happened: Dickens did not disappear, but the line between Dickens and Wardour collapsed, allowing Dickens to embody the "ideality" of Wardour's character. In *The Frozen Deep*, a fissure in the performance allowed the two figures—Dickens and Wardour—to collapse into one another, allowing audience members and actors, possibly even Dickens himself, to glimpse only Dickens's/Wardour's "real" suffering. It is at this precise moment, when actors cried for Dickens/Wardour without knowing precisely for whom they were crying, that the operations of surrogation remain visible.

As Joseph Roach argues: "In the life of a community, the process of surrogation does not begin or end but continues as actual or perceived vacancies occur in the network of relations that constitutes the social fabric. Into the cavities created by loss through death or other forms of departure [...] survivors attempt to fit satisfactory alternates" (2). One way that surrogation addresses these absences is through the creation and, often, destruction of effigies. Roach describes this process:

> The sacrificial victim must be neither divisive nor trivial, neither fully part of the community nor fully outside of it; rather, he or she must be distanced by a special identity that specifies isolation while simultaneously allowing plausible surrogation for a member of the community. This occurs in a two-staged process: the community finds a surrogate victim for itself from within itself; then it finds an alien substitute, like an effigy, for the surrogate. (40)

As evidenced by his impassioned response to John Rae's allegations, Dickens identified with Franklin. When Jane Franklin called on him to defend her husband's reputation, he responded with his scathing articles, articles that went so far beyond normal sympathy for the missing men that they prompt Dickens's biographer Peter Ackroyd to argue they "throw more light on his own excitable and anxious state of mind than upon the ostensible subject of his concern" (713). When these were not enough, Dickens nominated himself as a surrogate for the missing Franklin, determined to theatrically sacrifice himself so that public mourning for the real Franklin could take place. Since Dickens was unable and unwilling to actually die in order to fulfill this duty, he created an effigy—Wardour—to be sacrificed instead. Roach's formulation provides the language to articulate how Dickens responded to the loss of the Franklin expedition: nominating himself as a surrogate and then creating an effigy, an alien substitute, to be publicly sacrificed.

There are always gaps between the absent member of the community, the surrogate, and the effigy: "The intended substitute either cannot fulfill expectations, creating a deficit, or actually exceeds them, creating a surplus" (Roach 2). This is because performed effigies, effigies that "consist of a set of actions that hold open a place in memory into which many different people may step according to circumstances and occasions," are "fabricated from human bodies and the associations they evoke" (36). Wardour did not need to be Franklin, he only had to resemble the missing man by performing specific actions in order to act as an effigy and allow surrogation to occur. Wardour is not the commander of the expedition but is a second lieutenant: considering Dickens's arguments concerning naval rank, social class, and cannibalism, it was enough that both men were officers.[15] As an officer, Wardour would never resort to cannibalism and is capable of heroic self-sacrifice in dire circumstances. Wardour is not cheerful and friendly, as Franklin was, but moody and antisocial. He is also, unlike Franklin, heteronormative surplus: unlike other officers in the play, he has no woman or family at home and this marks him as outside of the play's normative social order. These differences from Franklin allowed Dickens to further counter Rae's allegations. Wardour is unfriendly, extremely jealous, and morally suspect: in all ways, he appears a villain. He is tempted to kill his rival Aldersley; he knows he will not be caught; he goes mad from hunger and exhaustion; he finds himself adrift in an open boat with Aldersley: despite temptation, desperation, and opportunity, Wardour neither kills Aldersley nor resorts to cannibalism. Despite his shortcomings, Wardour is ultimately an officer in the British Navy and the noble character this dictates leads him to nurse Aldersley back to health and sacrifice his own life for his fellow officer. Dickens and Collins's argument about Wardour as a potential cannibal is clear: no British officer, no matter how tempted and desperate he became, no matter how much of a rogue, would ever give into the desire to consume human flesh.

In order to function as an effigy, Wardour not only had to reject cannibalism—as Franklin, according to Dickens, must have—but also had to die. The disappearance of the Franklin expedition left a persistent dual absence: without written records or actual bodies, it was impossible to know what happened or to fully mourn the lost men. In order to fill this space, the public needed to know what happened and required a "real" death to mourn. By producing an event that was comprehensible and conclusive, Dickens filled the narrative absence left when the expedition disappeared. Likewise, by producing a death scene audience members could bear witness to, weep for, and then leave behind, Dickens as Wardour filled a space that had been held open by melancholic attachment to the missing men. States argues: "The ritual in theater is based in the community's need for *the thing* that transpires in theater and in the designation, or self-designation, of certain individuals who, for one reason or another, consent to become the embodiment of this thing" (157). The audience and actors needed to mourn Franklin and his men's deaths and Dickens designated himself to embody those real deaths, by acting out Wardour's theatrical one. Though the event the audience witnessed was not "real," the sensations it generated were:[16] the audience cried not only for Wardour's death, which they could witness, but also for Franklin's death, which they could not. Cox notes that melodramatic realism provided audience members not with a view of how the world really was but with an authentic emotional experience: in melodrama "we come away having had a 'real' experience, having 'really' felt something while we were in the theatre" (171). Although the audience could not really witness Franklin's death, they gained the "real" experience of mourning it by mourning the loss of an effigy.

THE QUEEN'S TEARS

By making his final response to Rae's report in the theater rather than on the printed page, Dickens provided audience members in the communal space of the theater with a viscerally affecting experience that was otherwise impossible. His performance transformed audience members from passive spectators into witnesses who saw—and therefore knew—what happened. To completely overwrite Rae's narrative, however, the emotional truth of the events Dickens staged had to be validated by unimpeachably legitimate spectators: Rae's illegitimate Inuit witnesses had to disappear from public consciousness completely. While the audience at Tavistock House, comprising invited guests from the highest echelons of literary and artistic society, validated Dickens's vision through its tears and applause, its approval was not enough. At Tavistock House, Dickens's reality was shared but private, limited by the venue and by the type and number of spectators. For Dickens's vision to enter public consciousness as an official event commemorating the loss of the Franklin expedition, it had to be legitimated by a more powerful audience.

Although the Tavistock House performances were ostensibly private, Dickens invited reviewers from the *Times, Morning Chronicle,* and *Illustrated London News*, prompting the *Times* to comment that "it would be absurd to apply the term 'private' to the theatrical performances that take place at Tavistock-house" (7 January 1857). News of the production quickly reached Lady Franklin, who heard about the performance from Sir Roderick Murchison; on January 16 she wrote in her journal: "There were parts of Mr. Ch. Dickens story [...] so touching as to make Sir Rod. cry, & he wd have carried away a sad impression from the evening's entertainment, had it not been followed by a very amazing farce" (10). The "private" performances at Tavistock House were reviewed in major papers, which was highly unusual and ensured that by the time of the first "public" performance in July 1857, the play had generated considerable hype. The *Morning Herald* noted the "sensation created in private circles by the theatrical performances at Tavistock House has extended to the general public" and described how three public performances sold out almost instantly, despite the fact that tickets prices were higher than normal (13 July 1857). The *Daily News* concurred: "it may be imagined that on this, the first occasion of its being given before a general public, the greatest excitement prevailed, and that every stall and seat, although the tariff of prices was high, was engaged at the earliest opportunity. From the footlights of the little stage to the back of the hall was one 'vast sea of human faces,' and the audience included not only many of the aristocracy, but most of the celebrities in the literary, artistic, and musical circles" (13 July 1857). Even allowing for a bit of puffery among reviewers, press coverage indicates that although tickets were expensive, the performances were hotly anticipated. Although the *Daily News* does not link ticket price to audience composition, it does suggest that the "public" audience was, like the "private" audience at Tavistock House, composed of more sophisticated and higher-class spectators than melodrama typically drew.

Hype surrounding the first "public" performances of *The Frozen Deep* also stemmed from publicity surrounding the play's command performance on July 4. As early as February 3, rumors of a command performance of *The Frozen Deep* began circulating. Dickens told Angela Burdett-Coutts that "The wildest legends are circulating about town, to the effect that the Queen proposes to ask to have the Frozen Deep at Windsor. I have heard nothing of it otherwise, but slink about, holding my breath" (3 February 1857, *Letters* 273). On February 5, Dickens coyly described these speculations to Collins: "the Queen has a strong idea of following it [*The Frozen Deep*] up with some of the Crimean Amateur Performances" but added "I know nothing about it" (275). In June, Dickens entered into heated negotiations with the Palace mediated by Colonel Phipps: the Queen felt attending a public benefit would set an unpleasant precedent; Dickens argued that he and his actors could not perform at the palace because it would place them in an ambivalent social position.[17] Eventually, Phipps and Dickens agreed that the Queen would attend a private performance at the Gallery of Illustration before the play opened to the public.

The command performance was well publicized both before and after it occurred. The *Times* announced the performance on June 24: "Her Majesty has commanded a private representation of Mr. Wilkie Collins's drama *The Frozen Deep*. It will be given on Saturday week at the Gallery of Illustration." The *Times* then reported on July 6 that

> Her Majesty and the Prince Consort, accompanied by His Majesty the King of the Belgians, the Princess Royal, Princess Alice, Princess Charlotte of Belgium, the Prince of Wales, Prince Alfred, Prince Frederick William of Prussia, the Count of Flanders, and the Prince of Hohenzollern Sigmaringen, honoured the amateur performance, under the management of Mr. Charles Dickens, of Mr. Wilkie Collins's drama of *The Frozen Deep*, at the Gallery of Illustration in Regent-street, with their presence on Saturday evening.

The audience included not only Queen Victoria and Prince Albert but also representatives of virtually every European royal family: it was a veritable "who's who" of nineteenth-century imperial power. It was the most legitimate audience one could imagine for a play that repudiated accusations of cannibalism and attempted to restore Franklin's reputation as a hero.

Members of this select audience responded enthusiastically. Georgina Hogarth, who played Lucy, reported that "the Queen and her party made a most excellent audience—so far from being cold, as we expected, they cried and laughed, and applauded and made as much demonstration as so small a party (there were not more than fifty) could do" (qtd. in Brannan 67). Following the performance, the Queen sent for Dickens so that she could to thank him personally, but "[b]efore her messenger reached him, he had changed into comic dress for the farce [...] and he bluntly refused her first and then her repeated request to appear before her" (Brannan 67). Despite Dickens's refusal to see her, the next day the Queen instructed Colonel Phipps to write Dickens a letter of thanks. Colonel Phipps's letter told Dickens:

> It is no formal compliment to say that the Queen and Prince Consort, and the whole of the Royal party were delighted with the rich dramatic treat of last night. I have hardly ever seen her Majesty and HRH so much pleased. I cannot to yourself repeat all that was said of your own acting, but I may say that Mr. Mark Lemon's performance was particularly (and I may add from myself deservedly) admired. [...] The Queen commanded me particularly to express her admiration of the piece itself—not only on account of its interest, and striking situations, or of the very superior language in which it is written, but on account of the high tone which is preserved in it. There was every temptation to an Author to increase the effect of the play by representing the triumph of the Evil [*prophet*], but it was particularly pleasing to Her Majesty to find a much higher lesson taught in the Victory of the better and nobler feelings—and of the Reward—the only one he could obtain—to Richard, in his self-content before his death. (Qtd. in Storey and Tillotson 366)[18]

The presence of the Queen and her entourage, their evident enjoyment, and their tacit approval of the performance not only validated its aesthetic merit but also sanctioned its implicit closure of the question of what had happened to Franklin. When the most important eyes in the world gazed upon Dickens's representation of events, it legitimated the performance as the "real" narrative of what happened, supplanted illegitimate Inuit witnesses with the most legitimate spectators in the world, and effectively replaced Franklin's unknowable actual death with Wardour's emotionally real death.

Because the command performance of *The Frozen Deep* occurred before an extremely limited audience, members of the interested public had to content themselves with imagining the Queen's response. The British public was fascinated by watching the Queen watch theater. Michael Diamond notes that when the Queen watched Jenny Lind sing in May 1848: "The vast opera house was filled with the court and the aristocracy, and an audience who were equally anxious to see the Queen and to hear Jenny Lind. Each woman was basking in the approval of her own admirers, and in the adulation accorded to the other" (255). Diamond suggests that the relationship between the Queen and Jenny Lind was mutually beneficial: "Not only did the royal patronage add to Jenny Lind's glory, but the Queen [...] was associating herself with a unique standard of elegance" (255). Queen Victoria wielded an enormous amount of power as a spectator, modeling middle-class taste, as in Diamond's example, and appearing as "the mother of enjoyment, urging her subjects towards serious pleasure and rational play," as Emily Allen suggests (68). The Queen was also well aware of how her spectatorship itself constituted a performance: by watching Jenny Lind perform, the Queen demonstrated her difference from the King of France, who had lost his throne earlier that year, performing the "blessings of a well-balanced constitutional monarchy" (Diamond 254) by participating in the popular performance.

Rumors of how the Queen and her party responded to *The Frozen Deep*—of the Queen's laughter, tears, and applause, as noted by Georgina Hogarth—must have rapidly circulated among interested members of the middle class and the aristocracy. It seems likely that the Queen's imagined response influenced how later audiences approached the play. Imagining the Queen watching the performance meant imagining and enacting the models she set for how audiences were to respond to the play and for how the nation was to respond to the event of the Franklin expedition's disappearance. Emily Allen argues: "If the nation is not just a place, an imagined community, but a set of collective practices, or ritualized performances, then viewing the royals in celebration was an important and identifying practice" (73). *The Frozen Deep* produced an account of the loss of the Franklin expedition that the Queen, representing the British public, witnessed and mourned. The Queen's gaze transformed *The Frozen Deep* from a private amateur theatrical into an imperial spectacle, legitimating Dickens's vision as the "true" version of what happened and validating the emotions generated by Dickens's performance as official mourning. The Queen's presence and response to the play thus laid the groundwork for the public outpouring of grief that occurred at the Manchester performances. The responses were emotionally heightened not only because of increased publicity, not only because the performance served as a memorial for Jerrold, not only because the professional actors were more skilled, but also because the performance, a commemoration of the absent Franklin, had been sanctioned by the Queen as an outlet for public mourning. When the play closed in Manchester, it had allowed audience members to mourn the loss of Wardour not as a character in a melodrama but as an effigy for Franklin, providing both dramatic closure within the dramaturgical structure of the play and psychological closure of the greater question concerning what happened to Franklin's men.

Conclusion: Franklin Remains ❧

*T*he *Frozen Deep* is an appropriate end point to the series of performances considered here. Marking the transition from melancholic
engagement to mournful closure, it contained, erased, and overwrote histories proposed by other performances. Like *Zero, or Harlequin
Light,* it performed a disciplinary function, conditioning a specific public
response through affective verisimilar performance, flattering press coverage, Dickens's public persona, and the Queen's presence. By staging a
white Arctic utterly devoid of Inuit witnesses, *The Frozen Deep* erased the
possibility of intercultural collaboration and racial liminality that arose
in Qalasirssuaq's theatrical and extratheatrical transformation aboard the
Assistance and effectively obliterated the possibility of "playing" with race
suggested by Charles Francis Hall's actions while living among Inuit. Oral
histories of contact with Franklin's men—such as the stories preserved by
Owwer and Innookpoozheejook's mother-in-law—had no place in official
commemorations of Franklin. In a sense, *The Frozen Deep* laid to rest not
only Franklin and his men but also questions about racial and cultural difference, about competing epistemologies, and about the value of embodied
historical knowledge.

But Franklin and his men have not rested in peace; they remain as
spectral figures who engage us through their eerie endurance. In this book,
Franklin surfaces not as a historical figure so much as a ghost, haunting
the margins, failing to appear clearly. This is somehow appropriate: while
the search for Franklin began as a search for an individual man and those
under his command, the performances that intervened in the search and
responded to the loss of the expedition were not as much about Franklin
himself as about searching for and losing abstractions. The name Franklin
initially signified an idealized naval masculinity, the British colonial interest in the Arctic, and the victory of civilization over a savage land. As it
became clear that the expedition had ended in disaster, the sum of what

was lost included not only 129 men, but also these significations: Rae's report suggested that officers resorted to cannibalism, calling Franklin's heroism into question; Hall revealed that Inuit had indeed witnessed what happened, calling British exploratory dominance into question. Perhaps most significantly, the lack of written records meant it was impossible to *know* what happened.

Because what happens has remained unknown, Franklin's expedition continues to fascinate us. His ships, HMS *Erebus* and HMS *Terror*, are together designated as a Canadian national historic site, making them the only such site that remains "undiscovered." In the twentieth and early twenty-first centuries, dozens of scientific expeditions have descended on the central Arctic in search of traces of the lost expedition. In 2008, Parks Canada launched a series of underwater searches for traces of Franklin's missing ships; at the time of writing, the third search in this cycle was underway. Although these recent searches have uncovered some remarkable relics—notably the wreck of HMS *Investigator*, a British search ship abandoned in 1853—they have failed to uncover further traces of Franklin's expedition.

Margaret Atwood presciently remarks: "Because Franklin was never really 'found,' he continues on as a haunting presence; certainly in Canadian literature" (16). Modern and postmodern retellings of what happened remind us that the narratives produced in the 1850s and 1860s and epitomized by *The Frozen Deep* are unstable and problematic, exclusive and partial. Gwendolyn MacEwen's verse drama *Terror and Erebus*, broadcast by the CBC in 1975, includes an Inuk, Qaqortingneq, who reminds audience members that Franklin and his men were not, as Dickens and Collins suggested, alone in the Arctic. Mordecai Richler's 1989 novel *Solomon Gursky Was Here* imagines that a Jewish assistant surgeon, Ephraim Gursky, was the sole survivor of the expedition and lived among Inuit as the leader of a Jewish-Inuit religious sect; Richler points out the links between Arctic exploration and missionary impulses and questions the idea of a Christian (or convert-able) Arctic that has been normalized in exploration literature and in northern history. Geoff Kavanagh's play *Ditch*, first produced as part of the SummerWorks Festival in 1993, challenges the heteronormativity implicit in Arctic narratives, by imagining that the two men whose skeletons were found in the boat on King William Island by McClintock's expedition were lovers. By focusing on the mundane details of what two men likely suffered before they died, the play works against the historiographic impulse to reduce the end of the expedition to a list of skeletons found and to ignore the lived experience of the men. Finally, Don Druick's

Images C.1   Franklin Monument at Waterloo Place, London

play, *The Frozen Deep*, workshopped by Nightwood Theatre and produced at the National Arts Centre in Ottawa in 2003, examines Dickens's motives in producing the play and questions how the professional and personal relationship between Collins and Dickens has been represented in accounts of their individual and collaborative works. These works suggest the continuing ability of performance (and literature) to address what was

Images C.2   Franklin Memorial at the Royal Naval College, Greenwich

lost and the continuing potential for theater to challenge the heteronormative, Christian, civilizing narrative of what happened that *The Frozen Deep*
proposed.

   This is not to suggest that contemporary performance has unprob-
lematically rectified the violent racism implicit in Dickens's play or
reconciled the role that the search for Franklin played in the colonization of the Arctic. The complicated relationship between Inuit and
qallunaat cultures—which emerges in this project in the questions of

how visitors to the Arctic understood Inuit they encountered, of how Inuit experiences became historical evidence, and of how intercultural performance facilitated the search effort—has become a critical environmental, political, and cultural issue. That the problematics of intercultural contact that emerged during the Franklin search are alive and well today is apparent in a story that made international headlines in May 2009. Canadian Governor General Michaëlle Jean, in the wake of the European Union's ban of the import of seal products, ate a piece of seal heart during a visit to Rankin Inlet, Nunavut. Press coverage included a number of "graphic" images of Jean helping gut the seal and eating raw meat with blood on her fingers. Responses to her gesture were mixed, with officials from PETA and the European Union harshly criticizing her actions. The *Globe and Mail*'s Alexandra Panetta reported on May 30, 2009: "Ms. Jean's decision to help butcher the blubbery mammal at a festival was derided as 'bizarre' by the Belgium-based European Union, and compared by environmentalists to Neanderthalism and wife battery." In contrast, many "ordinary" Canadians praised Jean's cultural relativism and open-mindedness in letters to the editor and online comments. By eating seal meat to demonstrate her solidarity with Inuit and her recognition of Inuit traditional culture, Jean played out the trope of "acting Inuit" through her act of eating raw meat, reproducing Hall's performance of almost 150 years earlier. That Jean's act was capable of generating so much fascination in the press demonstrates that the role of performance in negotiating intercultural contact—and in producing a difference between "us" and "them" in relation to the north—is as powerful today as when Dickens argued against Rae's report by invoking differences between civility and savagery.

This book has shown, I hope, that Dickens's attempt at historical erasure was ultimately unsuccessful. Many of the stories and histories he rejected have indeed survived, albeit in highly mediated and often changed forms. The final survivors' experiences of desperation, anguish, and misery endure, surfacing in ghost stories, in remembered gestures, in tokens transformed by experience. While performances provide only limited access to the past, they allow one to understand something about the lived experiences of search parties, Inuit, and survivors that would otherwise disappear. The examples considered in this book testify to the remarkable power of performance to preserve cultural memory, but also reveal that this power can be dangerous: today one can read in Dickens's performances—in *Household Words* and in *The Frozen Deep*—an ethical injunction against the misuse of performance as a tool of historical revision.

Performances—enacted, erased, reproduced, and rediscovered—archive the desires and anxieties of the past and serve as a cultural repository holding open moments of absence, preserving unspeakable losses, capturing snapshots of quickly shifting political and social circumstances, and saving the remains of experience.

Notes ❧

INTRODUCTION: JANE FRANKLIN'S DRESS: ARCHIVES AND AFFECT

1. Jane Franklin's vehement denial of her husband's death may have resulted from financial and emotional motivations. As long as John Franklin lived, Jane retained control over his estate, which included considerable assets he had inherited from his first wife, Eleanor Porden. Upon his death, these assets would belong to his daughter Eleanor Gell. After March 1851, Jane Franklin's financial situation worsened when her father disinherited her. In 1854, Jane was relying on income from her husband's inheritance to fund search efforts; the Admiralty's decision to declare him dead had considerable financial implications for both Jane and the search. See Ken McGoogan, *Lady Franklin's Revenge* pp. 319–27.
2. The story is mentioned in the following works: Pierre Berton, *Prisoners of the North* pp. 153; Ken McGoogan, *Lady Franklin's Revenge* pp. 331; Francis Spufford, *I May Be Some Time* pp. 119–20; Jen Hill, *White Horizon* pp. 18.
3. Sir John Barrow, the Second Secretary of the Admiralty, initially wanted Edward Parry to lead the expedition. When he declined, Barrow considered James Clark Ross, James Fitzjames, George Back, and Francis Crozier before deciding to appoint Franklin (Sandler 65–74). Lady Franklin's behind-the-scenes machinations also helped her husband gain the command; see McGoogan *Lady Franklin's Revenge*, pp. 268–72, for details of Lady Franklin's involvement in her husband's appointment. Franklin's first voyage to the Arctic was as commander of the brig *Trent*, part of Captain David Buchan's 1818 attempt to sail over the North Pole. The first expedition under Franklin's command was his disastrous 1819–22 Coppermine expedition; his second Arctic command, undertaken from 1825–27, was an overland expedition that charted long sections of the Mackenzie River and Beaufort Sea coastlines.
4. The graves were exhumed by forensic anthropologist Owen Beattie in the 1980s; testing revealed that all three men were likely weakened by exposure to high levels of lead (likely from poorly soldered food tins), suffered from tuberculosis, and ultimately died of pneumonia (Beattie 124, 161).
5. The form includes a mistake: the ships wintered at Beechey Island during the winter of 1845–46, not 1846–47; Fitzjames made the same mistake on both forms.

6. See also Scott Cookman's *Ice Blink*, which hypothesizes that poor quality food was the primary cause of the expedition's failure and speculates about the deadly effects of food spoilage and lead poisoning.

7. At least one of the ships was badly damaged or destroyed by ice, but it is unclear whether this occurred before the 1848 abandonment. See chapter 5.

8. Inuk is the singular form of Inuit. While I have attempted to use Inuktitut spelling of Inuit names when possible, there are cases, as with Innookpoozheejook, when only the anglicized spelling survives in archival documents. I have relied on Dorothy Eber's *Encounters on the Passage* as an authority on contemporary spelling of Inuit names.

9. In 1855, the Hudson's Bay Company sent out an overland expedition to the Back River to confirm Rae's report. James Anderson and James Green Stewart met Inuit who reported that "one man died on Montreal Island, and that the balance of the party wandered on the beach of the mainland opposite. [...] The Esquimaux reported, further, that Indians far to the north of them, who had seen the ships of Franklin's party, and visited them, stated that they had both been crushed between the icebergs" (*Times* 9 January 1856). Anderson and Stewart retrieved iron kettles, English snowshoes, and a boat on which the word *Terror* was visible. Bad weather and leaking canoes forced them to turn around before reaching King William Island, but their findings confirmed what Rae's Inuit informants had reported.

10. The other significant nineteenth-century expedition to uncover Inuit stories of encounters with Franklin survivors and relics from the expedition was Frederick Schwatka's 1878–80 expedition. In the early twentieth century, echoes of Franklin stories were heard by explorer-anthropologists like Vilhjalmur Stefansson and Knud Rasmussen.

11. Hood was the only British member of the expedition to die; other than Teroahauté, one Inuk and nine voyageurs died.

12. For more information about events concerning the detachment, see "Dr. Richardson's Narrative" in Sir John Franklin, *Journey to the Shores of the Polar Sea*, vol. 4, pp. 97–122. For a literary rethinking of the events that occurred, see Rudy Wiebe, *Playing Dead*, pp. 20–45.

13. Other scholars, notably Russell Potter, Janice Cavell, and Jen Hill, have explored the ways that other forms of cultural production—visual art, print media, and literature, respectively—responded to the loss of the expedition.

1   DISCIPLINING NOSTALGIA IN THE NAVY; OR, HARLEQUIN IN THE ARCTIC

1. Personifying cold as "Zero" was common among British sailors posted to the Arctic: Robert McClure's published journal notes that "*Zero*, it must be

observed, was invariably referred to as a veritable foe having an actual existence, and was to be combated as they would do the Arch-Enemy" (101). The *Illustrated Arctic News*, published on the *Resolute*, included a song written by George McDougall in its November 30, 1850, issue that included the lines: "Don't let old Zero's tricks, /Perplex the brave Arctics" (12). The lyrics indicate that the figure of "Zero" as an Arctic trickster was familiar to the men before the play was performed.

2. At least two other original plays were staged during the search for Franklin: *Pantomime*, performed January 30, 1851, on the *Advance* (an American search vessel) and *King Glumpus*, performed February 1, 1853, on HMS *Resolute* (O'Neill, "Zero" 44).

3. *Aurora Borealis* and the *Illustrated Arctic News* were published on the *Assistance* and the *Resolute*, respectively.

4. The island is now known as Griffith Island; it was not unusual for such minor changes in nomenclature to occur throughout the nineteenth and twentieth centuries.

5. My use of homosociability in this chapter is indebted to Eve Kosofsky Sedgwick's articulation of this concept in *Between Men: English Literature and Male Homosocial Desire.*

6. Collinson would know: during his four years in the Arctic, he placed every one of his officers under arrest for disobeying orders (Barr 243).

7. According to Patrick O'Neill, a committee comprising solely lower-ranking officers was associated with antitheatricality on the part of the captain: he claims the example of Edward Belcher illustrates the link between incompetent leadership and antitheatrical prejudice ("North" 358). This argument is somewhat contentious, contradicted as it is by Belcher's own words: "to kill time, I shall use my best endeavours to promote them [shipboard performances] [...] The mere act of learning their parts frequently inculcates some moral which may prove the keystone to the future development of abilities" (Vol. 2, 64–65). Even the "antitheatrical" and much-maligned Belcher recognized that theater played an important role in preventing boredom and in educating common seamen, prompting skepticism about O'Neill's assessment of the link between antitheatricality, participation in performances, and arbitrary exercises of authority. I suspect, however, that the converse of O'Neill's argument is accurate: men enjoyed shipboard performances more when the captain was involved.

8. Surviving documents do not indicate whether the role of the officer was played by a member of the crew or an officer.

9. William Parker Snow notes that this easy authority characterized Austin and Ommanney's leadership as well. He found it notable that when their ships became stuck in autumn ice, they helped the men: "it was quite a pleasure to see how both officers and men worked at it. Captain Austin himself was as busy as any one; directing, and handling, and unceasingly working" (*Voyage* 183). He continues, mentioning Ommanney: "Often did I notice Captain Ommanney running up aloft, and out upon the topsail-yard-arm, glass in

hand, like a young reefer, intent upon personally examining the way before him" (184).

10. One quarter of the *Assistance*'s men were officers: their cabins took up a considerable amount of space and made the lower deck more crowded than usual. The crew's mess and sleeping quarters were in the forecastle of the ship; although informal performances took place in these spaces, staging a performance for officers in the forecastle was potentially problematic because it "belonged" to the crew.

11. This practice was introduced by Parry not only to save space but also so that if there were a fire on board the ship, supplies would be spared.

12. A widely circulated, though perhaps apocryphal, story concerns two chests of costumes apparently donated to the *Assistance* by Charles Kean. Patrick O'Neill, who mentions but does not attribute the anecdote, claims that the costumes on the *Assistance* in 1850–51 were "the finest employed in the Arctic" and that the fact that they were removed by Edward Belcher, who took command of the ship in 1852, demonstrates Belcher's antitheatricality ("North" 376, 358).

13. Oakum is a tarred fiber used for a variety of purposes on ships, including caulking and plumbing.

14. Day and Martin was a well-known brand of boot-blacking formula.

15. The idea that the men searching for Franklin were following in Parry's geographic and theatrical footsteps was expressed in the prologue spoken before *Charles the Second* was staged on HMS *Resolute* in 1852. Dr. Domville, playing the "Hyperborean King," reminded the audience that Parry "near this spot eleven months did tarry;/Ice-bound as you are now" (McDougall 159), drawing a parallel between the men in the audience and Parry in terms of both location and experience. The character describes how he forgave Parry's men for their "great intrusion" because of their cheerful attitudes, and tells audience members they were "welcome for their [Parry's men's] sakes [...] For you, your persevering predecessors do resemble/In everything" (McDougall 160); these lines make the claim that the audience inherited exploratory capital from Parry that would protect its members from the dangers of the Arctic. The men, as descendants of Parry, also inherited the ability to "take exercise, be cheerful, and care throw aside,/Cold, darkness, and monotony [they] may thus deride" (McDougall 160). The speech implies that Parry's legacy took material, epistemological, and disciplinary forms: the men inherited expressive theatrical practices, the knowledge that cheerfulness will triumph over adversity, and the self-discipline and respect for authority that would allow them to succeed in Arctic exploration.

16. When *Zero* was staged, pantomime was a doubly nostalgic genre, enticing audience members to fondly remember both the pre–Industrial Revolution British past and their own personal encounters with the genre. John O'Brien points out that urbanization and modernization in the eighteenth

and early nineteenth centuries brought "a sense of nostalgia for what had been lost. In such a context, characters such as Harlequin, Columbine and Pantaloon are best understood as stylized, stereotypical representations of the common folk, inhabiting a timeless pastoral world [...] the experience of returning to these characters and their stock situations offered a reassuring trip into an idealized past, into the kind of merry England for which they felt nostalgia only when they realized it was passing" (112). By mid-century, generic changes meant the genre itself could also be the subject of nostalgia: London audiences watching Clown-centered pantomimes that lacked the conventional pursuit structure of the harlequinade felt a longing not only for the good old days of England but also for the good old days of theater.

17. The *Illustrated Arctic News* includes an anecdote related to the failure to recognize cross-dressing: in discussing the November performances of *High Life Below Stairs* and *Done on Both Sides*, a reviewer mentions that Qalasirssuaq, the Inuk on board the ship, "was evidently deeply enamoured with the lovely English Koonah,—We understand he inquisitively inspected several two ton tanks the following day, for the purpose of ascertaining the whereabouts of the fair Lydia" (19). In this case, misreading the performance is explicitly linked to the lack of cultural refinement brought on by Qalasirssuaq's racial difference.

18. Sung to the tune of "Ivy Green," the North Polar Star's song would have immediately evoked home for audience members familiar with the ballad by Henry Russell, based on lyrics from Dickens's *Pickwick Papers*.

19. This citation of Nelson's famous signal command, issued immediately before the Battle of Trafalgar began, is not isolated: Russell Potter notes that "England Expects every Man to do his Duty" also appeared on a brass plaque at the wheel of HMS *Resolute* (112).

20. John Ross's *Victory* was trapped from 1829–33; he and his men were only rescued after abandoning their ships and traveling to Lancaster Sound in small boats. One reason the Admiralty was slow to search was because some members believed that an expedition could not be "summarily lost" in the Arctic because there were "no heavy seas which could prevent escape from a shipwreck; nor could any imaginable catastrophe, by the ice of these regions, suddenly overwhelm two entire crews [...] the very ice which might destroy the discovery ships, would yield a solid platform for refuge from the present danger" (Scoresby 12–13).

21. The lack of detail in reviews relates something critical about shipboard newspapers' intended audiences. Unlike urban reviews intended for readers who had not necessarily seen a play, shipboard reviews were read by those who had seen the play and helped audience members remember and relive a performance.

22. E.G. Blanchard, for example, doubled and even tripled roles to add novelty to pantomimes (Mayer, *Harlequin* 313–14).

2   "THE SLY FOX": READING
INDIGENOUS PRESENCE

1. Other naval practices, particularly "Crossing the Line" ceremonies that marked the crossing of the Equator, involved more blatant reversals of rank and disruptions of order.
2. Peter Freuchen describes stone fox traps used by Greenland Inuit: "flat stones are used to form a kind of cage which is hidden [...] The bait is at the bottom of the cage, and the fox can enter at its front. When the fox takes the bait, he releases a string which has been holding the stone which closes the cage, and there he sits" (68).
3. The *Illustrated Arctic News* remarked on February 28, that "The Original Pantomime of Zero, was again performed, and had been evidently much improved. A new Song or two was introduced & the indefatigable Mr Dean astonished the Audience by his clever imitation of a Bear & a Fox" (55). The vague "improvements" and the mention that Mr. Dean impressed the audience with his Fox allow speculation that the Fox may have been introduced in the second performance and that, therefore, the transformation sequence may also have been an addition.
4. Austin's ships converged on Cape York along with eleven other ships under the commands of Penny, De Haven, and John Ross. Beck was interviewed by a number of the officers.
5. See also Richard Cyriax "Adam Beck" pp. 35–51.
6. While the story was not about the Franklin expedition, David Woodman's *Unravelling the Franklin Mystery* suggests that Beck's story was based on real events (59).
7. There is some debate as to who constituted his family: according to William Parker Snow, Qalasirssuaq was an unmarried orphan (*Voyage* 226), while T.B. Murray claimed that his mother and sisters were with him at Cape York (12).
8. For a detailed analysis, see Kathleen Wilson, *The Island Race: Englishness, Empire and Gender in the Eighteenth Century*.
9. Spufford bases his comments, in part, on John Everett Millais's 1874 painting "The North-West Passage," which completely erases all signs of the region's indigenous inhabitants from its representation. See Spufford pp. 184–88.
10. See Renée Fossett, "Mapping Inuktut: Inuit Views of the Real World" for a discussion of Inuit approaches to mapping and navigation.
11. This was one of the only viable hopes for an expedition on the brink of disaster; this is illustrated by the example of Elisha Kent Kane's 1853–55 expedition. Kane and his men faced scurvy, defection, and shipwreck. After two winters trapped in the ice between Ellesmere Island and Greenland, Kane led him men on an eighty-three-day sledge and boat journey from Etah to Upernavik, a distance of approximately 1300 miles, during which they depended upon the assistance of Inuit (McGoogan, *Race* 284).

12. Mr. Muff was a recurring character in stories in *Punch*; readers of *Aurora Borealis* were likely familiar with the character from home.

3   GOING NATIVE: "PLAYING INUIT," "BECOMING SAVAGE," AND ACTING OUT FRANKLIN

1. Hall fails to mention that Hickey, who served under Elisha Kent Kane on the second Grinnell expedition, was a cabin boy, hardly a rank associated with authority. Despite this, and although Hall's opinion was unorthodox, he was not alone in his belief. William Parker Snow, for example, claimed: "I am, more than ever, convinced there is strong ground for believing that some of the Lost Expedition are alive and in captivity amongst the wild tribes of the North" ("A Paper on the Lost" 33). Snow, like Hall, believed that "close attention to all the information obtained from the natives, leads to a belief that the actual ground where the whole truth could be known has not yet been examined" (Committee 3) and argued: "Such information can be gained only by being on the spot for some time, and not merely passing hastily along by sledge or on foot" (Committee 2).
2. Hall hired Kudlago, an Inuk visiting the United States, as his interpreter. The expedition's complement was reduced to one—Hall—when Kudlago died on the way north.
3. Hall traveled north three times, from 1860–62, 1864–69, and in 1871. His second expedition led him to King William Island and made his most significant contribution to knowledge of what happened to the Franklin expedition. His third expedition was a short-lived quest for the geographic North Pole. Only months in, Hall died of arsenic poisoning. It remains unclear whether Hall's death was the result of deliberate poisoning by a disgruntled member of his expedition or the result of Hall's overzealous self-medication. See Loomis pp. 297–354.
4. Obviously, Ashcroft, Griffiths, and Tiffin provide only one definition of "going native." Another thread of scholarship interrogates the ways in which "going native" functions to define and reaffirm the boundaries of white culture in America. See Huhndorf, *Going Native: Indians in the American Cultural Imagination* and Deloria, *Playing Indian*.
5. In identifying "playing Inuit" and "becoming savage" as components of "going native," I am both indebted to and departing from the work of Shari M. Huhndorf and Phil Deloria. Huhndorf differentiates between "going native" and "playing Indian" (a concept explained by Deloria), arguing that "playing Indian," which she defines as "temporarily donning Native costume and emulating Native practices," was a practice that "historically aided European Americans in various quests for identity and authenticity since the Revolutionary Era" (7). In contrast, "going native" involved "the more

widespread conviction that adopting some vision of Native life in a more permanent way is necessary to regenerate and to maintain European-American racial and national identities" (Huhndorf 8).

6. Hall's decision to adapt to life in the Arctic by adopting indigenous practices was not unique. Hudson's Bay Company employees worked closely with indigenous peoples and frequently adopted their travel and camping practices. John Rae thrived in the Arctic by becoming an expert hunter, using dogsleds and snowshoes instead of man-hauled sledges, and learning to build igloos to avoid carrying heavy tents (*Arctic Correspondences* xciii–xcviii). William Kennedy, the son of a Hudson's Bay Company trader and a Cree woman, led a search expedition funded by Lady Franklin: he and his men survived an arduous 2000-kilometer trek by wearing skin and fur clothing and using dogsleds. Although Hall, like Rae and Kennedy, adopted Inuit practices, he differed from them because whereas they traveled independently, employing survival skills they learned, Hall relied on Inuit themselves and practiced what he saw his companions doing.

7. McClintock's better-equipped expedition arrived in the Arctic in 1857 and reached King William Island by 1859 after encountering fairly predictable weather delays: Hall's belief he could make the trip in weeks demonstrates his naiveté about overland travel.

8. This is clear in comparing Hall to an anonymous near-contemporary who wrote in an article entitled "Peuples ichtyophages et créophages": "The Eskimo, the Fuegians and, more rarely, the Hottentots, eat raw meat with an altogether bestial gluttony [...] The Fuegian devours anything he finds, rotten fish, great molluscs and octopuses that are entirely decomposed [...] These singular deviations from the habitual practices of civilization indicate that these nations have fallen to the last degree of mindlessness" (qtd. in Jahoda 18). The passage locates the desire to eat "rotten" food as a sign of "savagery," indicating that "savage" races had degenerated from an earlier state of civilization.

9. On January 10, 1861, Hall left the *George Henry* for his first extended trip with Inuit. He took some of his own food and bedding with him, but no tent, hunting gear, or gun. After ten days, the group's food supply ran dangerously low due to bad weather and poor hunting. Ebierbing, an Inuk man with whom Hall developed a close friendship, went back to the *George Henry* for supplies, and when he returned, Hall recognized that he had only survived because of Ebierbing: "I was by his side grasping his hand, and, with a grateful heart, thanking him for the really good deed he had performed in thus coming alone with the relief" (*Life* 180).

10. One of Hall's most significant discoveries during his 1860–62 expedition was identifying the site where Martin Frobisher's vessels had landed during his 1576–78 voyages. The landing spot, long forgotten in England, was preserved accurately by Inuit oral history.

11. His response to Koojesse was fairly typical; his normally sympathetic biographer Loomis notes that Hall "usually admired the Eskimo's independence,

but when it interfered with what he wanted to do, he was angered; independence then seemed irresponsibility" (124).

12. "Mimetic capital" refers to the "multiple sites of representation" linked to the "problem of the assimilation of the other" (Greenblatt 6). Greenblatt conveys the sense that "mimesis, as Marx said of capital, is a social relation of production [...] any given representation is not only the reflection or product of social relations but [...] it is itself a social relation" (6).

13. See the O.E.D. "dame" definitions 1 and 2. The word also had another connotation: that of the "dame" as a cross-dressed character in pantomime—calling the women "dames" may suggest that they were grotesque and unfeminine.

14. Robert Hood and George Back, who served under Franklin during his first expedition, apparently had romantic relationships with the same Inuk woman, Green Stockings, and allegedly dueled over her. Green Stockings apparently bore Hood's child. Neither the duel nor the child is mentioned in records of the expedition, however. John Hepburn, a seaman on the expedition, told William Kennedy and Joseph René Bellot about the events when they served together on the *Prince Albert*. See Wiebe pp. 34–38.

15. Legislation prohibiting marriage between blacks and whites was in place in all slaveholding and many free states prior to the Civil War; laws specifically prohibiting intermarriage between whites and Native Americans were in place in eight states when Hall left New London in 1860. While Hall was in the Arctic, three more states enacted similar legislation.

16. Between expeditions, Hall returned to the United States with Tookoolito and her husband; the shaman's accusation likely responded to her close association with Hall and the perception that she had "gone white."

17. *Angakkuit* ceremonies played a central role in Inuit life until the early twentieth century. As Dorothy Eber explains: "Shamans were the regulators of the Inuit world, the mediators between humans and the spirit realm. They were said to fly through the air to faraway places, assume animal forms, cure human sickness, and make animals plentiful when people were hungry. They gained their powers through inheritance or a 'calling' or rigorous initiation. They were assisted by *tuurngait*, their spirit helpers, who were the souls of animals but could also be souls of inanimate objects such as rocks, mountains, or icebergs" (xvii). Simon Inuksaq describes a shaman ceremony: "They would meet in a *qaggiq*; the shaman would be there [...] The shaman would do the performance at this time. We would see different things. The shaman would change in many ways—only half of his fingers would be there at times. The shamans are able to see what we normal people cannot see. They could do impossible things and they are able to take away the fears of the person who is not well" (qtd. in Bennett and Rowley 381–82). Although Inuksaq's account describes the ceremony as "performance," his focus is on how the shaman could change the material world through spiritual intervention. This contrasts Hall's emphasis on the theatrical elements of the ceremony in order to highlight what he sees as a fraudulent performance.

18. Although Hall refused Mingumailo's offer, he does not at this point openly criticize the Inuit practice of spousal exchange. During his second expedition, however, he implicitly critiqued the practice when he helped Tookoolito avoid becoming the object of one such exchange (Loomis 187–88).

19. Martha Tunnuq describes the function of the *qaggiq*: "We would have our celebrations in the *qaggiq*, and also we would all gather in the *qaggiq* when the weather was poor. They would have drum dances there and play *taptaujak* [blindman's bluff] before we were introduced to Christianity. We would do our celebrations in there and it was truly a part of our lives [...] After there was a good hunt we would gather in the *qaggiq* and have feasts there" (qtd. in Bennett and Rowley 363).

20. One also must recall another set of stories, concerning starving sailors with blackened mouths and noses caused by scurvy—Franklin's own men—circulating among Inuit at this time.

21. As Dale Cockrell illustrates, blackface performance originated in earlier folk traditions (33–56) and, as William Mahar argues, blackface comedy was often based on a critique of white culture and economic structures rather than derision of black culture (41). Lhamon, Cockrell, and Mahar all emphasize the importance of Lott's study as one reading of the minstrel scene, but each also points out the multiple perspectives on race informing both the production and the reception of blackface performance.

22. See Davis-Fisch "Girls in 'White' Dresses" for a detailed explanation of how square dancing facilitated interracial sexual liaisons.

23. The fear of "going native" was widespread among whalemen in contact with indigenous women. Margaret Creighton proposes that this concern sprang from the fear that sex with a native woman would corrupt a man who should remain chaste for his partner or potential partner at home (157–58).

24. Interracial sexual relationships held material and social benefits for Inuit families as well: women received clothing and goods they could not otherwise obtain and their relationships with whalers provided material and economic stability for their families.

25. See Kane, *Arctic Explorations: The Second Grinnell Expedition in Search of Sir John Franklin, 1853, '54, '55* and McGoogan, *Race to the Polar Sea* pp. 222–43.

4   AGLOOKA'S GHOST: PERFORMING EMBODIED MEMORY

1. One reason for this omission may be that the story was not included in the published account of Hall's second expedition, only in Hall's unpublished fieldnotes. In *Unravelling the Franklin Mystery*, David Woodman reprints the relevant text and spends considerable time addressing Owwer's testimony: his work is exceptional for considering the story. See Woodman pp. 123–38.

2. Teekeeta's earlier interview with Hall differs slightly. He says: "On *Ag-loo-ka's* first meeting with the Innuits he had a gun in his hand; on seeing him lay it down, the Innuits laid down their spears. Then Crozier walked up and said, '*Tijmo?*' '*Man-ik-too-mee?*' at the same time brushing his hand down their breasts and shaking hands, *Kob-lu-na*-way" (Nourse 406). This account suggests confusion about whether Aglooka and Crozier are the same person (this occurs throughout Hall's notes because Hall was so certain Aglooka was Crozier that he often substituted one name for the other) and concerning who carried the gun. Unlike Owwer, Teekeeta also explicitly remembered Inuit carrying spears when they went forward to meet the *qallunaat*. Finally, Teekeeta remembers the order of events a little differently: he has Crozier saying "Tijmo" immediately followed by "Man-ik-too-mee" and the gestures of friendship—brushing his hand down the Inuit's breasts and shaking hands. whereas on May 18, Owwer tells Hall that this man did other things before approaching closely enough to shake hands.
3. The word is also spelled as *teyma* or *taima* in contemporary documents.
4. John K. Washington's pocket-sized *Esquimaux and English Vocabulary* (1850), provided to expeditions in search of Franklin did not include any phrase that resembled this.
5. See, for example, Cooper pp. 121, Woodman pp. 107, and Cyriax, *Sir* pp. 153–57.
6. Inuit oral traditions include stories about visiting a ship or ships off the coast of King William Island; some involve meeting white men on these ships while others concern visiting an empty ship. See Nourse pp. 255–60 for stories from Pelly Bay Inuit about contact with Franklin survivors and Woodman pp. 209–26 for Inuit stories of visiting an abandoned ship and of witnessing a ship sinking.
7. Oo-me-en is Hall's translation of *umiaq*, the Inuktitut word for boat.

5   THE LAST RESOURCE: WITNESSING THE CANNIBAL SCENE

1. There is some debate concerning the location of the campsite: Frederick Schwatka identified it as Starvation Cove, a point at the "south end of the bay lying to the west of Point Richardson, on the American continent" (*Arctic Correspondence* 275); however, David Woodman suggests that the site was actually on King William Island, near Terror Bay, and that Schwatka's site was only where the last of Franklin's men died (150). Woodman argues that the Inuktitut term that Rae's interpreter translated as "continent" or "mainland" could also apply to King William Island, which was the main piece of land in relation to smaller islands nearby. Woodman claims, questioning the "standard reconstruction" of events, that after the ships were damaged by ice, the men moved ashore to a campsite on King William

Island, at a place called Toonoonee by Inuit, or Terror Bay by Europeans. Approximately forty of these men, led by Aglooka, left the campsite in an attempt to reach Repulse Bay, while "[d]iscipline broke down among those left behind [...] Those who remained at Toonoonee would all eventually die after being reduced to the last extremity" (246). Inuit stories, according to Woodman's argument, concern the bodies found at Toonoonee (Terror Bay). The question of where cannibalism occurred—like many raised by Inuit stories—is critical for one concerned with reconstructing what happened, but less pressing for one interested in how the cannibalism was experienced and remembered.

2. Rae used slightly different wording in the two letters: whereas his letter to the Hudson's Bay Company didn't use the word cannibalism, his letter to the Admiralty did.

3. McClintock's 1859 discovery of the Victory Point record contributed to this dismissal. Although it did not disprove the allegations, it placed Franklin's death before the 1848 abandonment and exonerated him personally from charges of cannibalism.

4. Dickens followed the press response to Rae's report and initially thought the report was "hasty in its acceptance of the details, particularly in the statement that they had eaten the dead bodies of their companions" ("Letter to Mrs. Richard Watson," 1 November 1854, qtd. in Stone, *Night* 5).

5. Grace Moore argues that "Dickens's stance on racial matters may have oscillated between contempt and pity by 1853, but by no means did he hold the extreme and reactionary views that he developed after the Indian Mutiny. The events of 1857 enabled Dickens to formulate a more consistent, but decidedly unpleasant attitude towards other races" (242–43).

6. The article might have been Dickens's response to controversy that arose in 1852 after he criticized Stowe's *Uncle Tom's Cabin* for "making out the African race to be a great race" (qtd. in Stone, "Charles" 188); the legal reformer Lord Denman published an article in the *London Standard* claiming that Dickens "exerts his powers to obstruct the great cause of human improvement [...] We do not say that he actually defends slavery or the slave-trade; but he takes pains to discourage, by ridicule, the effort now making to put them down" (qtd. in Stone, "Charles" 190). Grace Moore argues that "The Noble Savage" was Dickens's attempt to rebut Denman's criticisms by "adopting the voice that Denman had attributed to him in order to demonstrate the absurdity of his accusations" (239).

7. In an argument that seems to underline rather than deny Dickens's racism, Bernth Lindfors contextualizes his comment, arguing that Dickens was "striving to puncture an inflated Romantic conception of the dignity of 'primitive' peoples," and claiming Dickens was "was not really recommending genocide" but was advocating "cultural, not literal, genocide" (76–77).

8. For further elaboration on Dickens's views on savagery and civility, see Kristen Guest, "Cannibalism" pp. 112.

9. This story also inspired Dickens's characterization of Magwitch in *Great Expectations*.

10. The *Grosvenor* was wrecked off the coast of South Africa in 1782 on its way from Ceylon to England. Of the 123 people who survived the shipwreck, only eighteen made it to Cape Town.

11. Rae's December 23 response illuminates the flaws in Dickens's arguments about translation and gesture and attempts to vindicate Inuit testimony. Rae specifically claims that oral transmission constituted valid knowledge, using the example of hearing about John and James Ross from Inuit who had never met the men: "they described so perfectly the personal appearance of Sir John Ross and Sir James Ross—although the men spoken with had not seen these gentlemen—that any one acquainted with these officers could have recognized them" (435).

12. Rae responded to these questions easily, pointing out Dickens's deliberate misreading of his suggestion that the officer "lay down in this position as a precaution" (433) and noting that the men possessed sledge runners and cases that could have provided fuel (434).

13. Rae's experience in the Arctic, combined with his Scottish background, may have worked against him, positioning him as a racialized other: Dickens's "invocation of racialized stereotypes foregrounded Rae's own foreignness. As a Scot who worked for a commercial monopoly, he was not, in fact, English, nor was he pledged to the patriotic, empire-building aims of the military. [...] Thus when [...] Rae responded to each of Dickens's hyperbolically patriotic claims by pointing to his own experience in the Arctic, the shadow of the savage—perhaps even the cannibal—lay across his words" (Hill 123).

14. The *Peggy* was an American ship bound for New York from the Azores.

15. Dr. Rae argued that none of Dickens's examples were analogous to the situation Franklin and his men were in (458) and took issue with Dickens's characterization of Franklin's men as well-disciplined: even before they left Stromness, four sailors had attempted to desert after drinking smuggled whisky (Cavell 216–17). Rae noted that "their conduct at the very last British port they entered was not such as to make those who knew it, consider them very deserving of the high eulogium passed upon them in Household Words" (458). Finally, Rae criticized Dickens's assumption that men would have remained disciplined after abandoning the ships, warning "seamen generally consider themselves, when they have lost their ship and set foot on shore, as being freed from that strict discipline to which they would readily submit themselves when on board" (458). Though Rae's rebuttal seems convincing today, his insinuations that Franklin could not maintain order and that his crews were "a lustful rabble" would not have helped his case; Janice Cavell remarks that Rae's "gratuitous slurs against dead men did nothing to promote the idea that he would not make accusations without good reason" (217).

16. *The Wreck of the Golden Mary* was first published in a Christmas number of *Household Words* on December 6, 1856.

17. This story does not appear in McClintock's published narrative. The apparent omission may indicate that Inuit stories were censored for British consumption, either by explorers or their editors, in the years that immediately followed the *Household Words* debate.

18. While the human remains discovered by Owen Beattie in the 1980s produced convincing forensic evidence that cannibalism occurred, the story told by bones on a laboratory table is very different—and arguably more sterile—than that preserved in Inuit testimony.

19. Woodman notes that explorers used "Neitchille" to refer to the entire Boothia Peninsula (*Unravelling* 332).

20. Examples of these items are on display at the National Maritime Museum at Greenwich (UK) and the Scott Polar Research Institute Museum at Cambridge.

6 THE DESIGNATED MOURNER: CHARLES DICKENS STANDS IN FOR FRANKLIN

1. Lieutenant Pim spoke at Marylebone Institution in December 1856 on the subject of the expedition, arguing that "it was almost too revolting to speak about. Were Sir John Franklin, and such companions as sailed with him, likely men to eat one another? Look to antecedents. [...] And how was the original report substantiated? Why, by second-hand Esquimaux report. Its very vagueness ought to have induced caution in accepting such an idea; but no, Sir John Franklin and his companions are blazoned to the world as cannibals; and even supposing all were dead [...] such a stain must be removed from the honoured memory of that great and good traveler" (28).

2. Potter convincingly argues that the bone soup suggests accidental cannibalism, subtly referring to the cannibalism that occurred during Franklin's 1819–22 expedition, and claiming that although one presumes Want serves a soup made of animal bones, the line between animal and human remains is "a source of considerable and anxious ambiguity" (160–61).

3. The idea that failing to see in time is critical to trauma's structure of belated experience is central to Cathy Caruth's interpretation of Freud's and Lacan's story of the dream of the burning child. See *Unclaimed Experience* pp. 91–112.

4. This erasure frequently arose in response to the anxiety provoked by Inuit presence in relation to how polar exploration was imagined and idealized. Lisa Bloom argues that polar exploration narratives "literalized the colonial fantasy of a tabula rasa where people, history, and culture vanish" giving "polar exploration an aesthetic dimension that allowed the discovery of the North Pole to appear above political and commercial concerns"; this process of erasure reduced "the vital participation of Inuit men and women to subordinate 'native bearers' imagined either as 'primitive' or 'unspoiled' figures" (2–3). In

order to justify Arctic exploration as "pure" discovery, rather than an act of colonial possession, the Arctic had to be imagined as unpopulated.

5. On November 1, 1856, Dickens wrote to Wilkie Collins of his "care with creating 'reality,'" describing how designer Stanfield wanted to "cancel the chair altogether" in act three and to "substitute a piece of rock on the ground, composing with the Cavern. That, I take it, is clearly an improvement" (217).

6. See Nayder pp. 63–94 and Brannan pp. 34–49 for detailed discussions of how Collins's and Dickens's drafts differed. Dickens's changes to Collins's script are preserved in a manuscript Dickens labeled "The Prompt-Book," which was the basis of the fair copy used in the 1857 performances and is the copy text Robert Louis Brannan used in preparing his edition of the script (Brannan 3). In 1866, Wilkie Collins used this manuscript as a working draft for his revised version of the play; in preparing his edition of the play, Brannan distinguished between the 1857 text and the 1866 alterations.

7. The prologue was spoken by John Forster during the Tavistock House performances (Brannan 98).

8. The parallel between Clara and Sophia Cracroft, which Potter notes, is based on the fact that Francis Crozier was in love with Cracroft, who rejected him (143).

9. See Hill pp. 133 for a more detailed discussion.

10. While the wives of commanding officers sometimes accompanied their husbands to Stromness, it was less common for women to meet their husbands on their return. One exception occurred in 1846, when Jane Franklin travelled to the west coast of the United States hoping to meet her husband (McGoogan, *Lady* 276).

11. Interestingly enough, in "Insularities," a piece written for *Household Words*'s January 19, 1856, edition, Dickens linked the distinction between the two forms of acting to national tastes. Dickens wrote of the difference between a dramatic and a theatrical picture, noting that the French taste was for the theatrical and the English was for the dramatic. The difference lay in the consciousness of a spectator: "Conceiving the difference between a dramatic picture and a theatrical picture to be, that in the latter case the groups are obtrusively conscious of a spectator, and are obviously dressed up, and doing (or not doing) certain things with an eye to the spectator, and not for the sake of the story" (2).

12. Dickens began acting in minor and private theaters when he was only a teenager (Brookes Cross 86). In 1845 he started an amateur company, whose first production of Jonson's *Every Man in his Humour* was held at the Royalty that year. In 1848, his production of *The Merry Wives of Windsor* ran for nine performances, with Dickens playing Justice Shallow, and one of these performances was attended by Queen Victoria and Prince Albert (Brookes Cross 88).

13. Frédéric Lemaitre (1800–76) was a celebrated French actor and playwright, known for his performances as Edmund Kean in Alexandre Dumas, père's

Kean (1836) and as Ruy Blas in Victor Hugo's play of the same title (1838). The review suggests that he was a bit of a "has been" by 1857.

14. While this inability to remain distanced seems to be a sign of amateurism, one must note that Ternan was a professional actress hired to replace Dickens's daughter and that there is no account of the same phenomenon occurring when the play was staged at Tavistock House or the Gallery of Illustration with an amateur playing Clara.

15. The rank one attained was, to Dickens, more important than the social class into which one was born. Although the play specifies that Wardour is a gentleman's son, this does not necessarily imply anything positive about his character: Franklin himself was a merchant's son.

16. Ann Cvetkovich's discussion of how sensation novels generated affect is instructive here. She argues: "Sensationalism works by virtue of the link that is constructed between the concreteness of the 'sensation-al' event and the tangibility of the 'sensational' feelings it produces. Emotionally charged representations produce bodily responses that, because they are physically felt, seem to be natural and thus to confirm the naturalness or reality of the event" (23–24).

17. This was because Dickens and his company were amateurs; he wrote that he "should not feel easy as to the social position of my daughters at the Court under such circumstances" ("Letter to Angela Burdett-Coutts," 20 June 1857, 357).

18. The Queen's journal included the notes that The Frozen Deep was "most interesting, intensely dramatic, and most touching, and moving, at the end. The Play was admirably acted by Charles Dickens, (whose representation of Richard Wardour was beyond all praise and not to be surpassed) his 3 daughters [*one was in fact Helen Hogarth*] and son,—Mark Lemon, the author, etc. There was charming scenery and almost constant accompaniment of music, which adds so much to the effect of a melodrama. We were all kept in breathless suspense, and much impressed" (qtd. in Storey and Tillotson 366).

Works Cited ❧

PERIODICALS

Daily News (London)
Illustrated London News
Manchester Times
Morning Herald (London)
Observer (London)
Sun (London)
Times (London)

PRIMARY SOURCES

Arctic Miscellanies. Souvenir of the Late Polar Search. By the Officers and Seamen of the Expedition. London: Colburn and Co., 1852. (*Aurora Borealis*).

Armstrong, Alexander. *A Personal Narrative of the Discovery of the North-west Passage.* London: Hurst and Blackett, 1857.

Belcher, Edward. *The Last of the Arctic Voyages Being a Narrative of the Expedition in H.M.S. Assistance under the Command of Captain Sir Edward Belcher, C.B., in Search of Sir John Franklin, during the Years 1852–53–54*. Vol. 2. London: L. Reeve, 1855.

Borden, Lorris Elijah. *Memoirs of a Pioneer Doctor.* Typescript. Ottawa: Library and Archives Canada (MG30-B46).

Collins, Wilkie, and Charles Dickens. *The Frozen Deep.* Ed. Robert Louis Brannan. *Under the Management of Mr. Charles Dickens: His Production of "The Frozen Deep."* Ithaca, NY: Cornell UP, 1966.

———. *The Wreck of the Golden Mary.* London: A. Barker, 1955.

Collinson, Richard. *Journal of H.M.S. Enterprise: On the Expedition in Search of Sir John Franklin's Ships by Behring Strait, 1850–55* . London: Sampson, Low, Marston, Searle & Rivington, 1889.

Committee for Snow's Arctic Search. *Renewed Arctic Search for Journals, Records, or Other Traces of the Lost Franklin Expedition.* 1860. Scott Polar Reseach Institute, Cambridge, UK.

Dickens, Charles. "Insularities." *Household Words* 13.304 (19 January 1856): 1–4.

———. *The Letters of Charles Dickens*. Eds. Graham Storey and Kathleen Tillotson. Vol. 8 (1856–58). Oxford: Oxford UP, 1995.

———. "Letter to Angela Burdett-Coutts." 3 February 1857. In Storey and Tillotson.

———. "Letter to Angela Burdett-Coutts." 20 June 1857. In Storey and Tillotson.

———. "Letter to Angela Burdett-Coutts." 5 September 1857. In Storey and Tillotson.

———. "Letter to Frank Stone." 9 August 1857. In Storey and Tillotson.

———. "Letter to Mary Boyle." 6 February 1857. In Storey and Tillotson.

———. "Letter to Mrs. Richard Watson." 7 December 1857. In Storey and Tillotson.

———. "Letter to W. H. Wills." 6 April 1856. In *The Letters of Charles Dickens*. Ed. Walter Dexter. Vol. 2. London: Bloomsbury, 1938.

———. "Letter to Wilkie Collins." 1 November 1856. In Storey and Tillotson.

———. "The Long Voyage." *The Uncommercial Traveller and Reprinted Pieces, Etc.* London: Oxford UP, 1958. 369–78.

———. "The Lost Arctic Voyagers." *Household Words* 10.245–46 (2 and 9 December 1854): 362–65, 387–93.

———. "The Noble Savage." *Household Words* 7.168 (11 June 1853): 337–39.

Ede, Charles. *Zero, or Harlequin Light*. In *Franklin's Footsteps* by Clements Markham. 129–143.

FACSIMILE OF THE ILLUSTRATED ARCTIC NEWS, PUBLISHED ON BOARD H.M.S. RESOLUTE:CAPTN. HORATIO T. AUSTIN. C.B. IN SEARCH OF THE EXPEDITION UNDER SIR JOHN FRANKLIN. London: Ackermann & Co., 1852.

Fitzjames, James, and Francis Crozier. "Victory Point Record." National Maritime Museum, Arctic Collection, doc. 2/121. Greenwich, London, UK.

Fitzjames, James. *The Last Journals of Captain Fitzjames, R.N., of the Lost Polar Expedition*. Ed. William Conigham. Brighton: W. Pearce, no date.

Franklin, Jane. *Journal. 2 January to 26 December 1857*. Scott Polar Research Institute. MS 248/115; BJ Journal. Holograph. Cambridge, UK.

———. "Letter to Sir James Graham." 20 January 1854. Scott Polar Research Institute. MS 248/212/6. Cambridge, UK.

Franklin, John. *Journey to the Shores of the Polar Sea*. 4 Vols. London: John Murray, 1829.

Great Britain. Admiralty. *Arctic expedition return to an address of the Honourable the House of Commons, dated 21 March 1848, for, copies of instructions to Captain Sir John Franklin, R.N., in reference to the Arctic Expedition of 1845 ; to any officer or officers appointed by the Admiralty on any expedition in search of Captain Sir John Franklin, R.N., and, copies or extracts of any proceedings and correspondence of the Admiralty in reference to Arctic expeditions, from 1845 to the present time, together with copies of charts illustrating the same.* London: HMSO, 1848.

Hall, Charles Francis. *Fieldnotes from 18 May 1869.* Book 38 of 62. Item 103. National Museum of American History, Behring Centre, Smithsonian Institution, Washington D.C.

———. *Life with the Esquimaux: A Narrative of Arctic Experience in Search of Survivors of Sir John Franklin's Expedition.* 1864. Edmonton: M.G. Hurtig, 1970.

Kane, Elisha Kent. *Arctic Explorations: The Second Grinnell Expedition in Search of Sir John Franklin, 1853, '54, '55.* London: T. Nelson and Sons, 1861.

King, Richard. *The Franklin Expedition from First to Last.* London: John Churchill, 1855.

Markham, Clements. *Franklin's Footsteps: A Sketch of Greenland, along with the Shores of Which His Expedition Passed, and of the Parry Isles, Where the Last Traces of It Were Found.* London: Chapman and Hall, 1853.

McClintock, Francis Leopold. *The Voyage of the "Fox" in the Arctic Seas: A Narrative of the Discovery of the Fate of Sir John Franklin and his Companions.* London: J. Murray, 1869.

McClure, Robert. *The Discovery of a North-West Passage by H.M.S. Investigator, Capt. R. McClure During the Yeares 1850–1851–1852–1853–1854.* Ed. Sherard Osborn. 4th ed. London: William Blackwood and Sons, 1865.

McDougall, George. *The Eventful Voyage of H.M. Discovery Ship "Resolute" to the Arctic Regions in Search of Sir John Franklin and the Missing Crews of H.M. Discovery Ships "Erebus" and "Terror", 1852, 1853, 1854, to which Is Added an Account of Her Being Fallen in with by an American Whaler after Her Abandonment in Barrow Straits, and of Her Presentation to Queen Victoria by the Government of the United States.* London: Longman, Brown, Green, Longmans, & Roberts, 1857.

Murray, Thomas Boyles. *Kalli: The Esquimaux Christian, A Memoir.* London: Society for Promoting Christian Knowledge, 1856.

Nourse, J.E., ed. *Narrative of the Second Arctic Expedition Made by Charles F. Hall.* Washington D.C.: U.S. Naval Observatory, Government Printing Office, 1879.

Osborn, Sherard. *Stray Leaves from an Arctic Journal; or, Eighteen Months in the Polar Regions, in Search of Sir John Franklin's Expedition, in the Years 1850–51.* London: Longman, Brown, Green and Longmans, 1852.

Pim, Bedford. *An Earnest Appeal to the British Public on Behalf of the Missing Arctic Expedition.* London: Hurst and Blackett, 1857.

Rae, John. *John Rae's Correspondence with the Hudson's Bay Company on Arctic Exploration, 1844–55.* Ed. E.E. Rich. London: The Hudson's Bay Record Society, 1953.

———. "The Lost Arctic Voyagers." *Household Words* 10.248–49 (23 and 30 December 1854): 433–37, 457–59.

Rasmussen, Knud. *The People of the Polar North.* London: K. Paul, Trench, Trubner & Co., 1908.

Rink, Hans. *Tales and Traditions of the Eskimo with a Sketch of Their Habits, Religion, Language and Other Peculiarities.* Edinburgh; London: W. Blackwood, 1875.

Scoresby, William. *The Franklin Expedition: or, Considerations on Measures for the Discovery and Relief of Our Absent Adventurers in the Arctic Regions.* London: Longman, Brown, Green, and Longmans, 1850.

Simmonds, P.L. *Sir John Franklin and the Arctic regions: With Detailed Notices of the Expeditions in Search of the Missing Vessels under Sir John Franklin. To Which is Added an Account of the American Expedition, Under the Patronage of Henry Grinnell, Esq., with an Introduction to the American Edition, by John C. Lord, D.D.* 1852. Rev. ed. Glouchestershire: Nonsuch Publishing, 2005.

Snow, William Parker. *A Paper on the Lost Polar Expedition and Possible Recovery of its Scientific Documents. With an Introduction and Supplementary Remarks, Containing an Analysis and Critical Examination of Facts and Opinions on the Subject, Demonstrating the Probability of Survivors Yet Being Found.* London: Edward Stanford, 1860.

———. *Voyage of the Prince Albert in Search of Sir John Franklin; A Narrative of Every-day Life in the Arctic Seas.* London: Longman, Brown, Green, and Longmans, 1851.

Stefansson, Vilhjalmur. *Friendly Arctic: The Story of Five Years in Polar Regions.* New York: Macmillan, 1922.

Washington, John K. *Esquimaux and English Vocabulary, for the Use of the Arctic Expeditions.* London: John Murray, 1850.

White, W. "Probable Fate of Sir John Franklin and Crew, or, the Scurvy in the Arctic Seas, and Correspondence of Captain W. White with the Lords of the Admiralty, and the Principle Commanding Officers of the Late Arctic Expeditions, on Its Prevention and Cure." London, 1852. Scott Polar Research Institute, Cambridge, UK.

SECONDARY SOURCES

Ackroyd, Peter. *Dickens.* New York: Harper Collins, 1990.

Allen, Emily. "Communal Performances: Royal Ritual, Revolution and National Acts." *The Performing Century.* Eds. Tracy C. Davis and Peter Holland. Houndsmills, Basingstoke, Hampshire; New York: Palgrave Macmillan, 2007. 60–79.

Ashcroft, Bill, Gareth Griffiths, and Helen Tiffin. *Post-colonial Studies: The Key Concepts.* London: Routledge, 2007.

Atwood, Margaret. *Strange Things: The Malevolent North in Canadian Literature.* Oxford: Clarendon Press, 1995.

Bakhtin, Mikhail. *Rabelais and His World*. Trans. Helene Iswolsky. Cambridge, MA; London: MIT Press, 1965.

Barr, William. *Arctic Hell-Ship: The Voyage of HMS Enterprise, 1850–1855*. Edmonton: University of Alberta Press, 2007.

Beattie, Owen. *Frozen in Time: Unlocking the Secrets of the Franklin Expedition*. Saskatoon, SK: Western Producer Prairie Books, 1988.

Benjamin, Walter. *Illuminations*. Ed. Hannah Arendt. Trans. Harry Zorn. London: Pimlico, 1999.

Bennett, John, and Susan Rowley, eds. *Uqalurait: An Oral History of Nunavut*. Montreal; Kingston: McGill-Queen's UP, 2004.

Berton, Pierre. *The Arctic Grail: The Quest for the North West Passage and the North Pole, 1818–1911*. Toronto: McClelland and Stewart, 1988.

———. *Prisoners of the North*. Toronto: Anchor Canada, 2004.

Bhabha, Homi K. *The Location of Culture*. London: Routledge, 1994.

Bloom, Lisa. *Gender on Ice: American Ideologies of Polar Explorations*. Minneapolis: University of Minnesota Press, 1993.

Boas, Franz. *The Central Eskimo*. Lincoln: University of Nebraska Press, 1964.

Booth, Michael R. *Theatre in the Victorian Age*. Cambridge, UK: Cambridge University Press, 1991.

Brannan, Robert Louis. *Under the Management of Mr. Charles Dickens: His Production of "The Frozen Deep."* Ithaca, NY: Cornell UP, 1966.

Brookes Cross, A.E. "The Fascination of the Footlights." *The Dickensian* 23 (1927): 85–91; 161–66; 243–49.

Carlson, Marvin A. *The Haunted Stage: The Theatre as Memory Machine*. Ann Arbor: University of Michigan Press, 2001.

Caruth, Cathy. *Unclaimed Experience: Trauma, Narrative, and History*. Baltimore: Johns Hopkins UP, 1996.

Cavell Janice. *Tracing the Connected Narrative: Arctic Exploration in British Print Culture, 1818–1860*. Toronto: University of Toronto Press, 2008.

Cockrell, Dale. *Demons of Disorder: Early Blackface Minstrels and Their World*. Cambridge UK: Cambridge UP, 1997.

Cooke, Alan, and Clive Holland. *The Exploration of Northern Canada 500 to 1920: A Chronology*. Toronto: Arctic History Press, 1978.

Cookman, Scott. *Ice Blink: The Tragic Fate of Sir John Franklin's Lost Polar Expedition*. New York: John Wiley and Sons, 2000.

Cooper, Paul Fenimore. *Island of the Lost*. New York: Putnam, 1961.

Cox, Jeffrey. "The Death of Tragedy; or, the Birth of Melodrama." *The Performing Century*. Eds. Tracy C. Davis and Peter Holland. Houndsmills, Basingstoke, Hampshire; New York: Palgrave Macmillan, 2007. 161–80.

Creighton, Margaret S. *Rites & Passages: The Experience of American Whaling, 1830–1870*. Cambridge, UK: Cambridge University Press, 1995.

Cvetkovich, Ann. *Mixed Feelings: Feminism, Mass Culture, and Victorian Sensationalism*. New Brunswick, NJ: Rutgers UP, 1992.

Cyriax, Richard. "Adam Beck and the Franklin Search." *Mariner's Mirror* 48 (1962): 35–51.

———. *Sir John Franklin's Last Arctic Expedition. The Franklin Expedition. A Chapter in the History of the Royal Navy.* London: Methuen & Co., 1939.

Davis-Fisch, Heather. "Girls in 'White' Dresses, Pretend Fathers: Interracial Sexuality and Intercultural Community in the Canadian Arctic." *Theatre Research in Canada* 32.1 (Spring 2011): 84–106.

Deloria, Philip. *Playing Indian.* New Haven: Yale UP, 1998.

Dening, Greg. *Mr. Bligh's Bad Language: Passion, Power, and Theatre on the Bounty.* Cambridge, UK: Cambridge UP, 1992.

———. *Performances.* Chicago: University of Chicago Press, 1996.

Diamond, Michael. *Victorian Sensation: Or, the Spectacular, the Shocking and the Scandalous in Nineteenth-Century Britain.* London: Anthem, 2003.

Druick, Don. *The Frozen Deep.* MS. 2006.

Eagleton, Terry. *Literary Theory: An Introduction.* Oxford: B. Blackwell, 1983.

Eber, Dorothy. *Encounters on the Passage: Inuit Meet the Explorers.* Toronto; Buffalo: University of Toronto Press, 2008.

Eng, David L., and David Kazanjian, eds. *Loss: The Politics of Mourning.* Berkeley, CA; London: University of California Press, 2003.

Fossett, Renée. *In Order to Live Untroubled: Inuit of the Central Arctic, 1550 to 1940.* Winnipeg: University of Manitoba Press, 2001.

———. "Mapping Inuktut: Inuit Views of the Real World." *Reading Beyond Words: Contexts for Native History.* Eds. Jennifer S.H. Brown and Elizabeth Vibert. 2nd ed. Peterborough, ON: Broadview, 2003. 111–32.

Freuchen, Peter. *Book of the Eskimos.* Cleveland: World Pub. Co., 1961.

Freud, Sigmund. "Mourning and Melancholia." *The Standard Edition of the Complete Psychological Works of Sigmund Freud.* Vol. 14. London: Hogarth Press, 1966. 237–58.

Garber, Marjorie. *Vested Interests: Cross-Dressing & Cultural Anxiety.* New York: Routledge, 1992.

Gikandi, Simon. *Maps of Englishness: Writing Identity in the Culture of Colonialism.* New York: Columbia UP, 1996.

Greenblatt, Stephen. *Marvelous Possessions: The Wonder of the New World.* Oxford: Clarendon, 1988.

Guest, Kristen. "Are You Being Served? Cannibalism, Class, and Victorian Melodrama." *Eating Their Words: Cannibalism and the Boundaries of Cultural Identity.* Ed. Kristen Guest. Albany, NY: SUNY Press, 2001. 107–27.

Hadley, Elaine. *Melodramatic Tactics: Theatricalized Dissent in the English Marketplace, 1800–1885.* Stanford, CA: Stanford UP, 1995.

Hill, Jen. *White Horizon: The Arctic in the Nineteenth-Century British Imagination.* Albany, NY: SUNY Press, 2008.

Huhndorf, Shari Michelle. *Going Native: Indians in the American Cultural Imagination.* Ithaca NY: Cornell UP, 2001.

Jahoda, Gustav. *Images of Savages: Ancient Roots of Modern Prejudice in Western Culture*. London; New York: Routledge, 1999.

Kavanagh, Geoff. *Ditch*. Toronto: Playwrights Union of Canada, 1990.

LaCapra, Dominick. "Trauma, Absence, Loss." *Critical Inquiry* 25.4 (Summer 1999): 696–727.

Lamb. G.F. *Franklin, Happy Voyager: Being the Life and Death of Sir John Franklin*. London: Benn, 1956.

Levi-Strauss, Claude. "The Culinary Triangle." *Partisan Review* 33 (1966): 586–95.

Lhamon, W.T. *Raising Cain: Blackface Performance from Jim Crow to Hip Hop*. Cambridge, MA: Harvard UP, 1998.

Lindfors, Bernth. "Charles Dickens and the Zulus." *Africans on Stage: Studies in Ethnological Show Business*. Ed. Bernth Lindfors. Bloomington; Indianapolis: Indiana UP, 1999. 62–80.

Loomis, Chauncey. *Weird and Tragic Shores: The Story of Charles Francis Hall, Explorer*. New York: Knopf, 1971.

Lott, Eric. *Love and Theft: Blackface Minstrelsy and the American Working Class*. New York: Oxford UP, 1993.

MacEwen, Gwendolyn. *Terror and Erebus. Staging the North: Twelve Canadian Plays*. Eds. Sherrill Grace, Eve D'Aeth, and Lisa Chalykoff. Toronto: Playwrights Canada Press, 1999. 115–34.

Mahar, William. *Behind the Burnt Cork Mark: Early Blackface Minstrelsy and Antebellum American Popular Culture*. Urbana: University of Illinois Press, 1999.

Marlow, James E. "English Cannibalism: Dickens after 1859." *Studies in English Literature, 1500–1900* 23.4 (Autumn 1983): 647–66.

———. "Sir John Franklin, Mr. Charles Dickens, and the Solitary Monster." *Dickens Studies Newsletter* 12.4 (Dec. 1981): 97–103.

Mayer, David. "Encountering Melodrama." *The Cambridge Companion to Victorian and Edwardian Theatre*. Ed. Kerry Powell. Cambridge, UK: Cambridge UP, 2004. 145–63.

———. *Harlequin in His Element: The English Pantomime, 1806–1836*. Cambridge, MA: Harvard UP, 1969.

McGoogan, Ken. *Fatal Passage: The Untold Story of John Rae, the Arctic Adventurer Who Discovered the Fate of Franklin*. Toronto: Harper Perennial, 2001.

———. *Lady Franklin's Revenge: A True Story of Ambition, Obsession, and the Remaking of Arctic History*. Toronto: Harper Collins, 2005.

———. *Race to the Polar Sea: The Heroic Adventures and Romantic Obsessions of Elisha Kent Kane*. Toronto: Harper Collins, 2008.

McClintock, Anne. *Imperial Leather: Race, Gender, and Sexuality in the Colonial Conquest*. New York: Routledge, 1995.

Moore, Grace. "Reappraising Dickens's 'Noble Savage.'" *The Dickensian* 98.3 (2002): 236–44.

Moss, Sarah. *Scott's Last Biscuit: The Literature of Polar Travel.* Oxford: Signal Books, 2006.

Nayder, Lillian. *Unequal Partners: Charles Dickens, Wilkie Collins, and Victorian Authorship.* Ithaca, NY: Cornell UP, 2002.

O'Brien, John. "Pantomime." *The Cambridge Companion to British Theatre, 1730–1830.* Eds. Jane Moody and Daniel O'Quinn. Cambridge, UK: Cambridge UP: 2007. 103–14.

O'Neill, Patrick. "Theatre in the North: Staging Practices of the British Navy in the Canadian Arctic." *Dalhousie Review* 74.3 (Fall 1994): 356–84.

———. "*Zero* and the Arctic Dramatic Tradition." *Canadian Drama* 16.1 (1990): 42–48.

Panetta, Alexandra. "Seal ceremony makes Jean an Arctic star." *Globe and Mail,* 30 May 2009. 11 June 2009. <http://www.theglobeandmail.com/news/national/seal-ceremony-makes-jean-an-arctic-star/article1160838/>.

Pascoe, Peggy. "Race, Gender, and Intercultural Relations: The Case of Interracial Marriage." *Frontiers: A Journal of Women Studies* 12.1 (1991): 5–18.

Pearson, Mike. "'No Joke in Petticoats': British Polar Expeditions and Their Theatrical Presentations." *TDR* 48.1 (Spring 2004): 48–59.

Pearson, Roberta. *Eloquent Gestures: The Transformation of Performance Style in the Griffith Biograph Films.* Berkeley: University of California Press, 1992.

Phelan, Peggy. *Unmarked: The Politics of Performance.* London; New York: Routledge, 1993.

Potter, Russell A. *Arctic Spectacles: The Frozen North in Visual Culture, 1818–1875.* Montreal; Kingston: McGill-Queen's UP, 2007.

Pratt, Mary Louise. *Imperial Eyes: Travel Writing and Transculturation.* London; New York: Routledge, 1992.

Rayner, Alice. *Ghosts: Death's Double and the Phenomena of Theatre.* Minneapolis: University of Minnesota Press, 2006.

Richler, Mordecai. *Solomon Gursky Was Here.* Toronto: Penguin, 1989.

Roach, Joseph. *Cities of the Dead: Circum-Atlantic Performance.* New York: Columbia UP, 1996.

Robinson, Michael F. *The Coldest Crucible: Arctic Exploration and American Culture.* Chicago; London: University of Chicago Press, 2006.

Ross, W. Gillies. *Whaling and Eskimos: Hudson Bay 1860–1915.* Ottawa: National Museum of Man, Publications in Ethnology, No. 10, 1975.

Sandler, Martin. *Resolute: The Epic Search for the Northwest Passage and John Franklin, and the Discovery of the Queen's Ghost Ship.* New York: Sterling, 2006.

Schechner, Richard. *Between Theatre and Anthropology.* Philadelphia: University of Pennsylvania Press, 1985.

Schneider, Rebecca. "Performance Remains." *Performance Research* 6.2 (2001): 100–08.

Sedgwick, Eve Kosofsky. *Between Men: English Literature and Male Homosocial Desire.* New York: Columbia University Press, 1985.

Senelick, Laurence. *The Changing Room: Sex, Drag, and Theatre.* London: Routledge, 2000.

Spalding, Alex (trans). *Eight Inuit Myths.* Ottawa: National Museum of Man; Cultural and Linguistics Section, Department of Indian and Northern Affairs, 1979.

Spivak, Gayatri Chakravorty. *A Critique of Postcolonial Reason: Toward a History of the Vanishing Present.* Cambridge, MA: Harvard UP, 1999.

———. "Translator's Preface." *Of Grammatology.* Baltimore: The Johns Hopkins UP, 1976. ix-lxxxvii

Spufford, Francis. *I May Be Some Time: Ice and the English Imagination.* London: Faber and Faber, 1996.

States, Bert O. *Great Reckonings in Little Rooms: On the Phenomenology of Theater.* Berkeley; Los Angeles: University of California Press, 1987.

Stocking, George. *Victorian Anthropology.* New York: Macmillan, 1987.

Stoler, Ann Laura. *Carnal Knowledge and Imperial Power: Race and the Intimate in Colonial Rule.* Berkeley: University of California Press, 2002.

Stone, Harry. "Charles Dickens and Harriet Beecher Stowe." *Nineteenth-Century Fiction* 12.3 (Dec. 1957): 188–202.

———. *The Night Side of Dickens: Cannibalism, Passion, Necessity.* Columbus: Ohio State UP, 1994.

Taussig, Michael. *Mimesis and Alterity: A Particular History of the Senses.* New York: Routledge, 1993.

Taylor, Diana. *The Archive and the Repertoire: Performing Cultural Memory in the Americas.* Durham, NC: Duke UP, 2003.

Taylor, Millie. *British Pantomime Performance.* Bristol, UK: Intellect Books, 2007.

Toll, Robert C. *Blacking Up: The Minstrel Show in Nineteenth-Century America.* New York: Oxford UP, 1974.

Vizenor, Gerald. *Fugitive Poses: Native American Indian Scenes of Absence and Presence.* Lincoln, NE: University of Nebraska Press, 1998.

———. *Manifest Manners: Postindian Warriors of Survivance.* Hanover: Wesleyan UP, 1994.

Vizenor, Gerald, ed. Introduction. *Survivance: Narratives of Native Presence.* Lincoln: University of Nebraska, 2008.

Wiebe, Rudy. *Playing Dead: A Contemplation Concerning the Arctic.* Edmonton: NeWest, 1989.

Wilson, Kathleen. *The Island Race: Englishness, Empire, and Gender in the Eighteenth Century.* London; New York: Routledge, 2003.

Woodman, David C. *Unravelling the Franklin Mystery: Inuit Testimony.* Montreal: McGill-Queen's UP, 1991.

Woodward, Frances. *Portrait of Jane: A Life of Lady Franklin.* London: Hodder and Stoughton, 1951.

Wright, Noel. *Quest for Franklin.* London, Heinemann: 1959.

Index